FATHERS TO SONS
Advice Without Consent

FATHERS

 TO SONS

Advice Without Consent

EDITED AND WITH AN INTRO-
DUCTION BY ALAN VALENTINE

UNIVERSITY OF OKLAHOMA PRESS · *Norman*

By Alan Valentine

The Age of Conformity (Chicago, 1954)
Vigilante Justice (New York, 1955)
Trial Balance (New York, 1956)
1913: Between Two Worlds (New York, 1962)
Lord George Germain (Oxford, 1962)
Fathers to Sons: Advice Without Consent (Norman, 1963)

Library of Congress Catalog Card Number: 63–18075

Copyright 1963 by the University of Oklahoma Press, Publishing Division of the University. Composed and printed at Norman, Oklahoma, U.S.A., by the University of Oklahoma Press. First edition.

☞ *Acknowledgments*

THE COLLECTING AND EDITING of these letters was a less onerous task than that of trying to make sure that all copyright claims in America, England, and several European countries were discovered and met. No copyright holder whom I was able to locate refused the requested permission, but there were a few complicated cases in which I was unable to track down every possible interested party. If any rightful claim has not been dealt with, I offer sincere apology, with the assurance that I have done my best, and with the conviction that no man of good will would have refused my request for a purpose so obviously non-commercial.

For the use of copyrighted or possibly copyrighted material I gratefully make acknowledgment to the following:

To Her Majesty Queen Elizabeth for her gracious permission to republish two extracts from letters written by King George V to his sons, later King Edward VIII and King George VI.

To the Public Trustee of Great Britain and the Macmillan Company of New York for permission to republish a letter from Queen Victoria and Prince Albert to their son, later King Edward VII, appearing in Sir Sidney Lee's *Life of Edward VII.*

To Prime Minister Jawaharlal Nehru and the Asia Publishing House of Bombay and London for a letter to Mr. Nehru from his father, printed in *A Batch of Old Letters.*

To Lord Tennyson for an extract from *Tennyson: A Memoir,* by Hallam Tennyson, published by Macmillan and Company, Ltd. of London.

To Professor Bonamy Dobrée for charming letters approving my printing of a letter from Lord Chesterfield in his edition of *Letters of ... Chesterfield,* published by Her Majesty's Printers, Eyre and Spottiswood, Ltd.

v

To Her Majesty's Stationery Office and the Royal Historical Manuscripts Commission for the brief extract from the Pepys Manuscripts containing the letter from the Duke of Northumberland printed by the Commission.

To Ives Hendrick and Doubleday and Company for a letter from *The Life and Letters of Walter Hines Page*, by Burton J. Hendrick.

To the Clarendon Press of Oxford University for an extract from *James Brydges, First Duke of Chandos*, edited by C. H. C. and M. I. Baker; and to the Oxford University Press for an extract from *Further Letters of Gerard Manley Hopkins*, edited by C. C. Abbott.

To Lawrance Thompson and The Macmillan Company of New York for a letter from *Young Longfellow*.

To Professor Brainard Mears, George E. Mears, and Holt, Rinehart and Winston, Inc., for a letter from *Life and Letters of Stuart P. Sherman*, by Jacob Zeitlin and Homer Woodbridge.

To the Harvard University Archives for a letter written by John Lowell.

To the Philosophical Library for a letter by Dagobert D. Runes in *Letters to My Son*.

To the University of South Carolina Press for a letter from *The Letters of William Gilmour Simms*, edited by Oliphant Odell, and Eaves.

To the state of North Carolina Department of Archives and History for a letter from *The Correspondence of Jonathan Worth*, and for a letter from *The Papers of William A. Graham*, both edited by J. G. de Roulhac Hamilton.

To the Carnegie Institution of Washington for a letter from Andrew Jackson in *Correspondence of Andrew Jackson*, Institution Publication 371, edited by John Spencer Bassett.

To the University of Texas Press for a letter from Sam Houston in *Writings of Sam Houston*, edited by A. W. Williams and E. C. Barker.

To the Princeton University Press and the American Philosophical Society, holders of the copyright, for extracts from *Letters of Benjamin Rush*, edited by C. H. Butterfield.

To Simon and Schuster, Inc., for a letter from Benjamin Franklin in *A Treasury of the World's Great Letters,* and one from Lorenzo de Medici in *A Second Treasury of the World's Great Letters.*

To George Allen and Unwin, Ltd., for a letter from *The Works of John Ruskin,* edited by Cook and Wedderburn; and for extracts from *The Private Letters of William Wilberforce,* edited by A. M. Wilberforce.

To James Clarke and Company, Ltd., and the anonymous author, for a letter from *Letters to a Ministerial Son.*

To I. Andersen and The Fleming H. Revell Company for extracts from *The Letters of General Nicholas Longworth Andersen.*

To Routledge and Kegan Paul, Ltd., for a letter by Camille Pissarro from *Letters to His Son,* edited by John Rewald; and for a letter from *Shelley in England,* by Roger Ingpen.

To John Murray, London, for extracts from *The Life of Disraeli,* edited by Monypenny and Buckle; from *The Private Letters of Sir Robert Peel,* edited by George Peel; and from Lord Bute in *A Prime Minister to His Son,* edited by E. Stuart Wortley.

To G. Bell and Sons, Ltd., for a letter from *Memoirs of Coventry Patmore,* edited by Basil Champneys.

To Edward Arnold, Ltd., for a letter from *The Autobiography of Dean Merivale,* edited by J. A. Merivale.

To Faber and Faber, Ltd., for extracts of letters from *The Works of Sir Thomas Browne,* edited by Geoffrey Keynes.

To Jonathan Cape, Ltd., for extracts from letters in *The Pembroke Papers,* edited by Lord Herbert.

To Curtis Brown, Ltd., for a letter from Kenneth Grahame in *Kenneth Grahame,* by P. A. Chalmers.

To The Bodley Head, Ltd., for an extract from *The Life and Letters of William Cobbett,* by Lewis Melville.

To the Houghton Mifflin Company for extracts from *John Jay Chapman,* by M. A. DeWolfe Howe; from *Letters of Horace Howard Furness,* edited by H. H. Jayne; from *Letters and Journals of S.F.B. Morse,* edited by E. L. Morse; and from *A Cycle of Adams Letters,* edited by W. C. Ford.

To Putnam's and Coward-McCann for extracts from *Memoirs,*

by Jane C. Croly; and from *The Life of Charles Carroll*, by K. M. Rowland.

To Little, Brown and Company for extracts from pages 153, 154, and 157 of *Letters of Sherwood Anderson*, edited by Howard Mumford Jones and Walter B. Rideout.

To David Higham Associates, Ltd., for extracts from *Letters to his Nephew*, by Arnold Bennett; and to that company and Sir Osbert Sitwell and Macmillan and Company of London for extracts from Sir Osbert's *Great Morning* and *Laughter in the Next Room*.

To the W. W. Norton Company for extracts from *The Bach Reader*, edited by H. T. David and A. Mendel.

To Charles Scribner's Sons for an extract from *Letters of Richard Harding Davis*, edited by C. B. Davis; and for a letter reprinted with the permission of Charles Scribner's Sons from *Theodore Roosevelt's Letters to His Children*, by Theodore Roosevelt, copyright 1919 by Charles Scribner's Sons, renewal copyright 1947 by Edith K. Carow Roosevelt.

To William Heinemann, Ltd., for the letter from Philip Gosse in *The Life and Letters of Sir Edmund Gosse*, by E. Charteris.

To J. M. Dent and Sons, Ltd., for an extract from *The Works of Hazlitt*, edited by F. P. Howe and in connection with the use of extracts from *The Bach Reader*, edited by H. T. David and A. Mendel.

To Farrar, Strauss and Cudahy for an extract from *Goethe*, by Ludwig Lewisohn.

To Harcourt, Brace and World, Inc., for an extract from *The Letters of Lincoln Steffens*, edited by Ella Winter and Granville Hicks, copyright 1938 by Harcourt Brace and World, Inc., and reprinted with their permission.

To the William L. Clements Library of the University of Michigan for a letter from its collection of the papers of Lord Shelburne.

To the Bodleian Library of Oxford University for a letter from Philip Henry in its English Letters Collection, and for a letter from William Harris in its Rawlinson Collection.

To E. P. Dutton and Company for an extract from *Life and Letters of Phillips Brooks*, by A.V.G. Allen.

Acknowledgments

To the Viking Press for extracts from *The Letters of Sacco and Vanzetti*, edited by Frankfurter and Jackson.

To Jackson Son and Company, Ltd., for an extract from *The Letters of Thomas Osborne, Earl of Derby and Duke of Leeds*, edited by A. Browning.

To Macmillan and Company, Ltd., and the St. Martin's Press for extracts from translation from *Beethovens' Letters*, edited by Emily Anderson.

To Stanley Paul and Company, Ltd., of the Hutchinson Publishing Group, and the Duke of Argyll, for extracts from *Intimate Family Letters*, edited by the Duke of Argyll.

To Duell, Sloan and Pearce of the Meredith Press for selections from *FDR: His Personal Letters*, edited by Elliott Roosevelt.

To John Murray, London, for a letter from *The Life of Castiglione*, by Julia Cartwright.

To André Maurois for an extract from *The Titan*, published by Harper, New York.

To Mrs. Leonard Huxley for parts of two letters from *Life and Letters of T. H. Huxley*, by Leornard Huxley, published by Macmillan and Co., Ltd.

Alan Valentine

NORTH HAVEN, MAINE
AUGUST 21, 1963

☞ Contents

Contents

Contents

xv

Contents

Mr. Justice Oliver Wendell Holmes of the Supreme Court, going through his father's papers in 1908, wrote to a friend: "I feel a humorous filial piety, and, by the way, chuckled to come on a letter from *his* father to *him* at school inculcating virtue in the same dull terms that he passed on to me. If I had a son I wonder if I should yield to the temptation to twaddle in my turn." Holmes should have been too wise to wonder on that score; he would have been a rare father had he not yielded to temptation and then been a little hurt that his son did not appreciate his efforts. Only a few men have been able to make virtue seem interesting and desirable to their sons. Holmes's father, the "Autocrat of the Breakfast Table," was an affectionate and devoted parent whom all Boston thought witty and wise, yet his distinguished son could in full maturity pronounce his father's mild exhortations to be "twaddle." "I find this same problem exists in all fathers and sons," Sherwood Anderson wrote to his own son in 1941. "There is something about the relationship that is pretty difficult to put your finger on. I think fathers realize this and have it on their minds a good deal more than their sons realize."

Many men remember their fathers with a mixture of admiring affection and rebellious irritation, and recall their moments of resentment more clearly than their hours of happiness. At the age of fifty-one, Verlaine pictured his father as an over-strict disciplinarian, yet "we know," wrote Harold Nicolson, "that when Verlaine was at school his father would come to see him every day for eight years with cakes and chocolate in his pocket," and that "he was adored and petted by both his parents."

Sons have the last word, and sometimes they have taken unfair advantage of it. Henri Beyle changed his name to Stendhal partly in defiance of an affectionate though stuffy father. Throughout his life he referred to that father as his *"bâtard de père"* and said that his own last words as a suicide would be, "My father will achieve old age amid the hoots of decent men." Samuel Butler's characterization of his father as "Mr. Pontifex" was unjust, unless Butler thought that paternal oversight should not be The Way of All Flesh. Such examples make it clear that paternal love does not preclude filial resentment, and that the father-son relationship tests understanding and patience at least as much as marriage does.

Indeed, the relationship of father and son suffers under handicaps marriage does not present, for marriage is usually a free choice and, in theory at least, a pact between equals, but no son can choose his father or claim full equality with him from the start. What is more, fathers and sons, unlike husbands and wives, must cope with the inevitable incompatibilities of their different generations. To every generation the succeeding one seems to be ignoring essential truths and values; to every new age its predecessor seems stodgy or hypocritical. For thousands of years father and son have stretched wistful hands across the canyon of time, each eager to help the other to his side, but neither quite able to desert the loyalties of his contemporaries. The relationship is always changing and hence always fragile; nothing endures except the sense of difference. A father can barely stomach his son's heresies; a son can only pretend to worship his father's sacred cows. Inevitably the younger wins, for the future is with him. Even the Chinese, those notable admirers of their ancestors, have an adage which says: "What we call the spirit of the age, our fathers called the end of the world."

Though the future is with the sons, the past is with their fathers, and for purposes of argument and indoctrination the past is more useful than the future. Adam probably told his sons that their values were far inferior to those of his own youth in Paradise and that therefore they would do well to defer to his experience. Homer nodded when he failed to have Odysseus, immediately on revealing himself to Telemachus, ask his son whether he had been diligent to his studies and obedient to Penelope.

Yet despite infinite precedents to console him, every father thinks his own paternal problem unique and his own son particularly difficult. To the current generation of fathers, precedents are cold comfort, since the world has discarded tradition. The break in cultural continuity between themselves and their children is the greatest in history. Modern life, modern psychology, Marxian democracy, and nuclear fission have made today's young man more remote from the values and ways of thought of his grandfather than his grandfather was from those of Erasmus and Plato. The man born in 1900 could communicate on more common ground with John Bunyan or Benjamin Franklin than with his own teen-age son. Today's angry young men are angry in different ways than their predecessors; today's "beat generation" may have suffered from not being beaten in the traditional place.

The letters of twentieth-century fathers should reflect this widened breach. In a way they do, but not enough of them are available to prove the point. This is not an age in which fathers write long letters to their sons inculcating abstract virtues, baring their own souls, or urgently trying to save the souls of their children. Or if they write such letters, their sons do not preserve or perhaps even read them. The future biographies of contemporary great men will be based less on their personal letters than on their telegrams, recorded telephone calls, dictations, and press clippings. Such mechanized communication impairs intimacy as well as depth of thought: a dictating machine and a typist's notebook are as poor media for letters to sons as for letters to sweethearts.

There have always been reticences between fathers and sons, but the twentieth-century reticences are of a different kind. Earlier fathers were reserved because they were too sure of themselves to bother to explain, and earlier sons at least pretended deference. The current reticence is that of a father uncertain of both his wisdom and his authority. No matter how well he may dress his exchanges in chummy equality or genial palsmanship, the modern father rarely dares to risk the reactions of a son to assertions of authority or discourses on religion, ethics, sex, or sin. He fears his son will receive such intimacies with amusement if not with resentment as intrusions on his private life. If we should write to our sons as many an earlier father did, our sons would probably reply, if at all, with the suggestion that father consult a psychiatrist.

A modern boy of fourteen, at least in the Western world, now demands from his parents recognition of his full equality with them in matters of opinion; he is not inclined to defer to age or experience. To him the greatest paternal sins are authoritarianism and hypocrisy. In this lies our greatest break with the past. Through the centuries fathers assumed and stated their superior wisdom and authority, and usually got away with it. "The advice that is given you comes from a father, and therefore carries with it love and authority." "When you are a man you will, I trust, be safely left to your own judgment in such matters. In the meantime you will be contented with mine." "Form no plans. Your mama and I have been thinking and planning for you. I shall disclose our plan to you when I see you." What father in his right mind would today risk writing thus to a son of eighteen or twenty?

However a modern father may estimate his rights and duties, he is aware that to his children firm paternal authority is no more than a vestigial remnant of ancient tyranny, like sweatshops and slavery. He avoids raising the issue of his ultimate power, legal or moral, as cautiously as a president avoids that issue with Congress, the king with the Commonwealth, or a dean with his university students. Only in moments of anger or last resort does he invoke his traditional powers. First he reasons or pleads: he appeals to affection, loyalty, or filial gratitude. He can still, perhaps, enforce his will—more or less—through his control of the family purse, but he knows that in families, as with nations, economic sanctions endanger good will, bring down iron curtains, and generate cold wars.

Fathers have lost their old authority partly because most of them do not want it except in moments of final resort. They have lost it also because they have lost control of their sons' environment, activities, and thoughts. Motor cars, movies, radio, television, magazines, and jam sessions have set up values to compete with those of the home. But fathers have abdicated authority primarily because they have lost certainty. They are no longer sure of their own wisdom or of their right to impose it. Their self-confidence has been weakened by the demonstrated fallacy of much they once believed true and by the constant impingement of the doctrines of modern psychology in garbled versions. Those doctrines insist that parents must be sensitive to their children's emotional reactions, independent personalities, and need for security. Psychology and weaker family control of environment have softened and humanized domestic discipline, but they have also confused and frustrated many a father, who now vacillates between tender consideration of a son's ego and resentment at his son's lack of any consideration of his own.

Yet there is nothing new under the sun, even in child psychology. The Greeks preached the doctrine of "know thyself" long before Freud and Jung, even if the Greeks did not suggest that parental self-knowledge should include parental abdication. The Earl of Bedford, in 1602, offered his son a regimen for self-analysis as modern as any textbook on applied psychology—but the Earl of Bedford was a bit of a scoundrel! James II anticipated progressive educators, Oxford Groupists, and modern novelists with his frank confessions to his son of his own amatory misadventures, though with doubtful beneficial results. In 1802 the Reverend Richard Cecil begged for his son's full confidence and intimacy as ardently as any twentieth-century psychoanalyst, but there is no evidence that he got it. Steeven Guazzo wrote in the sixteenth century a dialogue that might have taken place between two fathers at a Parent-Teacher meeting in Pasadena or Bronxville:

> ANNIBAL: The life of the father is no pattern for the young son to shape his doings by: and besides, in time he will accuse his father, for that having opportunity to send him abroad to get wealth and estimation, he kept him at home, and thereby hindered his preferment.
>
> GUAZZO: The child ought rather to think well of him for it, and to attribute it to too much love.
>
> ANNIBAL: Nay, rather too little love, for disordinate affection is not to be counted true love.

Of the ills of "disordinate affection" Carl Maria von Weber the musician wrote in terms that might have been spoken on the couch of a contemporary mental analyst: ". . . my father cherished me but too fondly, and in spite of all the love and esteem I bear him, this deprived him of my confidence, for I often felt how weak he was toward me."

Although these letters add little that is new to social history, they reflect it in interesting ways. Lorenzo de' Medici revealed between his lines to his son how far from first-century Christianity the fifteenth-century papacy had strayed, and thereby adumbrated a Reformation he would not have approved. When Elizabethan nobles coached their sons how to rise and rule, they were recording England's sudden expansion of riches and power. When Puritans preached to their sons, they were laying repressive hands on gaiety and cultivation as well as on luxury and sin, and were putting an enduring stamp on English and American culture. Many of the eighteenth-century advices to sons disclose the continuing conflicts between the values of Renaissance and Reformation, between reason and faith, between artisan and aristocrat. Meanwhile those same diversities had been transplanted in America with only a few sea changes. Charles Carroll of Carrollton perpetuated cavalier values amid his revolutionary doctrines; Morse later echoed Puritan authoritarianism; and Franklin, like Chesterfield, made the best of both worlds.

Every man makes his personal adjustment between God and Mammon, but the men of earlier centuries were often clearer than we just which was which. Their letters might begin and end with religious sentiments, but in between their advice was frankly worldly, whether its objective was a crown, a mitre, or a rich wife. In that respect cavaliers and Puritans, aristocrats and artisans, bishops and warriors were all alike. They advised, with no sense of dichotomy, their sons how to ingratiate themselves with men as well as with God, how to use friends as well as how to make them, how to marry shrewdly, and how to seem if not to be models of modesty and virtue; but they were usually clear in their distinction between the spiritual and the mundane spheres.

By the nineteenth century many men, eager to reconcile faith with reason and God with Mammon, had created confusion between them and passed those confusions on to their successors. They could not resist golden opportunities to accumulate and enjoy the things of this world and tried to justify doing so in terms of the spirit. Since, they argued, industry was a virtue, then the fruits of industry must be virtuous, and the richer those fruits the greater the virtue. Those Victorian soul searchings were often emotionally sincere but intellectually confused, and sons cannot be blamed for viewing the results, which endure today, with somewhat cynical eyes. But although the nineteenth century brought spiritual rebellion to a few sons and sectarian narrowness to others, it also created, at its best, a new breadth and warmth of spirit in the letters of men like Hope and Meredith.

It was also Victorianism that embarked on courses that have since shattered its own social and moral systems, and with them the omnipotence of fathers. Darwinism and democracy fostered forces many Victorians would have thought anarchic if they had recognized them in time. Among those forces were religious agnosticism, economic democracy, social egalitarianism, and racial equality. The tradition of the infallible father collapsed before the new equality of the sexes, the birth of juvenile self-expression, and the death of docility.

Through the centuries fathers have vacillated between the two horns of the educational dilemma. Should they give precedence to indoctrination or self-development, to discipline or sympathy, to preserving tribal values thought to be good or to encouraging progress toward values that might be better but were as yet unproved? Should a son be tailored to fit society or to improve it, to adjust or to assert? These questions lead all the way back to original sin, which is too far to follow them. But the advocates of both alternatives merit a hearing.

Plato insisted that discipline was the first essential:

> When the day breaks, the time has arrived for youth to go to their schoolmaster. Now neither sheep nor any other animals can live without a shepherd, nor can children be left without tutors, or slaves without masters. And of all animals the boy is the most unmanageable; inasmuch as he has the fountain of reason within him not yet regulated, he is an insidious and sharp-witted animal, and the most insubordinate of them all. Wherefore he must be bound with many bridles; in the first place when he gets away from mother and nurses, he must be under the management of tutors on account of his childishness and foolishness; then again, being a freeman, he must be controlled by teachers, no matter what they teach, and by studies; but he is also a slave, and in that regard any freeman who comes in his way may punish him

and his tutor and his instructor, if any of them does anything wrong; and he who comes across him and does not inflict upon him the punishment which he deserves, shall incur the greatest disgrace.

Plato would have had the boy conform to the ways of the tribe, the individual to the state, the private ego to the social will; but Erasmus questioned the method if not the end and invoked Christianity to confute Plato's priority on discipline:

> The office of fashioning of childhood resteth in many parts, of the which, as it is first, so it is the chief: that the tender wit drink the seeds of love to God and his parents. Secondly, that he love and learn the liberal sciences. Thirdly, that he be instructed to the order of his living. Fourthly, that from the beginning of youth he be brought up in civility and nurture.

Roger Ascham also stressed gentleness and affection rather than discipline in his *Scholemaster* of 1570:

> Chide not hastily, for that shall both dull his wit and discourage his diligence, but monish him gently, which shall make him both willing to amend, and glad to go forward with the love and hope of learning. . . . love is fitter than fear, gentleness than beating, to bring up a child rightly in learning.

Although Erasmus and Ascham had the later word, it was by no means the last. To many a harassed father, his son's psyche seems more akin to Plato's coltish insubordinate than to Ascham's sensitive young plant. Parents and schoolmasters, except the rare ones, are likely to fall into the system least demanding upon themselves, and routine rules and penalties require less daily effort than perceptive flexibility. Most elders have been more inclined to bridle their young mustangs than to turn them loose and then try to lure them home with lumps of sugar. The Elizabethan schoolmasters did not follow the precepts of their contemporary Ascham, but regarded their charges as "insidious and sharp-witted animals." The schoolroom was a potential battleground, as Edmund Coote made very clear in his *Englische Scholemaster* of 1596:

xxvi

> *Your cloathes unbuttoned do not use,*
> *Let not your Hose ungartered be,*
> *Have Handkerchief in readinesse,*
> *Wash Hands and Face, or see not mee.*
>
> *Lose not your Books, Ink-horn, or Pens,*
> *Nor Girdle, Garters, Hat or Band,*
> *Let Shoes be tyed, pin Shirt-band close,*
> *Keep well your Hands at any hand.*
>
> *If that thou cry or talk aloud,*
> *Or Books do read, or rend with Knife,*
> *Or Laugh, or Play, Unlawfully,—*
> *Then You and I must be at Strife.*

From then until very recent times authoritarian indoctrination was the general practice in home as well as school. It was preached in the Books of Conduct, many of them widely circulated, that were produced to improve the manners of the rising middle class. All of them glorified conventional virtues, with the implicit assumption that "Father Knows Best." Among them were *Instructions for a Son at Oxford,* by William Martyn (1612); the practical adages of William Cavendish, tutor to the prince who became Charles II ("to women you cannot be too civil, especially great ones"); the advices of the seventh Earl of Derby to his son (1651), which lifted whole paragraphs from earlier homilies; the *Father's Legacy* which Sir Henry Slingsby was said to have written just before he was executed for treason in 1658; and the Quakerly admonitions of William Penn called *The Fruits of a Father's Love.* More than we realize, tracts like those have influenced conduct and character ever since. The novels of Samuel Richardson are little more than Conduct Books in fictional form; so in a more intense sphere was *Pilgrim's Progress,* and Jane Austen and Thomas Hardy were among their legatees. Many a modern novelist who laughs at such outworn creeds unconsciously echoes thoughts and phrases derived from them.

Letters from fathers are concerned with the improvement of their sons, not of themselves. The quest for the perfect father has thus far ended only in Heaven, but many fathers have assumed that their paternal efforts have assured them a place there. Yet even in the centuries of firm paternal self-assurance, there was some soul-searching, for wise men have always recognized that of all professions fatherhood is the most demanding and the least apprenticed. The fine art of paternity must be learned from experience that usually brings its wisdom too late. It may be no coincidence that most of the more agonized letters were written to eldest or only sons: younger brothers got off more easily because by their time father had achieved either more wisdom or a clearer recognition of his own futility.

It is a pity that so many generations of experienced fathers have not left their successors a single dependable manual of the profession, and that with all its emphasis on vocational training modern society has done so little to prepare men for the most universal of vocations. It has done still less to educate sons for sonhood. With all the new books that instruct parents how to understand their child's emotions and play up to them, there is not even one slim volume on the psychology and placation of parents for the guidance of their children. Among all the books for boys it would be nice to find one on the care and management of fathers.

The virtues of fathers are either obvious or self-declared; let us therefore, like their children, take them for granted and ignore them. The faults of fathers are, however, sometimes the price of their virtues. Excessive ambition for a son is one of them. Stratford and Charles I faced the certainties of the scaffold more equably than the uncertainties of their sons' futures. The very strength of a father's emotional attachment often overwhelms his judgment in dealing with his son. It robs him of perspective and consequently of humor, and leads him into the very blunders he once resolved never to commit. Announcing that he will not preach, he preaches. Recognizing the unwisdom of over-urging, he continues to urge. Aware of how irrelevant comparisons with his own youth will seem to a son, he nevertheless embarks upon exemplary autobiography, ignoring what Baudelaire called "youth's hatred for the quoter of precedents." He talks of the wisdom of experience, but means only his own experience, and would discourage his son from gaining wisdom at first hand. And as a last resort he commends the youth to the guidance of an Almighty he is confident will duplicate his own paternal advice.

The difficulty often lies in the fact that a father's love is not as selfless as he likes to think it is. Long before modern psychology pointed this out, Goethe analyzed his father's unconscious egoism:

> All fathers entertain the pious wish of seeing their own lacks realized in their sons. It is quite as though one could live for a second time and put in full use all the experiences of one's first career. . . . My father wanted me, upon the whole, to pursue the same path that he had trodden, but more comfortably and to farther ends. He valued my innate gifts all the more since he lacked them. . . . In earlier and later years, seriously and in jest, he assured me that, had he had my talents, he would have borne himself quite otherwise and would not have been so shiftless and wasteful of them. . . . There was our father, loving and well disposed, but who, conscious of an extreme inner tenderness, played the part of iron strictness with unbelievable consistency, in order to give his children the best possible education, and not only to build, but to order and preserve, his well-established house.

Parents who feel they are giving so much and getting so little in return cannot fail to feel a bond with Goethe's father, or with Margaret Paston in the fifteenth century, wrestling unassisted with the problems of running the family estate in troubled times, when she wrote to her grown son enjoying the pleasures of London at her expense, "I have had little help or comfort from you yet!"

When it comes to the youth with real genius, it is difficult to say whether he or his parents suffer most from the relationship, and whether the greatest strains come from paternal disapproval or paternal overenthusiasm. Gautier wrote *Madamoiselle de Maupin* in six weeks, the story goes, because his father locked him in his room until he had finished the daily stint of ten pages, although his mother sometimes connived at his escapes through the window. Other fathers, instead of pushing genius too hard, cannot endure its unconventional by-products and may force the boy into defiance, as Sir Timothy Shelley did. Anatole France said he had formed most of his convictions by taking views opposed to those of his father, an ardent

Roman Catholic and royalist. Flaubert never forgave his father for falling asleep as he read him the manuscript of his *Sentimental Education*.

Fatherhood is a natural state of man, but in our time it seldom seems so. Few fathers are wholly natural with their sons. They depart from their normal personalities to fit their various concepts of what a father should be, or at least what a son should be. Many a man is consequently more at his ease and more successful with nephews and grandsons, for he accepts them more readily as personalities distinct from his own and feels less desire to present himself as other than he really is. He feels less responsible for the proper development of somone else's son and so treats him more casually and often enjoys him more. Happy is the son whose father can take their relationship easily enough to be consistently natural and play neither the censor nor the effortful "pal." Such fathers seldom leave a history of the relationship in letters, for their correspondence is so free of stresses that no one thinks of preserving it. Doubtless an infinite number of fathers have written to their sons letters that would warm and lift our hearts, if we could only find them. The happiest fathers leave no history, and it is the men who are not at their best with their children who are likely to write the heart-rending letters that survive.

Perhaps this collection should have been arranged according to the predominant subject matter or emotions of the situation, such as "Letters written in Anger," and "Letters of Encouragement," "Letters on Women" and "Letters on Extravagance." But the content of many of the best letters escapes easy classification, and they gain in continuity and contrast by arrangement in an order that is roughly chronological. In transcribing them, I have been arbitrary and technically inconsistent. My first objective has been to make them most easily readable without impairing their validity and spirit. For any affronts to pure scholarship that have resulted, I offer no defense except my own best judgment.

Those who read these letters may wish they knew the end of each story, and could trace some dependable correlation between the efforts or sins of the fathers and the characters and later careers of their sons. Did Lorenzo's letter make Giovanni a better pope? Did Charles II govern England more wisely as a result of his condemned father's admonitions? Did Edward VII and the empire profit from Victoria and Albert's message on a prince's royal duty? Was Ruskin's career more notable, or happier, because of his father's deferential devotion to filial talent? To most such questions there can be no sure answer, and in some cases none at all, since the facts have vanished. Where a son's later career is known and seems significant, I have mentioned it, but even so one cannot confidently trace in it the influence of his father.

Nor do the letters offer any sure generalizations for the universal guidance of future fathers—except perhaps one obvious lesson, already familiar but often forgotten. Of all the ingredients of successful fatherhood, unselfish affection seems to be the most precious. Without it all paternal systems, all wisdom, and all sacrifices are likely to be futile. With it, a father may make innumerable blunders and still end his days warmed by filial love and paternal pride. Plato may have been right that boys are the most insubordinate of all animals, but the experience of centuries supports Ascham that in breaking those fractious colts to society's bridle, "love is fitter than fear, gentleness than beating."

Young and old men who read these letters may alike be led to soften a little their own cherished resentments of some paternal sternness or apparent lack of sympathy. Much of such bitterness can be attributed to the inevitable cruelties of age and change. All the letters that might have led to tragedies did not do so; many sons have survived the sins of their fathers, and many fathers have received all the appreciation they deserved, even if sometimes at the eleventh hour. Ranier Rilke the poet, like many another son, never provided his father with a comforting answer to his troubled question: "Are you sure that you are keeping in mind an assured future, my dear Rene?" But after his father's death, the poet wrote in gratitude of

> *You who on my account*
> *Tasted so bitterly of life, my father;*
> *Who paid the price for the first troubled flow*
> *Of my necessities, as I grew up;*
> *Who with the tang of so obscure a future*
> *Preoccupied, my dim and upward gaze*

Tested, my father: you whose fear in me
I felt in all my hopes.

And since all fathers were once sons, and most sons will be fathers, then, in the words of Alexander Ross: "As dutiful children let us cover the Nakedness of our Fathers with the Cloke of a favourable Interpretation."

FATHERS TO SONS
Advice Without Consent

FATHERS TO SONS
Advice Without Consent

☞ *"Desist You from a Part So Shameful"*

IN the thirteenth century, marital alliances between royal families caused war as often as they produced peace. Edward II (1284–1327), who became king of England in 1307, married Isabella of France, but she soon openly defied him with her paramour Roger Mortimer (1287?–1330), who became the first Earl of March. Edward was long suffering, and when Isabella's brother Charles the Fair became king of France, he sent his fourteen-year-old son and heir, Prince Edward (1312–77), to France to pay Charles his royal compliments. That was in 1325, and Isabella took advantage of her son's mission to join Mortimer in France and there to try to enlist her son in her intrigues against her husband.

When Edward II heard of Isabella's activities, he wrote to Prince Edward urging him to leave this unholy menage and return to England. His letter was only partly successful. When the Prince came home, it was with Isabella and Mortimer, who promptly deposed Edward II, hanged his current favorite, Le Despencer, and eight months later had the deposed king brutally murdered in prison. They installed the young prince, then fifteen, as King Edward III, ruling under their regency, but the boy proved less amenable than they had hoped. Three years later he rebelled against his mother's direction, had Mortimer hanged, and took over a personal rule of England that continued for nearly fifty years.

[LICHFIELD, March 18, 1326]

EDWARD, MY FAIR SON,

We understand by your letters written in reply to ours that you remember well the charge we gave you; among other things, not to contract marriage, nor to suffer it to be contracted for you, without

3

our knowledge and consent; and also that at your departure from Dover you said "that it should be your pleasure to obey our commandments, as far as you could, all your days."

Fair son, if thus you have done, you have done wisely and well, and according to your duty, so as to have grace of God and us and all men; and if not, then you cannot avoid the wrath of God, the reproach of men, and our great indignation, for we charged you so lately and so strictly that you should remember well these things, and that you should by no means marry, nor suffer yourself to be married without our previous consent and advice; for no other thing that you could do would occasion greater injury and pain of heart to us. And inasmuch as it seems you say "you cannot return to us because of your mother," it causes us great uneasiness of heart that you cannot be allowed by her to do that which is your natural duty, and which not doing will lead to much mischief.

Fair son, you know how dearly she would have been loved and cherished, if she had timely come according to her duty to her lord. We have knowledge of much of her evil doings, to our sorrow; how that she devises pretenses for absenting herself from us, on account of our dear and faithful nephew, H. le Despencer, who has always so well and loyally served us, while you and all the world have seen that she openly, notoriously, and knowing it to be contrary to her duty, and against the welfare of the crown, has attracted to herself, and retains in her company, the Mortimer, our traitor and mortal foe, proved, attainted, and adjudged, and *him* she accompanies in the house and abroad in despite of us, of our crown, and the right ordering of the realm—him, the malefactor whom our beloved brother the King of France at our request banished from his dominions as our enemy! And worse than this she has done, *if* worse than *this* can be, in allowing you to consort with our said enemy, making him your counsellor, and you openly to herd and associate with him in the sight of all the world, doing so great a villainy and dishonor both to yourself and to us to the prejudice of our crown, and of the laws and customs of our realm, which *you* are supremely bound to hold, preserve, and maintain.

Wherefore, fair son, desist you from a part which is so shameful,

4

and may be to you perilous and injurious in too many ways. We are not pleased with you, and neither for your mother, nor for any other, ought you to displease us. We charge you by the faith, love, and allegiance which you owe to us, and on our blessing, that you come to us without opposition, delay, or any further excuse; for your mother has written to us, "that if you wish to return to us she will not prevent it," and we do not understand that your uncle the king detains you against the form of your safe conduct. In no manner, then, either for your mother, or to go to the duchy, nor for any other cause, delay to come to us. Our commands are for your good, and for your honour, by the help of God. Come quickly, then, without further excuse, if you would have our blessing, and avoid our reproach and indignation.

It is our wish to order all things for the good of the duchy, and our other dominions, for our mutual honour and benefit.

If John of Bretagne, and John of Cornwall, will come in your company, they will do their duty.

Fair son, trespass not against our commands, for we hear too much that you have done of things you ought not.

Given at Lichfield, the 18th day of March.[1]

[1] T. Rymer, *Foedera*, II, 623–30.

☞ *A Medici Advises a Teen-age Cardinal*

THE members of the Medici family who ruled Florence during the fifteenth century were no more unscrupulous than many of their rivals, but their success made them notorious and inspired Machiavelli's treatise on practical politics called *The Prince*. Their corruptions as well as their power were perhaps exceeded by the papal heirarchy, whose members schemed and poisoned with more unction, so that even a Medici could long to be a pope. While Columbus was finding America, the most magnificent of the Medici, Lorenzo (1449–92), was arranging the induction of his sixteen-year-old son, Giovanni (1475–1521), into the College of Cardinals. Returning to his palace from that ceremony, Giovanni found a long letter from his father. The outwardly amoral Lorenzo's exhortations to morality may have surprised Giovanni as much as it has surprised some later readers, but Lorenzo wrote it from what proved to be his death bed—often a remarkable inspiration to virtue. There is a story that in his last days Lorenzo begged the austerely righteous priest Savonarola to give him absolution, but was refused and died unshriven. It was a scene Thomas Mann recreated in his play *Fiorenza*.

[April, 1492]

You, and all of us who are interested in your welfare, ought to esteem ourselves highly favoured by Providence, not only for the many honours and benefits bestowed on our house, but more particularly for having conferred upon us, in your person, the greatest dignity we have ever enjoyed. This favour, in itself so important, is rendered still more so by the circumstances with which it is accompanied, and especially by the consideration of your youth and of our situation in the world.

The first thing I would therefore suggest to you is that you ought to be grateful to God, and continually recollect that it is not through your merits, your prudence, or your solicitude, that this event has taken place, but through His favour, which you can only repay by a pious, chaste and exemplary life; and that your obligations to the performance of those duties are so much the greater, as in your early years you have given some reasonable expectation that your riper age may produce such fruits. It would indeed be highly disgraceful, and as contrary to your duty as to my hopes, if, at a time when others display a greater share of reason and adopt a better mode of life, you should forget the precepts of your youth, and forsake the path in which you have hitherto trodden.

Endeavor therefore to alleviate the burden of your early dignity by the regularity to your life and by your perseverance in those studies which are suitable to your profession. It gave me great satisfaction to learn that, in the course of the past year, you had frequently, of your own accord, gone to communion and confession; nor do I conceive that there is any better way of obtaining the favour of heaven than by habitating yourself to a performance of these and similar duties. This appears to me to be the most suitable and useful advice which, in the first instance, I can possibly give you.

I well know that as you are now to reside in Rome, that sink of all iniquity, the difficulty of conducting yourself by these admonitions will be increased. The influence of example is itself prevalent; but you will probably meet with those who will particularly endeavor to corrupt and incite you to vice; because, as you may yourself perceive, your early attainment to so great a dignity is not observed without envy, and those who could not prevent your receiving that honour will secretly endeavor to diminish it, by inducing you to forfeit the good estimation of the public; thereby precipitating you into that gulf into which they had themselves fallen; in which attempt, the consideration of your youth will give them a confidence of success.

To these difficulties you ought to oppose yourself with the greater firmness, as there is at present less virtue amongst your brethren of the college. I acknowledge indeed that several of them are good and learned men, whose lives are exemplary, and whom I would recommend to you as patterns of your conduct. By emulating them you will be so much the more known and esteemed, in proportion as your age and the peculiarity of your situation will distinguish you from your colleagues. Avoid, however, as you would Scylla or Charybdis, the imputation of hypocricy; guard against all ostentation, either in your conduct or your discourse; affect not austerity, nor even appear too serious. This advice you will, I hope, in time understand and practice better than I can express it.

Yet, you are not unacquainted with the great importance of the character which you have to sustain, for you well know that all the Christian world would prosper if the cardinals were what they ought to be; because in such cases there would always be a good Pope, upon which the tranquility of Christendom so materially depends. Endeavor then to render yourself such, that if all the rest resembled you, we might expect this universal blessing. To give you particular directions as to your behaviour and conversation would be a matter of no small difficulty. I shall therefore only recommend that in your intercourse with the cardinals and other men of rank, your language be unassuming and respectful, guiding yourself, however, by your own reason, and not submitting to be impelled by the passions of others, who, actuated by improper motives, may pervert the use of their reason. Let it satisfy your conscience that your conversation is without intentional offense; and if, through impetuosity of temper, anyone should be offended, as his enmity is without just cause, so it will not be very lasting. On this your first visit to Rome, it will however be more advisable for you to listen to others than to speak much yourself.

You are now devoted to God and the church; on which account you ought to aim at being a good ecclesiastic, and to show that you prefer the honour and state of the church and of the apostolic see to every other consideration. Nor, while you keep this in view, will it be difficult for you to favour your family and your native place. On the contrary, you should be the link to bind this city closer to the church, and our family with the city; and although it be impossible to foresee what accidents may happen, yet I doubt not but this may be done with equal advantage to all; observing, however, that you are always to prefer the interests of the church.

You are not only the youngest cardinal in the college, but the youngest person that ever was raised to that rank; and you ought therefore to be the most vigilant and unassuming, not giving others occasion to wait for you, either in the chapel, the consistory, or upon deputations. You will soon get a sufficient insight into the manners of your brethren. With those of less respectable character converse not with too much intimacy; not merely on account of the circumstance in itself, but for the sake of public opinion. Converse on general topics with all. On public occasions let your equipage and dress be rather below than above mediocrity. A handsome house and a well-ordered family will be preferable to a great retinue and a splendid residence. Endeavor to live with regularity, and gradually to bring your expenses within those bounds which in a new establishment cannot perhaps be expected. Silk and jewels are not suitable for a person in your station. Your taste will be better shown in the acquisition of a few elegant remains of antiquity, or in the collecting of handsome books, and by your attendants being learned and well bred rather than numerous. Invite others to your house oftener than you receive invitations. Practice neither too frequently.

Let your own food be plain, and take sufficient exercise, for those who wear your habit are soon liable, without great caution, to contract infirmities. The station of a cardinal is not less secure than elevated; on which account those who arrive at it too frequently become negligent, conceiving that their object is attained, and that they can preserve it with little trouble. This idea is often injurious to the life and character of those who entertain it. Be attentive therefore to your conduct, and confide in others too little rather than too much.

There is one rule which I would recommend to your attention in preference to all others: rise early in the morning. This will not only contribute to your health, but will enable you to arrange and expedite the business of the day; and as there are various duties incident to your station, such as the performance of divine service, studying, giving audience, etc., you will find the observation of this admonition productive of the greatest utility.

Another very necessary precaution, particularly on your entrance into public life, is to deliberate every evening on what you may have to perform the following day, that you may not be unprepared for whatever may happen. With respect to your speaking in the consistory, it will be most becoming for you at present to refer the matters in debate to the judgment of His Holiness, alleging as a reason your own youth and inexperience. You will probably be desired to intercede for the favours of the Pope on particular occasions. Be cautious, however, that you trouble him not too often; for his temper leads him to be most liberal to those who weary him least with their solicitations. This you must observe, lest you should give him some offense, remembering also at times to converse with him on more agreeable topics; and if you should be obliged to request some kindness from him, let it be done with that modesty and humility which are so pleasing to his disposition. Farewell.[1]

Giovanni became a pope, and his easy-going nature more than his breadth of view permitted the development of the Reformation.

[1] W. Brockway and B. K. Winer (eds.), *A Second Treasury of the World's Great Letters*, 78–79.

☞ *"It Is Ordained . . .*
That We Reverence Our Parents
Next to God"

No man seemed to represent the fine flower of the Italian Renaissance better than Count Baldassare Castiglione (1478–1529), diplomat, papal nuncio, Bishop of Ávila, and author of that handbook of aristocratic manners *The Courtier* (1527). But even so admirable a character, representative of the new liberalism, thought it desirable to impress his parental authority upon his twelve-year-old son, Camillo. While on service in Spain he wrote in Latin to his children in Italy:

[MONZONE, July 11, 1528]

To My Dearest Children, Camillo, Anna, and Ippolita,

I am sure, my dearest son Camillo, that you, above all things desire my speedy return home. For it is ordained, alike by Nature and the laws of man, that we reverence our parents next to God. And you may be said to owe me a special debt, since I have remained content with one son, and have been unwilling to share either my fortune or my love with another. You are bound, therefore, to pay me this filial duty, lest I should repent my resolution. And, although I have no doubt that you recognize this, I wish you to understand that I do not regard this duty lightly, as other parents often do, but I exact it from you as my due. This debt you will best discharge by looking upon the admirable teacher whom your friends have given you, in the light of a father, and by obeying his voice as if it were my own. I can give you no better advice than this line of Virgil, which I repeat in no boastful spirit: "Learn, boy, from me, virtue and honorable toil; but good fortune from others." . . .

Your father,

BALDASSARE CASTIGLIONE.[1]

Camillo Castiglione (1517–98) profited by his father's example and presumably by his precepts. He entered the service of the Emperor when seventeen, fought with distinction in Germany and Flanders, married a countess and in 1573 acquired the noble castle of Isola da Piano, performed several important diplomatic missions for the Pope,

and won honors and a pension from Charles I before he died at the
ripe age of eighty-one.

[1] Julia Cartwright (Mrs. Henry Ady), *Castiglione: Life and Letters*, II, 393–94.

☞ *"All That I Have Must Be Yours"*

JOHN DUDLEY (1502?–53), Earl of Warwick, became the
favorite of the sickly boy-king, Edward VI (1537–53), who made him
Duke of Northumberland and Protector. Northumberland brought his
sons to court not only to make their fortunes but to forward his own
vaulting ambitions. This letter to his son John gives the impression of
a simple, honest, loyal man.

[1552?]

I had thought you had more discretion than to hurt yourself
through fantasies or care, specially for such things as may be reme-
died and holpen. Well enough you must understand that I know
you cannot live under great charges. And therefore you should not
hide from me your debts what so ever it be for I would be lothe but
you should keep your credit with all men. And therefore send me
word in any wise of the whole sum of your debts, for I and your
mother will see them forthwith paid and what so ever you so spend
in the honest service of our master and for his honour as you do not
let wild and wanton men consume it, as I have been served in my
days, you must think all is spent as it should be, and all that I have
must be yours and that you spend before, you may with God's grace
help it hereafter by good and faithful service. Wherein I trust you
will never be found slack and then you may be sure you cannot lack
such a master as you have toward whom the living God preserve and
restore you to perfect health and so with my blessing I commit you
to his tuition.

Your loving Father,
NORTHUMBERLAND

[Postscript in another hand]

Your loving mother, that wishes you health daily,
JANE NORTHUMBERLAND[1]

Young John became Earl of Warwick and Master of Horse to Edward VI, but whether in pursuit of family ambitions or of Protestant dominance or both, his father took steps that have put him down in history as a subtle intriguer, without principles. Anticipating death, the King named Lady Jane Grey, a Protestant, as his successor, and in 1553, Northumberland secretly married her to another of his sons, Lord Guilford Dudley, in the hope of making him virtual king. Upon Edward's death on July 6, 1553, Northumberland proclaimed Lady Jane queen, but received almost no support from other nobles, and Mary, a Roman Catholic, became queen instead. Northumberland was beheaded on August 22, 1553, and his son Lord Guilford and Lady Jane, on February 12, 1554. Young John was also sentenced to death but was pardoned in 1554.

[1]Royal Historical Manuscripts Series, LXX (1911), *Pepys Manuscripts*, 1–2.

☞ *The Refinements of Tudor Nobility*

IN letters to their sons, famous sinners have preached conventional morality as eloquently as the most virtuous men. Fathers whose own lives defied every religious principle have left letters urging their sons to embrace the true faith; men who ardently pursued war and vengeance have advocated peace and forgiveness to their heirs; promiscuous kings have advised their successors to forego mistresses; and cruel husbands have begged their sons to cherish and obey their mothers. Perhaps they thought, in their later years, that such gestures might unlock the closed gates of Heaven.

In the seventeenth and eighteenth centuries, paternal admonitions were so fashionable that even men who had no children composed and circulated them as they did sonnets, for literary exercise. Such essays almost invariably merged spiritual exhortations with more worldly formulas for success at court. Then, as puritanism and middle-class ambitions developed, their representatives pointed out to their sons that industry, honesty, and devotion to the Ten Commandments brought rewards in this world as well as in the next. Sermons comprised so large a part of the surviving letters of fathers to sons that, once samples of them have been offered here, the rest are omitted or deleted except for significant passages.

Yet good men wrote such letters, too, and sometimes deep affection, sincerity, and even humility shine through their conventional adages and phrases. They ring most true when the writer descended, with obvious relief, to the more practical aspects of morality and urged a son to virtue not only as a duty to God but to his family, his prosperity, and his good name. Such a letter was that written by Sir Henry Sidney (1529–86), three times Lord Deputy of Ireland and a leading courtier of Henry VIII and Edward VI, to his son Philip Sidney, then at school at Shrewsbury.

[*ca.* 1566]

I have received two letters from you, one written in Latin, the other in French, which I take in good part, and will you to exercise that practice of learning often; for that will stand you in most stead, in the profession of life that you are born to live in. And, since this is my first letter that ever I did write to you, I will not, that it be all empty of some advices, which my natural care of you provoketh me to wish you to follow, as documents to you in your tender age.

Let your first action be the lifting up of your tender mind to Almighty God, by hearty prayer, and feelingly digest the words you speak in prayer, with continual meditation, and thinking of Him to whom you pray, and of the matter for which you pray. And use this as an ordinary, and at an ordinary hour. Whereby the time itself will put you in remembrance to do that which you are accustomed to do.

In that time apply your study to such hours as your discreet master doth assign you, earnestly; and the time (I know) he will so limit, as shall be both sufficient for your learning, and safe for your health. And mark the sense and matter of all that you read, as well as the words. So shall you both enrich your tongue with words, and your wit with matter; and judgment will grow as years groweth in you. Be humble and obedient to your master, for unless you frame yourself to obey others, you shall never be able to teach others how to obey you.

Be courteous of gesture, and affable to all men, with diversity of reverence, according to the dignity of the person. There is nothing that winneth so much with so little cost. Use moderate diet, so as, after your meat, you may find your wit fresher, and not duller, and your body more lively, and not more heavy. Seldom drink wine, and

13

yet sometimes do, lest being enforced to drink upon the sudden, you should find yourself inflamed. Use exercise of body, but such as is without peril of your joints or bones. It will increase your force, and enlarge your breath. Delight to be cleanly, as well in all parts of your body as in your garments. It shall make you grateful in each company, and otherwise loathsome.

Give yourself to be merry, for you degenerate from your father, if you find not yourself most able in will and body, to do anything, when you be most merry, but let your mirth be void of all scurrility, and biting words to any man, for a wound given by a word is oftentimes harder to be cured, than that which is given with the sword. Be you rather a hearer and bearer away of other men's talk, than a beginner or procurer of speech, otherwise you shall be counted to delight to hear yourself speak. If you hear a wise sentence, or an apt phrase, commit it to your memory, with respect of the circumstances, when you shall speak it. Let never oath to be heard to come out of your mouth, nor words of ribaldry; detest it in others, so shall custom make to yourself a law against it in yourself.

Be modest in each assembly, and rather be rebuked of light fellows, for maiden-like shamefacedness, than of your sad friends for pert boldness. Think upon every word before you utter it, and remember how nature hath rampired up (as it were) the tongue with teeth, lips, yea, and hair without the lips, and all betokening reins, or bridles, for the loose use of that member. Above all things tell no untruth, no, not in trifles. The custom of it is naughty, and let it not satisfy you, that, for a time, the hearers take it for a truth; for after it will be shown as it is, to your shame; for there cannot be a greater reproach to a gentleman, than to be accounted a liar.

Study and endeavor yourself to be virtuously occupied. So shall you make such an habit of well-doing in you that you shall not know how to do evil, though you would. Remember, my son, the noble blood you are descended of, by your mother's side; and think that only by virtuous life and good action, you may be an ornament to that illustrious family; and otherwise, through vice and sloth, you shall be counted, *labes generis,* one of the greatest curses that can happen to man.

14

Well, my little Philip, this is enough for me, and too much I fear for you. But if I shall find that this light meal of digestion nourish any thing the weak stomach of your young capacity, I will, as I find the same grow stronger, feed it with tougher food. Your loving father, so long as you live in the fear of God.[1]

> Philip Sidney made himself remembered as the finest flower of Elizabethan nobility as well as a poet of distinction with his sonnet sequence *Astrophel and Stella.* He was a good soldier, too, and died of a wound when only thirty-two, after having helped to win victory at the battle of Zutphen. As he lay dying, he was offered a cup of water but, it is said, passed it to a wounded common soldier with the remark, "Thy necessity is greater than mine."

[1] James Montgomery, *The Christian Correspondent,* III, 160–63; W. B. Scoones, *Four Centuries of English Letters,* 223–24.

☞ "*Thou Canst Not Forbear to Love, Yet Forbear to Link*"

> THOUGH enshrined in history as a romantic figure in a romantic age, Sir Walter Raleigh (1552?–1618) invariably had his eye on a potential profit in his romantic undertakings. He could advise his son on how to win a golden crown in the next world, but wrote with more ease on how to gain gold or please a crown in this one. The first letter presented here was probably written for public consumption; the second rings more truly of personal disillusionment, and might have come from the unromantic pen of a Defoe or Benjamin Franklin's Poor Richard.

[First printed in 1632]

There is nothing more becoming any wise man than to make choice of friends, for by them thou shalt be judged what thou art. Let them therefore be wise and virtuous, and none of those that follow thee for gain; but make an election rather of thy betters than thy inferiors, shunning always such as are poor and needy; for if thou givest twenty gifts and refuse to do the like but once, all that thou hast done will be lost and such men will become thy mortal enemies.

. . . And be sure of this: thou shalt never find a friend in thy young years whose conditions and qualities will please thee after thou comest to more discretion and judgment. . . .

The next and greatest care ought to be in the choice of a wife, and the only danger therein is beauty, by which all men in all ages, wise and foolish, have been betrayed. And though I know it vain to use reason or arguments to dissuade thee from being captivated therewith, there being few or none that ever resisted that witchery, yet I cannot omit to warn thee, as of other things which may be thy ruin and destruction. . . . though thou canst not forbear to love, yet forbear to link. . . . Have therefore ever more care that thou be beloved of thy wife, rather than thyself besotted on her, and thou shalt judge of her love by these two observations: First, if thou perceive she have a care of thy estate and exercise herself therein; the other, If she study to please thee, and be sweet unto thee in conversation without thy instruction. . . .

Take care thou be not made a fool by flatterers . . . for they will strengthen thy imperfections [and] correct thee in nothing. . . . And because all men are apt to flatter themselves, to entertain the additions of other men's praise is most perilous. . . .

Be careful to avoid public disputation at feasts or at tables among choleric or quarrelsome persons . . . but if thou be once engaged carry thyself bravely so that they may fear thee after. . . . Jest not openly at those that are simple, but remember how much thou art bound to God who hath made thee wiser. Defame not any woman publickly though thou know her to be evil, for those that are faulty cannot endure to be taxed but will seek to be avenged of thee; and those that are not guilty cannot endure unjust reproach. . . . Take heed also that thou be not found a liar . . . a liar is commonly a coward [and] is trusted of no man; he can have no credit neither in publick nor private. . . .

Amongst all other things of the world, take care of thy estate, which thou shalt ever preserve if thou observe three things. First, that thou know what thou hast, what every thing is worth that thou hast, and to see that those are not wasted by thy servants and officers. The second is, that thou never spend any thing before thou have it, for borrowing is the canker and death of every man's estate. The third is, that thou suffer not thyself to be wounded for other men's faults and scourged for other men's offenses . . . paying the reckoning of another man's riot and the charge of other men's folly and prodigality: if thou smart, smart for thine own sins. . . .

Let thy servants be such as thou mayest command, and entertain none about thee but yeomen to whom thou givest wages, for those that will serve thee without thy hire will cost thee treble as much as they that know thy fare. . . . Exceed not in the humour of rags and bravery, for these will soon wear out of fashion, but money in thy purse will ever be in fashion; and no man is esteemed for gay garments but by fools and women. On the other hand, take heed that thou seek not riches basely, nor attain them by evil means; destroy no man for his wealth nor take any thing from the poor, for the cry and complaint thereof will pierce the heavens. . . .

Serve God; let him be the author of all thy actions; commend all thy endeavors to him. . . . Let my experienced advice and fatherly instructions sink deep into thy heart. So God direct thee in all his ways, and fill thy heart with his grace.

§   §   §

Above all things, be not made an ass to carry the burdens of other men: if any friend desire thee to be his surety, give him a part of what thou hast to spare; if he presses thee further, he is not thy friend at all, for friendship rather chooseth harm to itself than offereth it. If thou be bound for a stranger, thou art a fool; if for a merchant thou puttest thy estate to learn to swim; if for a churchman, he hath no inheritance; if for a lawyer, he will find an invasion by a syllable or a word to abuse thee; if for a poor man, thou must pay it thyself; if for a rich man, he needs not; therefore from suretyship, as from a manslayer or enchanter, bless thyself; for the best profit and return will be this, that if thou force him for whom thou art bound, to pay it himself, he will become thy enemy; if thou use to pay it thyself, thou will be a beggar.[1]

Sir Walter's greatest ventures were unfortunate, for his son as well as for himself. His attempt to establish the first settlement in Virginia

(1545?–1626?) and still less of his origins and family standing, but failed; his implication in a plot to dethrone James I in 1603 in favor of Arabella Stuart brought him thirteen years of imprisonment in the Tower of London, where he filled the long days and nights with writing a history of the world. Released in 1616, he led a venture to the Orinoco River in South America in search of gold, accompanied by his son Walter. Failing to find gold, Raleigh broke the King's peace with the Spaniards by attacking their towns there, and he was heart-broken when in one such raid his son was killed. Raleigh returned empty-handed and disgraced to England, where his old sentence was renewed and new charges made, and ostensibly in reparation to Spain for the violation of the peace agreement, Raleigh was executed.

[1] Sir Walter Raleigh and Others, *Instructions for Youth*, 9, 10, 13, 20, 22, 27, 30, 33, 34, 42.

☞ *Avoid Sloth, Women, and Lewd Fellows*

PURITANISM and resentment of aristocratic vices were always present in the English lower classes, and they had their spokesmen in Elizabethan times. Little is known of the private life of Nicholas Breton his moral professions were more those of the developing middle class than of the nobility. It was natural that a man who wrote not only verse but prose, not only tracts but romanticism, should emulate the contemporary fashion and compose moral admonitions addressed to a son who may never have existed. His letter illustrates bourgeois insistence on paternal authority and the Protestant virtues. To him, women were not the ideal creatures of chivalry but temptresses of the flesh and of the pocketbook; gambling was sinful partly because it was expensive; work, which to an aristocrat was an unbecoming activity, was to him a cardinal virtue as well as a necessity.

[*ca.* 1605]

MY DEAR SONNE,

As nothing can joy the heart of a Father more than the obedience of a loving child, so can there be nothing more grievous than a stubborn spirit of an ungracious Sonne. . . .

I am sorry to tell thee that I hear thy diligence doth not answer my desire. I would gladly have it otherwise, but I hope a kind admonition will suffice to work a good nature, and therefore will rather hope the best than doubt the contrary. And in the love of a father, let me entreat thee to avoid the company of a lewd fellow, as rather an enemy than a friend. The feminine sex are dangerous to affect for as they will be a loss of time, so with hindrance of study they will produce expense. The exercise of thy body I admit for thy health, but let thy love be in thy learning, else thou wilt never be a good Scholar. . . .

And therefore not out of the bitter humour of displeasure but the careful nature of affection, I write unto thee for thine own good, and so praying to God for thee, whom I beseech daily to bless thee with my heart's love, to the Lord's blessing, I leave thee.

Your Loving Father[1]

[1] Nicholas Breton, *A Poast with a Pacquet of madde Letters* (pamphlet).

☞ The Shrewd Decalogue of Elizabeth's Great Statesman

William Cecil (1520–98), Lord Burghley, founded one of the most distinguished families of England, almost unrivaled in its public services from the reign of the first Elizabeth to the reign of the second. Burghley's own origin and experience made him value the practical virtues, and his worldly wisdom reveals so clearly the mores of his time that this letter to his son is presented almost in its entirety. To a society which had but recently discovered the pleasures of moralizing, Burghley's phrases seemed less shopworn than to a reader of the twentieth century.

Robert Cecil (1563–1612) did not ignore his father's precepts and followed in his father's footsteps. He became a secretary of state and a chief minister to the crown, and more than any other man secured the succession of King James in 1603. He was made Earl of Salisbury in 1605 and died in 1612, "worn out with incessant labour," at the age of fifty-two. He had made up in energy and devotion what he lacked of his father's talents. James I called him, fondly, his "little beagle."

[*ca.*1580]

SON ROBERT,

The virtuous inclinations of thy matchless mother, by whose tender and godly care thy infancy was governed, together with thy education under so zealous and excellent a tutor, puts me in rather assurance than hope that thou art not ignorant of that *summum bonum,* which is only able to make thee happy as well in thy death as in thy life: I mean, the true knowledge and worship of thy Creator and Redeemer; without which all other things are vain and miserable. So that thy youth being guided by so sufficient a teacher, I make no doubt, that he will furnish thy life with divine and moral documents. Yet, that I may not cast off the care beseeming a parent towards his child, or that thou shouldst have cause to derive thy whole felicity and welfare from others than from whence thou receivedst thy breath and being, I think it fit and agreeable to the affection I bear thee, to help thee with such rules and advertisements for the squaring of thy life as are rather gained by experience than by much reading. To the end that, entering into this exorbitant age, thou mayest be the better prepared to shun those scandalous courses whereunto the world, and the lack of experience, may easily draw thee. And because I will not confound thy memory, I have reduced them into ten precepts; and, next unto Moses's tables, if thou imprint them in thy mind, thou shalt reap the benefit, and I the content.

And they are these following:—

1. When it shall please God to bring thee to man's estate, use great providence and circumspection in choosing thy wife; for from thence will spring all thy future good or evil. And it is an action of thy life like unto a stratagem of war, wherein a man can err but once. If thy estate be good, match near home and at leisure; if weak, far off and quickly. Enquire diligently of her disposition, and how her parents have been inclined in their youth. Let her not be poor, how generous[1] soever; for a man can buy nothing in the market with gentility. Nor choose a base and uncomely creature altogether for wealth; for it will cause contempt in others and loathing in thee. Neither make choice of a dwarf or a fool, for by the one thou shalt beget a race of

20

pygmies; the other will be thy continual disgrace; and it will yrike[2] thee to hear her talk. For thou shalt find it to thy grief, that there is nothing more fulsome than a she-fool.

And touching the guiding of thy house, let thy hospitality be moderate, and according to the means of thy estate, rather plentiful than sparing, but not costly; for I never knew any man grow poor by keeping an orderly table. . . . But banish swinish drunkards out of thine house, which is a vice impairing health, consuming much, and makes no show. . . . Beware thou spend not above three of four parts of thy revenues, nor above a third part of that in thy house; for the other two parts will do no more than defray thy extraordinaries, which always surmount the ordinary by much: otherwise thou shalt live, like a rich beggar, in continual want. . . . And that gentleman who sells an acre of land sells an ounce of credit; for gentility is nothing else than ancient riches. So that if the foundation shall at any time sink, the building must needs follow. So much for the first precept.

2. Bring thy children up in learning and obedience, yet without outward austerity. Praise them openly, reprehend them secretly. Give them good countenance, and convenient maintenance, according to thy ability; otherwise thy life will seem their bondage, and what portion thou shalt leave them at thy death they will thank death for it, and not thee. And I am persuaded that the foolish cockering[3] of some parents, and the over-stern carriage of others, causeth more men and women to take ill courses than their own vicious inclinations. Marry thy daughters in time, lest they marry themselves. And suffer not thy sons to pass the Alps; for they shall learn nothing there but pride, blasphemy, and atheism. And if by travel they get a few broken languages, that shall profit them nothing more than to have one meat served in divers dishes. Neither, by my consent, shalt thou train them up in wars; for he that sets up . . . to live by that profession can hardly be an honest man or a good Christian. Besides, it is a science no longer in request than use. For soldiers in peace are like chimneys in summer.

3. Live not in the country without corn and cattle about thee: for

21

he that putteth his hand to the purse for every expense of household, is like him that keepeth water in a sieve. And what provision thou shalt want, learn to buy it at the best hand: for there is one penny saved in four betwixt buying in thy need, and when the markets and seasons serve fittest for it. Be not served with kinsmen, or friends; or men intreated to stay; for they expect much and do little; nor with such as are amorous, for their heads are intoxicated. And keep rather too few, than one too many. Feed them well, and pay them with the most; and then thou mayest boldly require service at their hands.

4. Let thy kindred and allies be welcome to thy house and table. Grace them with thy countenance, and further them in all honest actions; for, by this means, thou shalt so double the bond of nature, as thou shalt find them so many advocates to plead an apology for thee behind thy back. But shake off those glow-worms, I mean parasites and sycophants, who will feed and fawn upon thee in the summer of prosperity; but, in an adverse storm, they will shelter thee no more than an arbour in winter.

5. Beware of suretyship for thy best friends. He that payeth another man's debt seeketh his own decay. But if thou canst not otherwise choose, rather lend thy money thyself upon good bonds, although thou borrow it. So shalt thou secure thyself and pleasure thy friend. Neither borrow money of a neighbor or a friend, but of a stranger; where, paying for it, thou shalt hear no more of it. Otherwise thou shalt eclipse thy credit, lose thy freedom, and yet pay as dear as to another. But in borrowing of money be precious of thy word; for he that hath care of keeping days of payment is lord of another man's purse.

6. Undertake no suit against a poor man without receiving[4] much wrong; for, besides that thou makest him thy compeer, it is a base conquest to triumph where there is small resistance. Neither attempt law against any man before thou be fully resolved thou hast right on thy side; and then spare not for either money or pains; for a cause or two so followed and obtained will free thee from suits a great part of thy life.

7. Be sure to keep some great man thy friend, but trouble him

not for trifles. Compliment him often with many, yet small gifts, and of little charge. And if thou hast cause to bestow any great gratuity, let it be something which may be daily in sight: otherwise, in this ambitious age, thou shalt remain like a hop without a pole, live in obscurity, and be made a football for every insulting companion to spurn at.

8. Toward thy superiors be humble, yet generous. With thine equals, familiar, yet respective. Towards thine inferiors show much humanity, and some familiarity: as to bow the body, stretch forth the hand, and to uncover the head; with such like popular compliments. The first prepares thy way to advancement,—the second makes thee known for a man well bred,—the third gains a good report; which, once got, is easily kept. For right humanity takes deep root in the multitude, as they are more easily gained by unprofitable courtesies than by churlish benefits. Yet I advise thee not to affect, or neglect, popularity too much. Seek not to be an Essex: shun to be a Raleigh.

9. Trust not any man with thy life, credit, or estate. For it were folly for a man to enthral himself to his friend, as though, occasion being offered, he should not dare to become an enemy.

10. Be not scurrilous in conversation, nor satirical in thy jests. The one will make thee unwelcome to all company; the other pull on quarrels, and get the hatred of thy best friends. For suspicious jests, when any of them savor of truth, leave a bitterness in the minds of those who are touched. And, albeit I have already pointed at this inclusively, yet I think it necessary to leave it to thee as a special caution; because I have seen many so prone to quip and gird, as they would rather lose their friend than their jest. And if perchance their boiling brain yield a quaint scoff, they will travail to be delivered of it, as a woman with child. These nimble fancies are but the froth of wit....[5]

[1] Well born.

[2] Irk.

[3] Overindulgence.

[4] Unless you have received.

[5] Montgomery, *The Christian Correspondent,* III, 153.

☞ *How a Scot Should Rule over Englishmen*

WHEN King James VI of Scotland (1566–1625), after years of shrewd maneuvering, left his country to become King James I of England on April 4, 1603, he sent a farewell letter to his eldest son, Prince Henry Frederick (1594–1612), nine years old, left at Stirling castle with his Danish mother.

My son, that I see you not before my parting impute it to this great occasion wherein time is so precious; but that shall by God's grace shortly be recompensed by your coming to me shortly, and continued residence with me ever after. Let not this news make you proud or insolent, for a King's son and heir was ye before, and no more are ye yet. The augmentation that is hereby like to fall upon you is but in cares and heavy burdens. Be therefore merry but not insolent; keep a greatness but *sine fastu;* be resolute but not willful; keep your kindness but in honorable sort; choose none to be your playfellows but them that are well born; and above all things give never good countenance to any but according as ye shall be informed that they are in estimation with me. Look upon all Englishmen that shall come to visit you as your loving subjects, not with that ceremony as towards strangers, and yet with such heartliness as at this time they deserve. This gentleman whom this bearer accompanies is worthy, and of good rank and now my familiar servitor; use him therefore in a manner homely loving sort nor otherwise. I send you herewith my book lately printed: study and profit in it as ye would deserve my blessing; and as there can nothing happen to you whereof you will not find the general ground therein, if not the very particular point touched, so ye may level every man's opinions or advices unto you as ye find them agree or discord with the rules there set down, allowing and following their advices that agrees with the same, mistrusting and frowning upon them that advises you to the contrary. Be diligent and earnest in your studies, that at your meeting with me I may praise you for your progress in learning. Be obedient to your master, for your own weal, and to procure my thanks; for in reverencing him ye obey me and honour yourself. Farewell.

Your loving Father,
JAMES R.[1]

Prince Henry, who shortly became Prince of Wales, followed his father southward to Windsor Castle on June 30. In the English court his honesty and courage made him more popular than his father, to whom he was decorous and dutiful, but he became a plaything of the politicians in the struggle between the Church of England and the Church of Rome. He died at eighteen in 1612, some thought from poison possibly administered by a jealous father, but such a theory has no grounds. His illness was almost certainly typhoid fever.

[1] Sir Henry Ellis (ed.), *Original Letters Illustrative of English History*, III, 78–79; Scoones, *Four Centuries of English Letters*, 44.

☞ *All Is Lost Save Honor*

EVEN in the close-knit Verney family, whose letters present one of the most authentic pictures of seventeenth-century life, politics could breed differences between father and son. Sir Edmund Verney (1590–1642), Knight Marshal and standard-bearer to King Charles I, ardent Protestant, and member of Parliament from 1624 until the Civil War, had a mind "accomplished in all active, useful and manly knowledge." His son, Sir Ralph Verney (1613–96), was equally able but more methodical and studious. He, too, was a member of both the Short Parliament and the Long Parliament. In 1639, before the struggle had reached the breaking point, Sir Edmund left his beloved family and acres and joined Charles I in his badly organized and badly led march on Scotland to subdue the Presbyterians who had refused to accept his new church ordinances. Charles soon found the Scots as stubborn as himself and far better prepared to fight. On that march Sir Edmund wrote to Sir Ralph:

[HEADQUARTERS OF CHARLES I AT YORK, April 1, 1639]
GOOD RAPHE,—

Since prince Henry's death I never knew soe much greefe as to part from you; and trewly because I saw you equally afflicted with it, my sorrow was the greater. It cannot bee longe ere by cource of nature wee must bee severd, and if that time bee prevented by accident, yet wee must resolve to beare it with that patience and courage as becomes men and cristians; and soe the great God of heaven send uss well to meete again, eyther in this woarld or in the next.

25

The King has been basly betrayd. All the party that hee hoped uppon all this while has basly left him. As wee are this day informed, the two cassels of Edenbrough and Dunbarton are yeelded upp without one blowe, and yett they were boath provided soe well as they were impregnable soe long as they had vittle, which they wanted not.

Dalkeeth, a place of great strength, wher the crowne and septer lay, is yeelded to, and the covenanters has taken awaye the crowne and septer, and a greate deale of armes and munition to; yett my lor tresorer of Scotland undertook to the king to keepe all that safe; and all thes are given upp without one blowe. . . . the king has been basly betrayde by them, and that wee shall all smart for. Say little of this to the woemen, least it fright them. You [shall] shortly heare from me againe. I heare noething of my armes

Your loving father,
Ed. Verney[1]

Yorke, this Monday

   3 of the clock after noone

     I praye putt your mother in meind to send mee thos papers of powder I gave her to keepe for mee, for they are excellent to prevente the gowte. As I came heather I was in soe much hope of a peace that I bought a fine hunting nagg by the waye. I would I had my monny in my purce again. . . .[2]

     A little later, Sir Ralph took the side of Parliament in opposition to his father, who with a heavy heart joined the King. At the Battle of Edgehill (1642), Sir Edmund was captured with the King's standard still in his hands. His captors offered him his life if he would yield up the standard. "My life is my own but the standard is the King's," he replied and fought until killed. It was said that he disposed of "sixteen gentlemen that day by his sword."

     Sir Ralph soon found that he could not stomach all the actions of Parliament, and in 1643 he went into exile rather than sign the Covenant. Ten years later he risked a return to England and was imprisoned by Cromwell until 1655. After the Restoration he devoted himself largely to his estate and to the ardent defense of his local liberties, and died "loved and honoured by all the country round."

[1] *Letters and Papers of the Verney Family* (ed. by John Bruce), 210–11.
[2] *Ibid.*, 84, 212–13.

☞ *"Never Suffer Thought of Revenge to Enter Your Heart"*

OF all the tragic noblemen of the English Civil War, none was more nobly tragic than Thomas Wentworth (1593–1641), first Earl of Strafford, victim of Parliament's excessive rancor and Charles I's weakness. Wentworth had served his king and his king's policy ably, courageously, and loyally as lord lieutenant of Ireland and as Charles' most outspoken adviser. He was too strong and too stubborn a man for Parliament to leave in power if Parliament were to have its way. When it accused him and put him on trial, Charles I, still king, promised him he should not suffer for his loyalty and conduct; when Parliament sentenced Strafford to death, Charles bewailed the act but made no firm effort to save him. The night before his execution Strafford wrote a letter to his only son, William, then fifteen.

TOWER [OF LONDON] this 11th May, 1641

MY DEAREST WILL,

These are the last lines that you are to receive from a father that tenderly loves you. I wish there were a greater leisure to impart my mind unto you; but our merciful God will supply all things by his his grace, and guide and protect you in all your ways. To whose infinite goodness I bequeath you; and therefore be not discouraged, but serve him and trust in him, and he will preserve and prosper you in all things.

Be sure you give all respect to my Wife, that hath ever had a great love unto you, and therefore will be well becoming you. Never be awanting in your love and care to your sisters, but let them ever be most dear unto you; for this will give others cause to esteem and respect you for it, and is a duty that you owe them in the memory of your excellent Mother and myself. Therefore your care and affection to them must be the very same that you would have of yourself, and the like regard must you have to your youngest sister, for indeed you owe it to her also, both for her Father's and Mother's sake.

Sweet Will, be careful to take the advice of those friends which are by me desired to advise you for your education. Serve God diligently morning and evening and recommend yourself unto him and have him before your eyes in all your ways. With patience hear the instructions of those friends I leave with you, and diligently follow their counsel: For 'till you come by time to have experience in the world, it will be far more safe to trust to their judgments than your own.

Lose not the time of your youth but gather those seeds of virtue and knowledge which may be of use to yourself and comfort to your friends for the rest of your life. And that this may be the better effected, attend thereunto with patience, and be sure to correct and restrain yourself from anger. Suffer not sorrow to cast you down, but with cheerfulness and good courage go on the race you have to run in all sobriety and truth. Be sure with an hallowed care to have respect to all the commandments of God, and give not yourself to neglect them in the least things, lest by degrees you come to forget them in the greatest. For the heart of man is deceitful above all things. And in all your duties and devotions towards God, rather perform them joyfully than pensively, for God loves a cheerful giver. For your religion, let it be directed according to that which you shall be taught by those which are in God's church the proper teachers therefor, rather than that you ever either fancy one to yourself or be led by men that are singular in their own opinions, and delight to go ways of their own finding out: for you will certainly find soberness and truth in the one, and much unsteadiness and vanity in the other.

The King I trust will deal graciously with you; restore you those honours and that fortune which a distempered time hath deprived you of together with the life of your Father: Which I rather advise might be by a new gift and creation from himself rather than by any other means, to the end you may pay the thanks to him without having obligation to any other.

Be sure to avoid as much as you can to enquire after those that have been sharp in their judgments towards me, and I charge you never to suffer thought of revenge to enter your heart; but be careful to be informed who were my friends in this prosecution, and to them apply yourself to make them your friends also; and on such you may rely, and bestow much of your conversation amongst them.

And God Almighty of his infinite goodness bless you and your

28

children's children; and his same goodness bless your sisters in like manner, perfect you in every good work, and give you right understanding in all things. *Amen.*

Your most loving Father,
T. WENTWORTH.

[*Postscript*] You must not fail to behave yourself towards my Lady Clare your Grandmother with all duty and observance; for most tenderly doth she love you, and hath been passing kind unto me. God reward her charity for it. And both in this and all the rest, the same that I counsel you, the same do I direct also to your sisters, that so the same may be observed by all. And once more do I, from my very soul, beseech our gracious God to bless and govern you in all, to the saving you in the day of his Visitation, and join us again in the communion of his blessed Saints, where is fullness of joy and bliss for ever more. *Amen. Amen.*[1]

> After Strafford's death, Charles I attempted restitution by restoring to William Wentworth (1626–95) the honors and estates that Parliament had taken from his father (December 1, 1641). But after the defeat of the King and his death, William was in danger of his own life until Charles II came to the throne, when he became again accepted as the second Earl of Strafford.

[1] Thomas Wentworth, first Earl of Strafford, "Letter to His Sonne," *Letters and Dispatches of the Earl of Strafford* (Somers Tracts, Quarto IV), 248–49.

☞ *"Forgive Those Who Have Deprived Me of All"*

THE execution of Strafford, whom Charles I (1600–49) had promised to save from punishment, was a warning to the King that Parliament might go to any lengths to assert its ultimate sovereignty. Charles ignored the warning or, as a matter of principle, was determined to maintain his prerogatives or die in the attempt. He fought far more stubbornly and gallantly in his own behalf than he had fought for Strafford, but was captured eight years later and sentenced to death. He devoted many of his last days to the composition of an essay on royal conduct in the form of last messages to his son Charles (1630–85), then eighteen, who had escaped with his mother the Queen to France. Young Charles regained the the crown in 1660. The *Eikon Basilikon* of Charles I, published soon after it was written, included these advices to his son:

. . . It is some kind of deceiving and lessening the injury of my long restraint when I find my leisure and solitude have produced something worthy of myself and useful to you . . . whom I have most cause to love, as well as myself, and of whose unmerited sufferings I have a greater sense than of mine own. . . .

I had rather you should be *Charles le Beau* than *le Grand*, good than great. I hope God hath designed you to be both. . . . With God I could have you begin and end. . . . the best government and highest sovereignty you can attain is to be subject to him, that the sceptre of his word and spirit may rule in your heart. . . . Above all I would have you, as I hope you are already, well-grounded and settled in your religion: the best profession of which I have ever esteemed that of the church of England in which you have been educated; yet I would have your own judgment and reason now seal to that sacred bond which education hath written, that it may be judiciously your own religion and not other men's custom or tradition, which you profess. . . .

When you have done justice to God . . . the next main hinge on which your prosperity will depend and move is that of civil justice, wherein the settled laws of these kingdoms, to which you are rightly heir, are the most excellent rules you can govern by, which by an admirable temperament give very much to subjects' industry, liberty and happiness, and yet reserve enough to the majesty and prerogative of any King who owns his people as subjects, not as slaves. . . . Your prerogative is best shewed and exercised in remitting, rather than exacting, the rigor of the laws then being nothing worse than legal tyranny.

In these two points, the preservation of established religion and laws, I may without vanity turn the reproach of my sufferings, as to the world's censure, into the honour of a kind of martyrdom, as to the testimony of my own conscience: the troublers of my kingdoms having nothing else to object against me but this: that I prefer religion and laws established before those alterations they propounded ... I have offered all for reformation and safety that in reason, honour and conscience I can, reserving only what I cannot consent unto without an irreparable injury to my own soul, the church, and my people, and to you also as the next and undoubted heir of my kingdom.

To which if the divine Providence, to whom no difficulties are insuperable, shall in his due time after my decease bring you, as I hope he will, my counsel and charge to you is: that you seriously consider the former, real or objected miscarriages which might occasion my troubles, that you may avoid them.

Never repose so much upon any man's single counsel, fidelity and discretion ... as to create in yourself or others a diffidence of your own judgments. ... Next, beware of exasperating any factions by the crossness and asperity of some men's passions, humours or private opinions, employed by you, grounded only upon the differences in lesser matters which are but the skirts and suburbs of religion. ...

It is all I now have left me, a power to forgive those who have deprived me of all, and I thank God I have heart to do it, and joy as much in this grace which God hath given me as in all my former enjoyments. ... the nobleness of your mind must raise you above the meditating any revenge or executing your anger upon the many. ... You will have more inward complacency in pardoning one than in punishing a thousand. ...

Thus I write to you, not despairing of God's mercy and my subjects' affections toward you, both which I hope you will study to deserve ... but if you never see my face again ... I do require and entreat you as your Father and your King that you never suffer your heart to receive the least check against or disaffection from the true religion established in the Church of England. ...

Farewell, till we meet, if not on earth, yet in Heaven.[1]

[1] *Eikon Basilikon: The Portraiture of His Sacred Majesty in Solitude and Suffering*, I.

☞ *A Condemned Cavalier's Farewell*

JAMES STANLEY (1607–51), seventh Earl of Derby, fought for Charles I against the forces of Parliament with more ardor than success. He, too, was sentenced to death, although his appeal was supported by Cromwell himself. He made an almost miraculous escape from the Tower of London, but was recaptured. Shortly before his execution on October 15, 1651, he wrote this letter to his children, who had escaped with their mother to his own possession, the Isle of Man. This "man of great honour and clear courage" was succeeded by his eldest son, Charles Stanley (1628–72), eighth Earl of Derby and probably the "Mall" and "Maleky" of the letter.

[1651]

MY DEAR MALL, MY NED, MY BILLY,—

I remember well how sad you were to part with me when I left the Isle for England, but now I fear you will be more sad to know that you can never see me more in this world. But I charge you all to strive against too great a sorrow; you are all of you of that temper that it would do you harm; and my desires and prayers to God are, that you may have a happy life; let it be as holy a life as you can, and as little sinful.

I can well now give that counsel, having in myself at this time so great a sense of the vanities of my life, which clodds my soul with sorrow; yet I rejoice to remember when I have sometimes blessed God with a pious devotion; and it is my chief and only delight, and must be my eternal happiness.

Love still the Archdeacon: he will give you good precepts: obey your mother with cheerfulness, for you have great reason so to do, for, besides that of mother, she is your example, your nurse, your councellor, your phisitian, your all under God; there was never, nor ever can be a more deserving person. The Lord my God bless you and guard you etc. So prays your father, that sorrows most at this time to part with Maleky, Neddy and Billy. Remember

J. DERBY[1]

---

[1] James Stanley, seventh Earl of Derby, *Private Devotions and Miscellanies of the Seventh Earl of Derby*, III, 3.

The Duke of Bedford to Francis Russell

☞ *"Lay Yourself Open to Yourself"*

FEW noblemen of the seventeenth century looked inward very deeply to understand their own motives and emotions, but the advice of William Russell (1613–1700), fifth Earl and first Duke of Bedford, to his son Francis might have come from an exponent of modern psychology. Perhaps in his later years the Duke put a premium on self-understanding because he had wavered so dramatically in his own political loyalties. In 1641 he broke with Charles I and became a general of horse in the army of Parliament. In 1643 he changed sides and supported Charles. The following year he returned his loyalty to Parliament, and after the restoration of the Stuarts in 1660, he managed to retain his title and his property until he died in 1700 at the age of eighty-seven. Francis, to whom he addressed this letter, died before him, and the Bedford dukedom passed to a grandson who was little troubled by intellectual uncertainties.

[*ca.*1654]

DEAR FRANK:

Ignorance and vice are the usual effects of an unlearned and undisciplined education. Of my passionate desire to free you from both these, I suppose I have given you and the world sufficient testimony, since I own, I have satisfied myself. You may guess how violent my longings are to advance your piety and understanding; that is, to render you a perfect man; in that death is only displeasing when I think of dying before I see my desire accomplished, or at least so far as my hopes may be greater than my fears. . . .

The most profitable and necessary in the world is to know and study thyself; wherefore, with all the plainness, sincerity and observation you can make in the best temper of mind and body, lay yourself open to yourself; take an impartial survey of all your abilities and weaknesses, and spare not to expose them to your eye by writing, which I conceive is the best done by framing your own character, and so to draw the picture of your mind, which I recommend to your yearly practice during your life. . . .

When you have found both your forces and infirmities, then look with one eye upon them, and with the other on the realms you live in, where by comparing yourself with the general state of affairs, you

33

shall soon discern whether there may be a corresponding and compliance between you and them; that you may thereupon either draw yourself within your private walls to enjoy the happiness of a holy, quiet and innocent repose, in case the times are rough and dangerous to sail in; or else, if calm and suitable to engage yourself in some public employment, for the service of your country and advancement of your family.

Though if I may guess at the future constitution of your mind by what I observe at present, were the times never so calm and inviting, you should not be easily enticed to embark yourself into the world or engage in busy and great employments. Your best course, in my judgment, Frank, were to say your prayers at home, manage your little affairs innocently and discreetly, and enjoy with thankfulness what God has bestowed upon me.

But it may so happen that your inclinations may be active and your parts correspondent, and that good fortune may find you out in your privacy and court you to employment. If she does, refuse her not, but embrace her with these cautions: first, be sure to ballast yourself well by calling in to your aid all the advantages of learning, art and experience: then consider to fit your sails to the bulk of your vessel. lest you prove a slug, or overset. And because commonwealths have their shelves and rocks, therefore get the skill of coasting and shifting your sails: I mean, to arrive at your journey's end by compassing and an honest compliance. Yet, if honesty be the star you sail by, doubt not of a good voyage, at least be sure of a good harbour.[1]

[1] John Russell, Earl of Bedford, *Life of Lord William Russell*, II, 213.

☞ *"Marriage Is a Clog Fastened to the Neck of Liberty"*

FRANCIS OSBORNE, a minor court official, published shortly before 1658 a treatise called *Advice to a Son*. It was another example of the current fashion of turning parental advice into a literary production, and it also smacks of the puritan attitudes fashionable under the Commonwealth. It was said by Pepys to be one of the three books most

34

read in England, and James Boswell much later told Samuel Johnson that Osborne was his favorite author. Dr. Johnson replied, "Were a man to write so now, the boys would throw stones at him." Osborne's chapter on marriage led the vice-chancellor to ban its sale in Oxford, but his threat to have the book burned was not fulfilled, and the treatise continued to sell widely.

[1656]

. . . Marriage, like a trap set for flies, may possibly be ointed at entrance with a little voluptuousness, under which is contained a draught of deadly wine, more pricking and tedious than the passions it pretends to cure, leaving the patient in little quieter condition in the morning than him that hath overnight killed a man to gratify his revenge.

Eve, by stumbling at the serpent's solicitations, cast her husband out of Paradise; nor are her daughters surer of foot, being foundered by the heat of lust and pride, and unable to bear the weight of so much of our reputation as religion and custom hath loaded them withal, that an unbalasted behaviour, without other leakage, is sufficient to cast away an husband's esteem.

Marriage . . . often comes so far short of [expectation] as to satisfy none, but rather aggravates the sins of solitude, making simple fornication to sprout into adultery. . . .

If none of my persuasions, nor others' woeful experience daily met with in the world, can deter you from yoking yourself to another's desires, make not a *Celebrated Beauty* the object of your choice, unless you are ambitious of rendering your house as populous as a confectioner's shop; to which the gaudy wasps, no less than the liquorish flies, make it their business to resort in the hope of obtaining a lick at your honey pot. . . . Neither can you, according to the loose custom of England, decently restrain her from this concourse without making demonstration of jealousy towards her (by which you confess yourself a cuckold in your own imagination already) or incivility to such as come to visit you. . . .

Marriage is a clog fastened to the neck of liberty by the juggling hand of policy, that provides only for the general necessities of all in gross, not for the particular conveniences of single persons, who by

35

this give stronger security to the commonwealth than sets with prudence or liberty. . . . therefore some take more content in sharing a mistress with others than they can find in the sole fruition of a wife: the reason is: strangers are taken for dainties, wives as physick. . . . Other courses weary us with change; this with continuance.[1]

[1] Francis Osborne, *Advice to a Son* (pamphlet).

☞ *"Be Not Fearful, but Adventure to Speak What You Can"*

WHEN the distinguished physician and author of *Religio Medici*, Sir Thomas Browne (1605–82), sent his son to France at the age of fourteen to gain a wider knowledge of the world, the boy was shy and uncertain of himself. For several years his father's letters encouraged him to "take up commendable boldness."

March the 10, style vetere

. . . write whether you like the place and how language goes down with you; be not fearful but adventure to speak what you can, for you are known a stranger and they will bear with you . . . let nothing discontent or disturb you; by this time you may attempt to hear the Protestant Preachers; live soberly and temperately . . . and keep within in the heat of the day.[1]

To the son at Cambridge, some three years later:

July, 1663

Honest Tom, be of good heart and follow thy business. I doubt not but thou wilt do well. God hath given thee parts to enable thee. If you practice to write you will have a good pen and style. It were not amiss to take the draught of the college or part thereof if you have time, but however omit no opportunity in your study. You shall not want while I have it,

Your loving father,
THO. BROWNE[2]

36

But after another four years, when Tom had taken to the sea with the Royal Navy, there was no further need to urge him to boldness, for Tom wrote to his father of the merits of blowing up the ship and its officers with it rather than surrendering it to the enemy. Sir Thomas replied:

Feb., 1667

... for though I know you are sober and considerate, yet knowing you also to be of great resolution, and having also heard from ocular testimonies with what undaunted and persevering courage you have demeaned yourself in great difficulties, and knowing your captain to be a stout and resolute man, and withall the cordial freindship [*sic*] that is between you, I cannot omit my earnest prayer unto God to deliver you from such temptation. He that goes to war must patiently submit unto the various accidents thereof. To be made prisoner by an unequal and over ruling power, after a due resistance, is no disparagement. . . . let God, that brought you into the world in his own good time, lead you through it, and in his own season bring you out of it, and without such ways as are displeasing to him.[3]

[1] *Works of Sir Thomas Browne* (ed. by Geoffrey Keynes), VI, 7–8.
[2] *Ibid.*, 19.
[3] *Ibid.*, 23–24.

☞ *An Angry Father Reproves a Prospective One*

THROUGHOUT the seventeenth century, the great families of England were in frequent jeopardy as the political pendulum swung from Stuart kings to Commonwealth, then back to the Stuarts in 1660, and finally to their dismissal in 1688. Sir Thomas Osborne (1632–1712) rose and fell and rose again as the political climate changed. He was lord treasurer of England and the first Earl of Danby under Charles II, but in December, 1668, he was impeached and dismissed on a charge of criminal correspondence with France. As popular resentment against King James II increased, Danby became in 1686 one of the seven lords who invited William of Orange to take the throne and save the nation from Roman Catholic domination. Under William and Mary he became Marquis of Carmarthen and a privy councilor. It was while he was prospering under Charles II that he addressed this letter to his recently married son, Viscount Latimer, "at Rycote or elsewhere."

WALLINGFORD HOUSE, CHRISTMAS DAY ATT NOONE [1676]

SON,

I know not whether to blame your carelessnesse, your ill manners, or your ill nature, but there is such a mixture of them all in staying from your wife till her labour, and att a time when I beleeve you scarse know what else to do with yourselfe, that I am truly ashamed of you for itt, and do most condemne myselfe, who suffer you to do so much you ought not, and so little you should, that I now find I have not educated you to that common civility which scarse anybody wants. I suppose this will bring you to towne, by which time your wife may either be a dead woman, or not beholding to you if shee be not; and women of less kindnesse to an husband than shee has to you does not use to want that satisfaction. Present my humble service to my Lord Norris, where I heare this is most likely to find you.

DANBY.[1]

[1]Andrew Browning, *Thomas Osborne, Earl of Danby and Duke of Leeds*, II, 39.

☞ *The Dangers of Academic Pride*

SOME fathers leave no record in history except through their sons; some sons are remembered only as the victims or beneficiaries of parental care. Neither the Reverend R. Lingard nor his son rose to eminence, but *A Letter to a Young Gentleman Leaving the University* found its way into print in 1673. That letter may have been one of those written more with an eye to publication than to the needs of a specific son at Oxford, but its warning against Oxford arrogance probably had sympathetic Cambridge readers.

You have been infinitely advantaged by your education in the University, which will have a perpetual good effect upon you, and give you lustre in the eyes of the world. But that you may be further useful and acceptable to mankind, you must pare off something you have contracted there, and add also to your own stores from observation and experience, a way of learning as far beyond that of precept as the knowledge of a traveller exceeds that which is gotten by the map.

As academick life is an horizon between two worlds; for men enter upon it children, and as such they must judge and act, though with difference according to their own pregnancy, the ingenuity of their teachers and the manner of their being taught; and when they pass from thence they launch into a new world, their passions at high water, are full of themselves as young men are wont to be, and such as are dipped in unusual learning, and if they so go on, they are lost. Besides that there is a husk and shell that grows up with the learning they acquired, which they must throw away, caused perchance by the childishness of their state or the formalities of the place, or the ruggedness of the retirement, the not considering of which hath made many a great scholar unserviceable to the world. . . .

I suppose you to understand the nature of habits and passions; I suppose you likewise what I know you to be, to be advisable, observant, and of a sedate temper: therefore you will be sufficiently instructed with a few intimations. For he that reflects upon himself and considers his passions and accommodates himself to the world cannot need many directions. I suppose you also to be principled with religion and morality, which is to be valued before any learning and is an ease and pleasure to the mind, and always secures a firm reputation, let the world be ever so wicked. No man ever gains reverence for his vice, but virtue commands it. Vicious men indeed have been popular, but never for being so, but for their virtues annexed. . . .

The advices I here lay down are negative rather than positive, for though I cannot direct you where you are to sail throughout your whole course, yet I may safely show you where you must not split yourself. And the first rock I discover, on which young scholars' ships wreck themselves, is vaunting of the persons and places concerned in their education. I therefore advise you to be sparing in your commendation of your university, college, tutor, or the doctor you most there admire, for either all is taken for granted or you only betray your affection and partiality, or you impose your judgment for a standard to others. . . .[1]

[1] R. Lingard, *A Letter of Advice to a Young Gentleman Leaving the University* (pamphlet).

☞ *The Hazards of Conjugal Indulgence*

JOHN EVELYN (1620–1706) was not only a great diarist but secretary of the Royal Society, and his advice to his son, John Evelyn, Jr. (1655–99), represented the informed scientific opinion of the late seventeenth century. On the eve of his son's marriage to Miss Martha Spencer, Evelyn advised him by letter with a frankness seldom imitated in later centuries. The text of the letter as given here has been expurgated. Young John survived only twenty years the dangers of which his father warned him, but that was long enough to become an officer in the Treasury and a commissioner of revenue in Ireland, and to translate books from Greek, Latin, and French, including portions of Plutarch's *Lives*.

[November, 1679]

. . . Take heed of those filthy lusts even with your own wife, nor delight to feed and satisfy your eyes or incite your fancy with nakedness, or unnatural figures & usages of yourselves, for they will breed impudence, loathing and contempt. . . . be none of those who brag how frequently they can be brutes in one night, for that intemperance will exhaust you, & possibly create importunate expectations when your inclinations are not so fierce. Such excesses do oft times dispose to . . . inconveniences through the straining of nature . . . which are sometimes incurable.

. . . It is likewise experimentally found that carnal caresses upon a full stomach, or in the daytime, or in the excessive heat and cold of weather are very pernicious, & too much frequency of embraces dulls the sight, decays the memory, induces the gout, palsies, enervates and renders effeminate the whole body & shortens life.

There should therefore repose succeed upon those wasting exercises, & therefore physicians permit it after the first concoction is made,

40

namely the first sleep; but rarely in the morning, never totally fast-
ing, as indisposing the body the whole day after.

These particulars I only touch, knowing that young married people
will hardly be reasoned into that temperance, & perhaps they are to
be indulged some liberties for a time, especially at first, But it is
profitable to know these things once, and much better to use moder-
ation. . . . I do not by these abridge you therefore any decent satisfaction; a man may eat . . . not only to satisfy hunger, but to cheer
him, & if there were not some gratification of the inferior sense ac-
companying this & other natural action, the world would cease.[1]

[1] *John Evelyn's Letter Book,* Evelyn MSS 39, in the British Museum.

☞ *"So Much Darkness in the Midst of So Much Light"*

LIKE many another impecunious country churchman, the
Reverend Philip Henry, rector of Broad Oaks, Shropshire, made sacrifices to advance his son's career beyond his own. Young Matthew
Henry had been put through the university and then financed onward
toward a legal career in London. His father could face more equably
the serious financial problems raised by the loss of the son's clothing in a
fire in his London lodgings than his alarm at the risks and temptations
the young man would face in the sinful metropolis. How could it be
otherwise when even in a Shropshire village, sex, superstition, and
papacy reared their ugly heads! All the worthy rector could do was
to warn and pray for a son exposed to even greater dangers.

Feb. 4, 1686/7

SON MAT,

We received the tidings this morning of God's goodness to you
in your journey, for which we desire to be thankful; also a further
account of the late Fire & your loss therein and do bless God it was
no worse. If your gown had been burnt it might have been looked on
as a *tacit supersedas* to your further progress in those studies, but 'tis
well it was not, however every Providence hath a voice and says something. . . .

Your tenant Pa . . . r's eldest son is scandalized by his mother's maid, who is with child, which almost breaks his mother's heart; he is little more than 17 years old. . . .

Your sister Elinor continues to gain ground, God be thanked, of her distemper; Ann walked afoot to Malpas to the burial of Widow Brinley & back again; when she was dying she asked was the money & the candle ready, the one whereof was put in the one hand and the other lighted in the other, at the time of her departure; they also sprinkled her & her bed & room with their holy water & fell a-sweeping of the room with besoms, as hard as they could, to sweep all her sins away. Oh, that ever there should be so much darkness in the midst of so much light! . . .

The Whitchurch curate took occasion on Monday last in his sermon to reflect upon the worthy Mr. Baxter by name. One of our greatest clergy-men lately being reproved for associating himself so much with Papists answered, To inquire what religion a man is of is as rude as to ask him what money he has in his pocket. . . .

We both send you our dear love & Blessing, making mention of you in daily Prayer, that you may be serious and sincere, humble and fruitful. Amen![1]

[1] Rev. Philip Henry, unpublished letter, Bodleian Library, English Letters, e29, fol. 30.

☞ *"Serve God in Your Station"— but Marry Well*

UNTIL the last century, local parsons of the Church of England received such small stipends (often only fifty pounds a year) that they were usually dependent upon the more affluent members of society to help them maintain the modest living standard expected of their station. It is not surprising that country churchmen were careful not to offend the local lord or squire and made spiritual compromises to gain some less meager living. To many a young vicar or curate, the only solution was to marry a wife with a good dowry. One such country rector was the Reverend Lewis Atterbury, rector at Milton in Buck-inghamshire. He had made serious sacrifices to send his son, Francis Atterbury (1662-1732), to Oxford, and the young man had done well there and secured a tutorship at Christ Church College. He, too, planned to take orders, but became more and more dissatisfied that his ambitions were not more quickly realized. There was also the question of money: was he also to spend a life restricted and embittered by the near poverty of his father and so many other guardians of the faith? To his complaint that at Oxford he was "weaved with this nauseous circle of small affairs," his father replied:

Nov. 1, 1690

I know not what to think for your uneasiness. It shows unlike a Christian, and savors neither of temper nor consideration. I am troubled to remember it is habitual. You used to say "When you had your degrees, you should be able to swim without bladders." You seemed to rejoice at your being Moderator, and of your *quantum* and sub-lecturer; but neither of these pleased you, nor was you willing to take those pupils the house afforded you, when Master, nor doth your lectures please, or noblemen satisfy you. But you make yourself and your friends uneasy—cannot trust Providence.

Do your duty and serve God in your station, until you are called to somewhat better. Man's ways are not in himself, nor can all your projecting change the colour of one of your hairs, which are num-bered; and a sparrow falls not to the ground without a divine over-sight. What may we think of our stations? You need not doubt but I could *wish* you all the great things you are capable of, but I can neither secure them to you nor to myself, but must leave all to time and providence.

I am not wanting in pains and prospect, and deny myself more in toiling than you ever did or will do; and all, I see, to little purpose, when it is of no better effect with you. . . .

There is no way for preferment like marrying into some family of interest, either Bishop or Archbishops, or some courtier, which may be done with accomplishments, and a portion to; but I may write what I will, you consider little, and disquiet yourself much . . . that

43

God would direct you and reason with you this fear is the earnest prayer of your loving father,

LEWIS ATTERBURY[1]

Francis became Bishop of Rochester and won dubious prominence as a supporter of the Stuart cause. He was imprisoned in 1720 for alleged participation in a plot to restore the Stuarts to the throne, but escaped to France and there threw in his lot openly with the Jacobites and played no further part in the English church or state.

[1] C. T. Williams, *Memoir of Bishop Atterbury*, 140.

☞ *The "Inconvenience" of Having Mistresses*

THE return of the Stuart kings with Charles II in 1660 brought drastic changes in the atmosphere of England. The French manners and morals that Charles and his supporters brought with them temporarily submerged the puritan spirit of the Commonwealth, and were welcomed by many Englishmen who had had enough of austerity and repression. But when James II (1632–1701) succeeded his brother in 1685, widespread fear that he would bring back Roman Catholicism resulted in his fall, in the Glorious Revolution, and the rule of William of Orange and his Stuart but Protestant wife, Mary. The deposed James hoped for the restoration of himself or his family and in 1692 wrote to his son, Prince James Francis Edward, a "final legacy" of advice.

In the first place serve God in all things as becomes a good Christian and a Zeleous Catholick of the Church of Rome, which is the only true Catholick and Apostolic Church, and let no human consideration of any kind prevail with you to depart from her. . . .

If it please God to restore me (which I trust in his goodness he will do) I may then hope to settle all things as may make it easier for you to govern all my Dominions with safety to the Monarchy, and the satisfaction of all the Subjects. . . . preserve your prerogative, but disturb not the Subjects in their property, nor conscience. . . . Be very careful that none under you oppress the people or torment them with vexations. . . . Live in peace and quiet with your neighbors, and know that Kings and Princes may be as great robbers as theeves and pirates . . . and be not carried away by Ambition . . . to enlarge your territorys by unjust acquisitions, be content with what is your own. . . .

Nothing has been more fatal to men and to great men, than the letting themselves go to the forbidden love of Women, of all the Vices it is most bewitching and harder to be mastered if it be not crushed in the very bud. . . . none ought to be more on their guard than you, since it has pleased God to lett you be borne what you are. . . . I must owne with shame and confusion, I let myself go too much to the love of Women, and my not being enough on my guard at the first attaques of so dangerous an enemy, and not avoiding, as one ought, the occasions which offer themselves every day, and relying too much on my own strength, having a better opinion of myself than I ought to have had. I have paid dear for it, and would have you avoyd those faults I have run into. . . .

What you ought to arm yourself most against, are the sins of the flesh. . . . when at a club of the mutinous and antimonarchial Lords and Commons, it was proposed by some to fall upon the [King's] mistresses, the Lord Mordaunt the father said, By no means, let us rather erect Statues for them, for were it not for them the King would not run into debt, and then would have no need for us. . . . had not the King your Uncle[1] had that weakness which crept in him insensibly and by degrees, he had been in all appearance a great and happy King, and had done great things for the glory of God and the good of his Subjects; for he had courage, judgment, witt, and all qualities fitt for a King. . . . I speak but too knowingly in these matters, having had the misfortune to have been led away and blinded by such unlawful pleasures. . . .

There is another great inconvenience . . . which attends Kings and great men having of Mistresses, which is the Children they have by those fair Ladys, who will never be at quiet till they are owned, have great titles given to them, which consequently require great establishments, and this is prest on by their relations, friends and most commonly even by flattering Ministers who are at the head of affairs. . . .

In the next place study the Trade of the Nation, and encourage it

45

by all lawfull means, tis that which will make you at ease at home and considerable abroad, and preserve the Mastery of the Sea, for without that England cannot be safe. . . .[2]

Edward, who later was known as the Old Pretender, continued the family efforts to regain the throne of England and landed in Scotland with ardent support from most Highlanders and some cautious assistance from France. But he was defeated and driven from Scotland, spent the rest of his life in futile intrigues and declining popularity in France, and died in 1766.

[1] Charles II.
[2] J. S. Clarke, *Life of James II*, II, 619ff.

☞ *Wormwood for the Stomach—*
Chocolate for the Spirits

IN the time of Queen Anne, medical care was still a mixture of quackery, superstition, old wives' tales, and ignorance only irregularly tempered by common sense and blossoming scientific knowledge. Even a leader of medical progress like Dr. William Harris, friend of great scholars, could prescribe curious remedies, as this letter to his son Edward Harris, Fellow of New College, Oxford, reveals.

Carriage is paid
LONDON, NOV. 27, 1707

DEARE NED,

I herewith send you six printed copies of my Oration, which I said, as once before, without once looking into my book, being willing to do my duty as I ought to give an example which I never saw followed or even attempted by any other since I have been of the College, about 29 years. And if you should be more tired with reading it than I was with speaking it, I have sent you 3 pounds of the best chocolate I think I ever made, being the best Nutts I have seen, at a time of scarcity of good Nutts, & with double refined sugar, which I hope may refresh your spirits after too long reading.

I would also in time send down your Cribb with empty bottles, but the strong we keep, the pale is almost gone. We often drink your health in it. I have got something of my Arrears, to help out this dull time of business, money being scarce, very scarce with the generality. You are the happy men, free from cares.

Have a can of strong beer, and put 2 handfulls of the tops of common wormwood dried, into a quart of rectified spirit, or, if you will, into a pint of it in a quart bottle. Let it lie a week in a cold infusion & then straine it off. And of this tincture you may often take 20 drops, or more, in a draught of water, to strengthen your stomach, when you find it in any way weake, especially considering your forebearance of strong liquors.

May you be able to write better Latin & better thoughts than

Yr. ever Loving Father,
W. HARRIS

[*Postscript*] I buy here rectified spirit at 6 sh. the gallon. If you put a little of it into a glass of fair water you'll taste or distinguish good from bad.

I send this parcel mentioned tomorrow by the coach at our Black Swan who goes to the King's Head, I think. Call for it, or send for it.[1]

[1] Dr. William Harris, unpublished letter, Bodleian Library, Rawlinson MSS, Letters, c.56, fol. 2.

☞ *The Trials of Building a Family Empire*

BY 1715, John Hervey (1665–1751) had by ability and shrewd adaptation to political winds become "the amiable first Earl of Bristol." His ambition to establish a noble family dynasty was stimulated by his production of twenty children by two wives. Most of those children lacked his own talents and durability, and when he died at the age of eighty-six, "having accumulated great wealth by living altogether in the country and by careful management of his estates," he had outlived all but six of them, and most of the survivors had disappointed him. Two of his sons had been spendthrifts, to him perhaps the worst of all faults, and on more than one occasion the Earl wrote sternly to them. One son, John Hervey of Ickworth, became Lord Privy Seal and left court memoirs invaluable to historians. His eldest son, Carr, Lord Hervey (1691–1723), promised well, and the Earl's letters to him were invariably affectionate, though they sometimes leaped rapidly from sentiment to politics.

[ICKWORTH PARK, NEAR BURY ST. EDMUNDS,] Sept. 17, 1715
TO MY SON CARR:

Your coming into the world this day 24 years was so sensible a pleasure to me that I then vowed never to forgett God's goodness in sending me and my family a son & heir; that you might live to prove both a blessing & ornament nott only to us but your country (too barren in present patriots) was always the predominant wish of my heart; but believe me, the modern scheme for augmenting standing armies and revenues can never produce that security to liberty in the conclusion, which I am sure you have (even now) as much at least at heart as your most affectionate father.[1]

But Carr as the eldest son had a responsibility to strengthen the security, if not the liberty, of his family, and the best way was a good marriage.

DEAR SON:

Altho' the answer you thought fitt to give me when I last spoke to you of marrying might have made any parent less zealously concerned than myself for the prosperity of our family resolve never to renew the mention of it any more, yet since you once told me, if I could find out such a party as would both build Ickworth & recruit again those necessary diminutions of my estate which suitable provisions for eleven younger children must occasion, that you would readily receive any such proposal, it has at last pleased Providence to afford us such an opportunity, there being a gentleman of £7000 per annum, who having an only daughter whom he would gladly dispose of into so honest a family & to a man of your merit and reputation, who offers me almost charte-blanche as to what part of it we would ask at present, & will settle the whole to descend at his death. This seeming to be the crisis of our family's fate, that God of his undeserved goodness to me would inspire you with such right resolutions as may determine you to true happiness, & that to a perpetual plenteous independency, shall be the fervent prayer of your most affectionate father.[2]

48

But Carr did not like the lady, and showed more interest in profit through speculation than through marriage, and the father wrote:

ICKWORTH, June 25, 1720

DEAR SON:

After having rejected so advantageous an opportunity as Providence had thrown into your power of making me, yourself & our family, not only easy, but great and independent for many generations notwithstanding the great number of children that must be provided for out of my estate, I cannot think the matter you desire my advice in can prove of much signification either; yet since you have thought fit to ask me it, I will give you my best thought upon it. In the first place, the value of money is so sinking & consequently that of land so rising, that the most foresighted men in these matters cannot at present guess where the proportion between one and t'other is likely to fix; & until that be known you must deal at random. But besides, what could you do with money now, when nobody knows how to employ any but by investing into Stocks, which are all near trebled above their original intrinsick values, & South Sea even farr exceeds these. . . . All of which considered I think your best way will be to keep as you are at least for the present.[3]

Three years later Carr died unmarried at the age of thirty-two, though there may be some truth to the rumor that he was actually the father of Horace Walpole. But seventeen years later the old Earl, having survived the uncertainties of inflation and the bursting of the South Sea Bubble, was still coping with the welfare of his fourth son, Henry Hervey, who had often troubled him by "reckless and extravagant conduct." Henry had married unwisely (which to his father was worse than not marrying at all), and at the age of thirty-six was still a drain on the family fortune as the impecunious rector of the small parish of Shotley. Henry was thrown into such extravagant grief by the death of a son that the Earl affectionately remonstrated.

ICKWORTH, Oct. 12, 1737

DEAR SON:

Your grief to me seems so offensively excessive to the great Rules of Providence, that I, who was early in life made acquainted with

49

the sharpest sorrow that ever afflicted a humane heart upon the death of the worthiest woman that ever lived, feel my self obliged to deal so freely with you as to tell you I can experimentally read the sin you too have been guilty of in its punishment, since I fear, as I of my wife, so you made an idol of the son you have lost,which God, who is represented in the Decalogue as a jealous Being and alone worthy of all our love, seldom fails to punish us for such unpardonable deviations from our duty by its privation, whenever we allow a greater share of our hearts to any creature than is consistent with that just subordination, which is due to the supreme Creator. If this is the case, you must humble your self with all contrition under His present correction by a thorough resignation to his declared will, lest a worse thing should happen to you. . . . You will of course then become as religiously inclined as I would have you; & if there be any room for taking into account the contentment of an aged parent in your present (I must own) commiserable situation, know that could I tell myself my instruction or advice had helped to make you a more dutiful servant of the Sovereign wise Disposer of all events, it would administer one of the most sensible satisfactions to the drooping mind of your affectionate father,

BRISTOL[4]

[1] John Hervey, first Earl of Bristol, *Diary and Letter Books of the First Earl of Bristol.*
[2] *Ibid.*
[3] *Ibid.*
[4] *Ibid.*

☞ *Domestic Economy in Early New England*

THE first governor of the Massachusetts Bay Colony was a John Winthrop, and for more than a century thereafter Winthrops were prominent in the history of New England. One of them was Wait Winthrop (1643–1717), a major general in the wars against the Indians and for thirty years a judge and chief justice in Boston. His son, another John Winthrop (1681–1747), moved to Connecticut and settled at New London, where he later served as a magistrate and displayed scientific ability that won him membership in the Royal Society. In the last year of his long life, the old General and Chief Justice wrote to his son:

Boston, Oct. 22d, 1717

Dear Son:

I have your letter and what you sent by Wilson. There was but nine fish: there was some maggots in them, it being hot weather. We had one of them at dinner today, which eat well. I hear nothing of Parker yet; if I cannot get away this winter, I know not what we shall do. A little butter and cheese will not do, nor 100 sheep. If I were shure of good weather, I would com in Mr. Pickets sloop. Shall send some gallons of Palm wine for present occation; its farr beyond Canary, and shall look out for strong locks. You say nothing about the fashion of the britches: the bucks skin you brought is drest with very good yellow lether of the ordinary color. Our Genll. Court sits in a few days: I would fain do something about the Tantiusque land before I leave this place, or we shall lose it all. I hear not of your letter by the Indian. Capt Sewalls wife died last Saturday. Mary sends duty, love, and thanks for the nutts, she is now at scoole. All friends well. Thay are to try pirates here tomorrow, I think. I pray God to bless and keep you all, and send your wife a good time.

Your loving father,
W. Winthrop[1]

[1] *Winthrop Papers*, part VI, p. 351.

☞ *You Lack the Talents to Be a Rake*

During the reigns of William and Mary and of Queen Anne, James Brydges (1673–1744) worked his way upward through the confused and shifting political currents, and from 1705 until 1713 held the post of paymaster general of Britain's armed forces—of all government posts the one best lending itself by opportunity and tradition to large-scale personal profit. He amassed a great fortune, became the first Duke of Chandos, and built a magnificent mansion in Middlesex where he was host for two years to Handel the musician.

In 1722 he wrote to his younger son, John, Lord Carnarvon (1703–1727), in Paris perfecting his education in worldly ways, who died at twenty-four and left no mark on history:

[July 21, 1722]

[Do not adopt] a negligent sauntering life and turning a down-right simple country gentleman, spending your time among horses & dogs, & howling with the meanest of the company: or else turn rake about town & run into all the extravagances of that race of people in which (should it be yor [sic] misfortune) remember what I tell you you have not vivacity enough (nor are your parts of a turn for it) to make any other than a contemptible figure. . . . My wife joins me in sending you our blessings.[1]

[1] C. H. C. Baker and M. I. Baker, *James Brydges, First Duke of Chandos*, 239.

☞ Bach Leaves His "Unruly Son to God's Mercy Alone"

EVEN as great a musician as Johann Sebastian Bach (1685–1750) could not bring harmony into the lives of most of his eleven sons. Two of them, it is true, became musicians of considerable repute, but the others proved disappointing. The fourth son, Johann Gottfried Bernhard Bach (1715–39), was a ne'er-do-well, though he had some musical talent. When he was twenty-three, his father secured him a post as organist of the town of Sangerhausen, but with results indicated in his father's letter—a mixture of dismay, flattery, and evasion. After the Sangerhausen fiasco, Gottfried went to Jena to study law, but died the following year.

To Herr Klemm, Gentleman, Most Respected Member of a Most Noble and Most Wise Council of the Town of Sangerhausen, My Most Particularly Esteemed Patron, in Sangerhausen:

LEIPSIG, May 24, 1738

MOST NOBLE, MOST HIGHLY ESTEEMED HERR KLEMM:

Your Honor will not take it unkindly that absence has prevented me from answering your most esteemed letter earlier than this, since I returned only two days ago from Dresden. With what pain and sorrow, however, I frame this reply, Your Honor can judge for yourself as the loving and well-meaning father of Your Honor's own most beloved offspring.

Upon my (alas! misguided) son I have not laid eyes since last year, when I had the honor to enjoy many courtesies at Your Honor's hands. Your Honor is also not unaware that at that time I duly paid not only his board but also the Mühlhausen draft (which presumably brought about his departure at that time) but also left a few ducats behind to settle a few bills, in the hope that he would now embark upon a new mode of life. But now I must learn again, with greatest consternation, that he once more borrowed here and there, and did not change his way of living in the slightest, but on the contrary has even absented himself and not given me to date any inkling as to his whereabouts.

What shall I say or do further? Since no admonition, nor even any loving care and *assistance* will suffice any more, I must bear my cross in patience, and leave my unruly son to God's mercy alone, doubting not that He will hear my sorrowful pleading, and in the end will so work upon him, according to His Holy Will, that he will learn to acknowledge that the lesson is owing wholly and alone to Divine Guidance.

Since I have now opened my heart to Your Honor, I am fully confident that you will not impute the evil conduct of my child to me, but will be convinced that a devoted father, whose children are close to his heart, seeks to do everything to help further their welfare.

This it was that impelled me, at the time Your Honor had the vacancy, to recommend him for it as best I could, in the hope that the more civilized Sangerhausen way of living and his eminent patrons would equally move him to a different behavior, and on this account I again express herewith my most dutiful thanks to Your Honor as the author of his advancement. Nor do I doubt that Your Honor will seek to move Your Most Noble Council to delay the threatened charge until it can be learned where he is keeping himself (God knoweth all things is my Witness that I have not seen him again since last year), so that it can be ascertained what he has decided to do in the future: to remain, and change his way of living;

or to seek his fortune elsewhere. I would not willingly have Your Most Noble Council burdened with this request, but for my part would only pray for patience until such time as he turns up, or it can be learned otherwise whither he has gone.

Since, moreover, various creditors have presented their claims to me, and I can hardly agree to pay those claims without my son's oral or written confession of them (in which I am supported by all laws), therefore I most obediently request Your Honor to have the goodness to obtain precise information as to his whereabouts, and then you need only to be good enough to give me definite notification so that one last effort may be made to see whether with God's help his impenitent heart can be won over and brought to a realization of his mistakes. Since, furthermore, he has hitherto had the good fortune to lodge with Your Honor, I will at the same time pray you to inform me whether he took with him the little furniture he had, or what there may be of it still on hand. Awaiting a most prompt reply, and wishing you a more joyous holiday than I shall have, I remain, with my most humble respect to your Honored Wife.

Your Honor's most devoted servant,
JOH. SEB. BACH[1]

[1] Hans T. David and Arthur Mendel (eds.), *The Bach Reader*, 160–61.

☞ *Marriage Is the Best Medicine, but an Elderly Mistress Is the Best Substitute*

WHEN Benjamin Franklin (1706–90) wrote the following letter, his son was only fourteen, so the beneficiary of this advice was another young man, unless Franklin wrote it merely as a literary exercise. Franklin was then only thirty-nine, with his great years still before him, but London as well as Philadelphia had already made him a man of the world.

June 25, 1745

MY DEAR FRIEND:—

I know of no medicine fit to diminish the violent natural inclination you mention, and if I did, I think I should not communicate it to you. Marriage is the proper remedy. It is the most natural state of man, and therefore the state in which you will find solid happiness. Your reason against entering into at present appears to be not well founded. The circumstantial advantages you have in view by postponing it are not only uncertain but they are small in comparison with the thing itself, *the being married and settled*. It is the man and woman united that makes the complete human being. Separate, she wants his force of body and strength of reason; he her softness, sensibility and acute discernment. Together they are most likely to succeed in the world. A single man has not nearly the value he would have in that state of union. He is an incomplete animal. He resembles the odd half of a pair of scissors.

If you get a prudent, healthy wife, your industry in your profession, with her good economy, will be a fortune sufficient.

But if you will not take this counsel, and persist in thinking a commerce with the sex is inevitable, then I repeat my former advice that in your amours you should *prefer old women to young ones*. This you call a paradox, and demand my reasons. They are these:

1. Because they have more knowledge of the world, and their minds are better stored with observations, their conversation is more improving and more lastingly agreeable.

2. Because when women cease to be handsome they study to be good. To maintain their influence over man, they supply the diminution of beauty by an augmentation of utility. They learn to do a thousand services, small and great, and are the most tender and useful of all friends when you are sick. Thus they continue amiable. And hence there is hardly such a thing to be found as an old woman who is not a good woman.

3. Because there is no hazard of children, which irregularly produced may be attended with much inconvenience.

4. Because through more experience they are more prudent and discreet in conducting an intrigue to prevent suspicion. The commerce with them is therefore safer with regard to your reputation; and regard to theirs, if the affair should happen to be known, considerate people might be inclined to excuse an old women, who would kindly take care of a young man, form his manners by her

good councils, and prevent his ruining his health and fortune among mercenary prostitutes.

5. Because in every animal that walks upright, the deficiency of the fluids that fill the muscles appears first in the highest part. The face first grows lank and wrinkled; then the neck; then the breast and arms; the lower parts continuing to the last as plump as ever; so that covering all above with a basket, it is impossible of two women to know an old from a young one. And as in the dark all cats are grey, the pleasure of corporal enjoyment with an old woman is at least equal and frequently superior, every knack being by practice capable of improvement.

6. Because the sin is less. The debauching of a virgin may be her ruin, and make her life unhappy.

7. Because the compunction is less. The having made a young girl *miserable* may give you frequent bitter reflections; none of which can attend making an old woman *happy*.

8th and lastly. They are so grateful!!!

This much for my paradox. But I still advise you to marry immediately; being sincerely,

Your affectionate Friend,
BENJ. FRANKLIN.[1]

It was forty-four years later that Franklin wrote in mood and circumstances less light-hearted to his son, Sir William Franklin (1731–1813). William had been appointed crown governor of the colony of New Jersey in 1763, and when his father sided with the revolutionists twelve years later, William remained loyal to the King. After some difficulties he found refuge in England, but the political break brought a personal rift with his father, and during the war years they did not communicate. Eight years after the war had ended, Sir William was still in England, although his illegitimate son, William Temple Franklin, was acting as personal secretary to his grandfather in Paris.[2] Sir William made a dutiful if hardly a contrite attempt at reconciliation with his father, then eighty-three and United States ambassador in Paris. Franklin's reply, more philosophical than warm, was that of an old man who knows the past cannot be altered and is too tired to try to salvage the present.

Benjamin Franklin to Sir William Franklin

Dear Son:

I received your letter of the 22nd ultimo, and am glad to find that you desire to revive the affectionate intercourse that formerly existed between us. It will be very agreeable to me; indeed, nothing has ever hurt me so much, and affected me with such keen sensations, as to find myslf deserted in my old age by my only son; and not only deserted, but to find him taking up arms against me in a cause wherein my good fame, fortune and life were all at stake. You conceived, as you say, that your duty to your King and regard for your country required this. I ought not to blame you for differing in sentiment with me in public affairs. We are men, all subject to errors. Our opinions are not in our own power; they are formed and governed much by circumstances that are often as inexplicable as they are irresistible. Your situation was such that few would have censured your remaining neuter, though there are natural duties which precede political ones, and cannot be extinguished by them.

This is a disagreeable subject. I drop it: and we will endeavor, as you propose, mutually to forget what has happened relating to it, as well as we can. I send your son over to pay his duty to you. You will find him much improved. He is greatly esteemed and beloved in this country, and will make his way anywhere. It is my desire that he should study the law, as the necessary part of knowledge for a public man, and profitable if he should have occasion to practice it. I would have you therefore put into his hands those law-books you have, viz. Blackstone, Coke, Bacon, Viner etc. . . .

I did intend returning this year; but the Congress, instead of giving me leave to do so, have sent me another commission, which will keep me here at least a year longer; and perhaps I may then be too old and feeble to bear the voyage. I am here among a people that love and respect me, a most amiable people to live with; and perhaps I may conclude to die among them, for my friends in America are dying off, one after another and I have been so long abroad that I should now be almost a stranger in my own country.

I shall be glad to see you when convenient, but would not have you come here at present. You may confide to your son the family affairs you wished to confer upon with me, for he is discreet; and I trust that you will prudently avoid introducing him to company that it may be improper for him to be seen with. I shall hear from you by him; and letters to me afterwards will come safe under cover directed to Mr. Ferdinand Grand, banker, at Paris. Wishing you health, and more happiness than it seems you have lately experienced, I remain your affectionate father.[3]

[1] M. L. Schuster (ed.), *A Treasury of the World's Great Letters*, 146–47.
[2] He later edited his grandfather's collected works.
[3] *The Complete Works of Benjamin Franklin* (ed. by John Bigelow), IX, 43.

☞ *"It Was Not for You to Work to Weaken the Doctrines of Our Holy Religion"*

THE father of Denis Diderot (1713–84) was "a man of the antique character, firm and righteous . . . one of the bravest, most upright, most patient, most sensible of men," according to Diderot's biographer, John Morley.[1] He was greatly respected in the town of Langres, where he managed the cutlery factory which had for generations given his family local standing and conservative prosperity. The ideas and conduct of his son Denis, who had escaped family supervision to lead a highly unconventional life in Paris, had long troubled his father, whose concern naturally reached a climax when Denis was imprisoned for three months in solitary confinement at Vincennes for publishing a pamphlet voicing antireligious sentiments that offended the French court and sneering lightly at the mistress of a powerful court minister. The following letter from his father did not alter Denis' sentiments or way of life. He published plays and novels that, to the conservative at least, were mildly subversive, and was the chief editor of the great encyclopedia that, with its liberal sentiments, was a precursor of advanced thought and of the French Revolution.

LANGRES, September 3, 1749

MY SON,

I have received the two letters which you wrote me recently, informing me of your detention and its cause.

58

But I cannot help saying that there absolutely must have been other reasons aside from the ones given in one of your letters, for your being put inside four walls.

Everything coming from the Sovereign is respectable and must be obeyed. . . .

But since nothing happens without God's consent, I do not know which is better for your moral well-being: that the imprisonment which you have had in that pebble-box should be ended, or that it should be prolonged for several months during which you could reflect seriously on yourself.

Remember, that if the Lord has given you talents, it was not for you to work to weaken the doctrines of our Holy Religion, which you must certainly have attacked for such a large number of ecclesiastical persons to protest against one of your works, or, at least, against those that are imputed to you.

Until then, I have given you sufficient proof of my love. In giving you an education, it was in the hope that you would make good use of it and not that its results should throw me, as they have done, into the most bitter sorrow and chagrin, on learning of your disgrace.

Forgive, and I shall forgive you.

I know, my son, that no one is exempt from calumny, and that they may impute to you works in which you have had no share.

But to give proofs to the contrary to the influential people whom you know, give to the public some Christian production of yours which will free your pen of all contrary thoughts they may have concerning it, I mean about your way of thinking.

This work will bring you the blessings of Heaven, and will keep you in my good graces. However, I warn you that you will never receive any consideration from me until you have informed me, truly and unequivocally, whether you are married, as they have written me from Paris, and whether you have two children. If this marriage is legitimate and the thing is done, I am satisfied. I hope you will not refuse your sister the pleasure of bringing them up, and me the pleasure of seeing them under my own eyes.

You ask for money.

What!

A man like you who is working on immense projects, as you are, can need money?

And you have just spent a month in a place where it cost you nothing to live!

Besides I know that his Majesty, out of his kindness, gives an honorable sustenance to those who, as a result of his orders, are placed where you are.

You have asked me to send you paper, pens and ink. I invite you to make better use of them than in the past.

Remember the memory of your poor mother. In the reproaches that she made to you, she told you several times that you were blind. Give me proofs to the contrary. Once again, and above all, be faithful in the execution of your promises.

You will find enclosed a draft for one hundred and fifty *livres* on the account of Maitre Foucou which you will spend as you see fit.

I await impatiently the happy day which will calm my worries by informing me that you are free. As soon as I can find out I shall go and render thanks to the Lord.

Meanwhile, my son, with all the love that I owe you.

Your affectionate father,
DIDEROT[2]

[1] John Morley, *Diderot and the Encyclopaedists,* I, 12.

[2] Lester G. Crocker, *The Embattled Philosopher: A Biography of Denis Diderot,* 86–88.

☞ *Vanity as a Goad to Power*

OF all the surviving letters from fathers to sons, those from Philip Dormer Stanhope (1694–1773), fourth Earl of Chesterfield, are the best known in the English language and are famous examples of the spirit and values of the eighteenth century. They have been compared with *The Prince* of Machiavelli as examples of aristocratic cynicism, but not all of Chesterfield's letters are solely concerned with worldly matters, and some of them breathe sincere affection for the illegitimate son, Philip (1732–68), to whom they were written. Chesterfield had made his way to a high place in English society and politics by the judicious use of his own maxims, and was ambitious that the boy should do likewise.

BATH, November 15, 1752

MY DEAR FRIEND:

Vanity, or to call it by a gentler name, the desire of admiration and applause, is perhaps the most universal principle of human actions. I do not say that it is the best; and I will own that it is sometimes the cause of both criminal and foolish effects. But it is so much oftener the principle of right things, that, though they ought to have a better, yet, considering human nature, that principle is to be encouraged and cherished in consideration of its effects. Where that desire is wanting, we are apt to be indifferent, listless, indolent, and inert; we do not exert our powers, and we appear to be as much below ourselves as the vainest man living can desire to appear above what he really is.

As I have made you my confessor, and do not scruple to confess even my weakness to you, I will fairly own that I had that vanity, that weakness, if it be one, to a prodigious degree; and what is more, I confess it without repentance; nay, I am glad I had it; since, if I have had the good fortune to please in the world, it is to that powerful and active principle that I owe it. I began the world, not with a bare desire, but with an insatiable thirst, a rage for popularity, applause, and admiration. If this made me do some silly things, on one hand, it made me, on the other hand, do almost all the right things that I did; it made me attentive and civil to the women I disliked, and to the men I despised, nor would I have accepted the favours of the one nor the friendship of the other. I always dressed, looked, and talked my best, and, I own, was overjoyed whenever I perceived that by all three, or by any one of them, the company was pleased with me. To men, I talked whatever I thought would give them the best opinion of my parts and learning, and to women, what I was sure would please them—flattery, gallantry, and love.

And, moreover, I will own to you, under the secrecy of confession, that my vanity has very often made me take great pains to make many a woman in love with me, if I could, for whose person I would not

61

have given a pinch of snuff. In company with men, I always endeavored to out-shine, or, at least if possible, to equal, the most shining man in it. This desire elicited whatever powers I had to gratify it; and where I could not perhaps shine in the first, enabled me, at least, to shine in a second or third sphere. By these means I soon grew in fashion; and when a man is once in fashion all he does is right. It was infinite pleasure to me, to find my own fashion and popularity. I was sent for to all parties of pleasure, both of men and women, where, in some measure, I gave the tone. This gave me the reputation of having had some women of condition; and that reputation, whether true or false, really got me others. With the men I was a Proteus, and assumed every shape in order to please them all: among the gay I was the gayest, among the grave the gravest; and I never omitted the least attentions of good breeding, or the least offices of friendship, that could either please, or attach them to me, and accordingly I was soon connected with all the men of any fashion or figure in town.

To this principle of vanity, which philosophers call a mean one, and which I do not, I owe a great part of the figure which I have made in life. I wish you had as much, but I fear you have too little of it; and you seem to have a degree of laziness and listlessness about you, that makes you indifferent as to general applause. This is not in character at your age, and would be barely pardonable in an elderly and philosophical man. It is a vulgar, ordinary saying, but it is a very true one, that one should always put the best foot foremost. One should please, shine, and dazzle, whenever it is possible. . . . Let me then recommend this principle of vanity to you; act upon it *meo periculo;* I promise you it will turn to your account. Practice all the arts that ever coquette did, to please; be alert and indefatigable in making every man admire, and every women in love with you. I can tell you, too, that nothing will carry you higher in the world.[1]

It is highly likely that Chesterfield stressed ambition, address, and manners to his son because Philip—a "mediocre person" who "completely disregarded" his father's precepts—was notably lacking in all three. Philip's death at the age of thirty-six gave his father a final blow by bringing to light the fact that he had long been secretly married to "a lady of humble origin," thus defying all Chesterfield's worldly wisdom. The lady was avaricious enough to sell and make public, for a large sum, the letters written by Chesterfield for Philip's eyes alone. A few years later Chesterfield adopted his distant cousin, a youth also named Philip Stanhope (1755–1815), who inherited his estate, succeeded to his title, and did his maxims far greater credit.[2]

[1] Philip Dormer Stanhope, fourth Earl of Chesterfield, *Letters of . . . Chesterfield* (ed. by Bonamy Dobrée), V, 1974–76.
[2] Schuster, *A Treasury of the World's Great Letters*, 146–48.

☞ *A Scot Protests the Irresponsibility of Presumptive Genius*

JAMES BOSWELL (1740–95) made Samuel Johnson immortal and himself in the process, and no one can be sure which was his primary intention. Modern scholarship has made him as important to literature as his hero, "the Great Cham," and shown him to be even better equipped with interesting frailties. But Boswell's father, Alexander Boswell (1707–82), eighth Laird of Auchinleck in Ayrshire, advocate, judge, and large landowner, suffered many a blow to his family pride and stern morals as well as to his pocketbook as he tried to guide his errant son to a career in Scotland like his own and worthy of his inheritance. Alexander combined and reconciled integrity with shrewdness, affection with dourness, and generosity with caution as neatly as any other lowland Scot. He yielded only reluctantly though repeatedly to young James's extensions of his desire to see the world and learn its sophisticated ways in London and on the Continent. For a Scot, such places and dissipations were full of false values that his son was all too enthusiastically adopting.

AUCHINLECK, 30 May, 1763

JAMES.

My last letter, which was wrote in February, let you know how much I was displeased with some particulars of your conduct which had come to my knowledge. The answer you wrote me was telling me in pretty plain language that you contemned what I could say or do. When I thereafter came to the country, I found that what I represented would probably be the consequences of your strange journals actually had happened. Mr. Reid[1] came here, informed as he had seen them, and, having a good memory, repeated many things from them. He made these reflections, that he was surprised a lad of sense and come to age should be so childish as to keep a register of his follies and communicate it to others as if proud of them. He added that if the thing were known, no man would choose to keep company with you, for who would incline to have his character traduced in so strange a manner, and this frequently after your receiving the greatest civilities and marks of friendship? When I went on my circuit to Jedburgh, I received a fresh mortification. The news were brought me, and therein was contained an account of the publishing some letters of yours; and one of them was insert as a specimen. I read it, and found that though it might pass between two intimate young lads in the same way that people over a bottle will be vastly entertained with one another's rant, it was extremely odd to send such a piece to the press to be perused by all and sundry. The gentleman at Jedburgh imagined and endeavored to persuade me that it had been somebody who put in that article in the news by way of jest, for they could not suspect the letter to be genuine. At the same time they said it was a cruel jest, as it was exposing you. From Jedburgh I came to Dumfries, where I found that while you were in that country you had given yourself up to mimicry, and had at different times and places taken off (as you called it) Lord Dumfries, Sir George Preston and Logan. This, too, you may believe behoved to give me vast pain. To make a mock of others is not praiseworthy; besides, such things are seldom concealed. You create enemies to yourself and even to your friends, it being the way of the world to resent such impertinences against all who show any countenance to the person guilty of them. To all which I may add that mimicry has been justly considered as the lowest and meanest kind of wit.

After mentioning these particulars, if you'll at all reflect, you must be sensible what I suffer by your means. Is it not hard that after all the tenderness I have shown you and the expense and labour I have bestowed upon you, you should not only neglect your own reputation, but do what you can to bring me to shame on your account?

The offices I hold entitle me to some respect, and I get it beyond my merit from all that know me except from you, who by the laws of God, nature and gratitude, and interest are bound to do what you can to make me happy, in place of striving, as it were, to find out the things which would be most galling to me and making those your pursuit. What I have said will account for my not having wrote you for these three months. Indeed, finding that I could be of no use to you, I had determined to abandon you, to free myself as much as possible from sharing your ignominy, and to take the strongest and most public steps for declaring to the world that I was come to this resolution. But I have been so much importuned by your excellent mother, the partaker of my distress and shame on your account, again to write to you, and your last letter, which I received at Ayr when on the circuit, is wrote in a strain that is becoming and speaks out that you are satisfied of some of your errors; therefore it is that you receive this from me in answer to those you sent me since the Session rose.

As in yours you desire me to give you my advice with freedom, you cannot be dissatisfied with the introduction to this letter. Every wise man would rather be informed for what things he is censured, that he may correct them, than be flattered when he don't deserve it; and he alone is a true friend who informs us of our faults. It is true such a friend is rarely to be met with, but you have had such a friend in me.

You are under a mistake in your last when you write I have been struggling for authority over you. I have a right to it, indeed, but it is a thing I never wished or desired. And every step in my conduct has shown that to be the case. I have always used you with lenity and tenderness; and though you were behaving in a way highly disrespectful to me, settled an annuity upon you for life and so put you in a state of independency. You say that you was struggling for independency. What you mean by becoming independent I am at a loss to conceive, for it would seem to be something very different from what anybody else could aim at. Your notion of independency seems to consist in contemning your relations and your native country, where and from you have a natural right to receive regard and friendship, and live in dependence upon strangers in another country, where you have no title to notice, and from whom you have nothing to expect but fair words. They have their relations to provide, their political connections to keep up, and must look on one who comes from Scotland as an idle person to have no right to share of their bounty; in the same way that we here would never think of bestowing anything upon a vaguing[2] Englishman except a dinner or a supper. When you left this, I told you that you would find this to be true on trial. You would not then believe it, but now you candidly own that you have found the thing turn out according as I said it would do.

You desire my advice as to your after schemes in life. As to this, I have already told you I have no authority; and the mention I have made of sundry things in your conduct that vex and distress me and every friend and acquaintance of yours who has common sense, is not from authority but friendship. I am bound by the ties of nature to love you; and though it is disagreeable still to be finding fault, I should be wanting in my duty to tell you my mind. If you'll call to remembrance sundry of your past schemes which I advised you against and were happily disappointed, you must be sensible how dangerous it is for a young man to propose to give himself up to be governed by whims. You have escaped from a variety of ruinous snares that you were quite bent upon, and now are convinced were such as behoved to have brought you misery. This should make you cautious in time coming. The poet says, *"Felix quem faciunt aliena pericula cautum,"*[3] but he must be unhappy indeed who won't learn from his own past dangers. To come more closely to the point in your letter wherein you ask my advice as to what scheme of life you should follow, I shall convince you that I do not insist on authority, for though you tell me you will return to Scotland if I tell you your absence from it makes me unhappy, I will not insist either on one thing or another, but fairly and candidly lay matters before you. All that I ever insisted upon was that you should behave as the young gentlemen of your station do and act with prudence and discretion. If you set up the character of my eldest son, you may expect regard and respect, but in the style of a vagrant must meet with the reverse. Be assured of this; for even I, who am your father and who, while you

66

trod the paths of virtue and discretion was bound up in you and carried on all my projects with a view to you in whom I flattered myself to find a representative worthy of this respectable family—I say, even I by your strange conduct had come to the resolution of selling all off, from the principle that it is better to snuff a candle out than to leave it to stink in a socket. And this purpose, though interrupted at present by your last letters being wrote in a strain that gives hopes of amendment upon my being disappointed in that hope, I should certainly carry into execution.

As for your manner of life, I never declared positively against any kind of life except that of dissipation and vice, and as a consequence against your going into the Guards. But I told you if you chose to be a soldier and make that your business in good earnest, though I did not like the business, I should procure you a commission in a marching regiment, and had one pressed upon me by my good friend General Sinclair, now no more. But you signified your unwillingness to serve in a marching regiment, so that scheme went over and you fell to the study of the law; and I can say with truth, showed as much genius for it when you applied as ever any I knew. Be assured that your following the study of the law, whether as a lawyer or as a gentleman, to fit you to be useful in the world, is what to me is most agreeable and what I verily think is the only thing that will make you go through life agreeably; for as you well observe, without some pursuit that is rational, one of your turn can never be happy. In the plan I propose you to have for your objects being respected, being useful with your advice, getting into Parliament, and having the power of conferring places instead of going about begging one. And to these may I add, you have the satisfaction of making your parents happy and adding more lustre to the family you have the honour to be come of. And if you were truly fixed on this plan, I would make no difficulty, when you were a little settled from your reelings, to let you go abroad for a while. But if you are bent on the Army, as you say you have the offer of an ensigncy in a marching regiment, though I am far from liking the thing, if better cannot be, take it, and hold by that as your business for life. But be more on your guard for the future against mimicry, journals, and publications, still acting with prudence and discretion, which is as necessary for a soldier as for a man of any other employment. I would further recommend to you to endeavor to find out some person of worth who may be a friend, not one who will say as you say when with you and when he is away will make a jest of you as much as of any other.

Your mother is in her ordinary, so is Johnny. Both remember you with affection.

Farewell. It is in your power to make us happy and yourself too. May God dispose you to the best.[4]

[1] The Reverend George Reid, minister of Ochiltree.
[2] Wandering.
[3] "He's a lucky man who learns caution from other people's dangers."
[4] Boswell's *London Journal, 1762–1763* (ed. by Frederick A. Pottle), 337–42.

☞ *A Grandfather is Caught Circumventing Parental Discipline*

THE Livingstons were one of the leading families in colonial New York and played important roles when the colony became a state of the new republic. They were American-style aristocrats, but they did not pamper or overindulge their sons, especially in financial matters. But a grandfather, feeling a little less responsible than a father for a grandson's frugality and therefore a little more human, could occasionally connive to ease a grandson's financial path. This letter from Robert Livingston of Livingston Manor, at the age of eighty-one, to Robert R. Livingston (1746–1813), then a law student of twenty-three in New York City and later a statesman and a jurist, tells its own story.

CLAREMONT, the 29th March 1769

DEAR GRANDSON ROBT.,

I recd. yrs. of the 6th March; but your good father opened it by mistake: consequently he knew you had apply'd to me, in pursuance of my orders, for a little money in case you should be straighten'd, wch I take in good part. Yr daddy was a little out of humour, alledging you was a little too lavish; but I told him you could not receive cash for law, till bills were taxt, and then not to be too hasty,

68

wch. would look necessitous and griping, wherein he acquiesced. I should immediately have enclosed you a 10 lb. bill, but he told me you would receive about £50 or £60 of his money, whereout you could deduct that amount; so I gave him the £10.[1]

[1] Charles Havens Hunt, *Life of Edward Livingston,* 19–20n.

☞ *Political Principles Versus Legal Ethics*

ONE of the events that most embittered relations between the British government and the American colonists in the decade before the Revolution was the Boston Massacre. A handful of British soldiers became involved in a melee with some resentful Bostonians who were arrantly baiting them and, under orders from Captain Preston, fired upon them. There were several casualties, and most Boston citizens were determined that Captain Preston should be convicted of murder. Josiah Quincy, Jr. (1744–75), then twenty-six, was a young lawyer of a leading family that was opposing British impositions and was himself an ardent advocate of colonial rights. Nevertheless, when asked to defend Captain Preston and the accused British soldiers, he accepted the brief. Most of Josiah's friends were shocked and angry at his action, and his father, a prosperous retired merchant living in Braintree, wrote to his son as follows:

BRAINTREE, March 22, 1770

MY DEAR SON,

I am under great affliction, at hearing the bitterest reproaches uttered against you, for having become an advocate for those criminals who are charged with the murder of their fellow citizens. Good God! Is it possible? I will not believe it.

Just before I returned home today from Boston, I knew, indeed, that on the day those criminals were committed to prison a sergeant had inquired for you at your brother's house—but I had no apprehension that it was possible an application would be made to you to undertake their defense. Since then I have been told that you have actually engaged for Captain Preston; and I have heard the severest reflections made upon the occasion, by men who had just before manifested the highest esteem for you, as one destined to be a saviour of your country.

I must own to you, it has filled the bosom of your aged and infirm parent with anxiety and distress, lest it should not only prove true, but destruction of your reputation and interests; and I repeat, I will not believe it, unless it be confirmed by your own mouth, or under your own hand.

Your anxious and distressed parent,
JOSIAH QUINCY[1]

The son replied: "These criminals, charged with murder, are *not yet legally proved guilty*, and, therefore, however criminal, are entitled, by the laws of God and man, to all legal counsel and aid. . . . To inquire my duty, and to do it, is my aim."[2] Captain Preston and his men were finally acquitted of murder, and young Quincy was soon again regarded as a potential leader of the cause of colonial freedom. A young man of such wisdom and moral courage might indeed have made a great contribution to the founding of the nation, but he died in 1775.

[1] Josiah Quincy, *Memoir of the Life of Josiah Quincy, Jun., of Massachusetts,* 34–36.
[2] *Ibid.*

☞ *"Preserve a Habit of Giving," but "Never Give More Than They Do"*

EDMUND BURKE (1729–97) was a leading Whig advocate of reform and of conciliation with the American colonies, but he made no protest when his merchant constituents in Bristol bought the votes that re-elected him to Parliament, and more than once he solicited unorthodox and profitable favors from Lord North, whom he bitterly attacked in Parliament for corruption. But that was the spirit of the times, and Burke's advice to his son Richard, then fifteen and traveling on the Continent, showed the same blend of virtue and shrewdness.

[1773]

. . . While I do most earnestly recommend you to take care of your health and safety, I would not have that care degenerate into

70

an effeminate and over-curious attention, which is always disgraceful to a man's self, and often troublesome to others. So you know
my meaning, when I wish you again and again to take care of yourselves for our sake. So when I wish you to avoid superfluous expenses,
as giving the mind loose and bad habits, be aware that I wish you
to avoid everything that is mean, sordid, illiberal, and uncharitable,
which is much the worst extreme. Do not spare yourselves nor me
in this point. As you are now a little setting up for yourselves, suffer
me to give you a little direction about the article of *giving*. When
others of decent condition are giving along with you, never give more
than they do; it is rather an affront to them, than a service to those
that desire your little bounty. Whatever else you do, do it separately.
But always preserve a habit of giving (but still with discretion), however little, as a habit not to be lost. When I speak of this, the funds
of neither of you are large, and perhaps never may become so. So
that the first thing is justice. Whatever one gives, ought to be from
what one would otherwise spend, not from what he would otherwise
pay. To spend little and give much is the highest glory a man can
aspire to. . . .

Your ever affectionate father,
EDM. BURKE[1]

Richard Burke (1758–94) spent his short life in the admirable but
unsuccessful effort to emulate his father's distinction. In spite of his
father's influence he failed to make a name in either law or politics.
Like his father he opposed the French revolutionaries and in 1791 spent
some time in Coblentz with the French *émigrés*. In 1794, on the very
eve of his election to Parliament and appointment as chief secretary to
the new Lord Lieutenant of Ireland, he died suddenly and unmarried.

[1] *Correspondence of Edmund Burke* (ed. by Earl Fitzwilliam and Sir Richard
Bourke), I, 425–26.

☞ ## "Be a Servant Now . . .
That You May Be a Master Hereafter"

UNTIL the eighteenth century it was chiefly the members of
the upper classes whose advice to their sons was written and preserved.

Their values and hence their instructions represented aims which in many cases only aristocrats could afford. But as merchants and artisans improved their economic position and their capabilities with a pen, a new kind of letter from fathers to sons appeared, not only in authentic private correspondence but in printed tracts that reflected the rise of middle-class status and ambitions. The son of a lord or wealthy squire had little need to observe industry, frugality, and deference to his betters, but artisans exalted those virtues because they were essential to their sons' success. One of the first of such tracts was from the industrious pen of Caleb Trenchfield. About his life little is known, except that he seems to have been a professional writer of pamphlets, including *Historical Contemplations, Christian Chymistrie,* and *Scriptural Observations.* In *A Cap of Grey Hairs for Green Heads,* he addressed himself to a real or imagined apprenticed son.

[1777]

Son,

Having been at so much cost and care to set you fairly out, to act your part upon the stage of this present world, I was consulting what might be further done to give assistance to your fair come-off. . . .

And though some fathers, and some of them, too, persons of great note, have undertaken to give advice unto their sons, whose works are yet extant, and therefore this may seem more needless; yet there are not any that I know of who have stooped so low as to give advice to an apprentice, but did direct their thoughts to such a pitch as lay not in the level of the greatest part of persons, to whom advice was not less needful. However, you'll find here some store of things not touched by their observation . . . what concerns you most is not the doctrine but the use. . . .

Now as I have made it my care to dispose you to such a master as hath a good report of all men, and I hope of the truth itself, that he is an honest, good man, and able in his way, from whom you will receive daily examples of the exercise of virtue; and who, as he will expect the duty of a servant from you in your service of him; so I know he will perform the duty of a master to you, in your improvement and instruction. So it behooves you now to answer the end that was designed in your being so disposed of, and so to take care to be a servant now, as that you may be a master hereafter. To which end it is not a little conducing to come off the stage with the clear applause of having acted the part of a servant well. For he that is furnished with that report goes a great way in the second part, I mean the setting up for himself.[1]

[1] Caleb Trenchfield, *A Cap of Grey Hairs for Green Heads*, 3, 4, 22, 23.

☞ *The Ingratitude of Filial Genius*

JOHANN GEORGE LEOPOLD MOZART (1719–87), the father of Johann Chrysostom Wolfgang Amadeus Mozart the composer (1756–91), was himself a professional musician of good repute—conductor of the ducal orchestra at Salzburg, composer, and author of a treatise on the violin. When his son displayed, at the age of four, a remarkable musical talent, Leopold gave up his own career except his court duties, some say to exploit ruthlessly his son's talents; others, to advance the cause of genius at great personal sacrifice. Before Wolfgang was ten years old, he had played with *réclame* in Munich before the Elector, in Versailles before Louis XV, and in London before George III.

Under his father's ardent management, Wolfgang continued his musical studies and conquests, though not always with the single-minded devotion his father wished. At the age of twenty-one he was lightheartedly visiting the courts of various German princes in quest of a good musical post, but also with obvious enjoyment of their distracting social pleasures. In this diversion from duty he was abetted by an adoring mother who accompanied him and fell in with his volatile plans and enthusiasms. Leopold, compelled to remain in Salzburg and going heavily into debt to support these expensive travelers, showed his adoration of his son to be increasingly tempered by his annoyance at Wolfgang's irresponsibility.

[SALZBURG,] November 24, 1777

MON TRÈS CHER FILS!

Your long and quite unnecessary sojourn[1] has ruined all your prospects. . . . So far you have just had a holiday and have spent the time in enjoyment and amusement. . . . You must adopt quite a

73

different manner of living and an entirely different outlook. There must be attention and daily concentration on earning some money. . . . Where there is no money, friends are no longer to be found, and that too even if you give a hundred lessons for nothing, compose sonatas and . . . play the fool every evening from ten o'clock until midnight. . . . For in the long run everything recoils on your poor old father.[2]

Without waiting for a reply, the lonely, ill, bankrupt, and largely disregarded father returned, three days later, to the charge:

SALZBURG, November 27, 1777

MON TRÈS CHER FILS!

. . . not a syllable about your plans for your next journey. I keep on racking my brains—and write myself blind. I do want to arrange things in advance. You, however, make light of everything, you are indifferent, you tie my hands when I want to advise and help, since you do not say a word about where you are going to next. I shall give you a clear instance of an unpardonable piece of thoughtlessness on your part. . . . A little meditation and common sense should convince you that it is most necessary to think things out and to take these wearisome and constant precautions, and that fruitless over-anxiousness is not prompting me to write as I do, nor timorous melancholy imaginings, but simply experience. . . . God bless you and keep you well!

MZT.[3]

Wolfgang's reply was, as often of late, deferential, affectionate, and noncommittal—full of hopes of concerts in Mannheim and of accounts of his social conquests there. His only comment on financial matters was, "We spend nothing beyond what is necessary." Further long letters were exchanged weekly, in which the father apologized for his criticisms, and the son accepted the apology. Wolfgang offered his father pledges of deep affection, but no plans except vague talk of going to Paris with his mother and settling there—still with no income in view. Then suddenly he discovered in the sixteen-year-old daughter of a friend in Mannheim what he believed to be a rare musical talent and wrote to Leopold all too specifically about his new plans. He would

74

take the girl with him to Italy and there make her an immediate operatic sensation. That broke the dam of Leopold's patience:

SALZBURG, Feb. 11th, 12th, 1778

MY DEAR SON!

I have read your letter of the 4th with amazement and horror. I am beginning to answer it today, the 11th, for the whole night long I was unable to sleep and am so exhausted that I can only write quite slowly, word by word, and so gradually finish what I have to say by tomorrow.

Up to the present, thank God! I have been in good health; but this letter, in which I only recognize my son by that failing of his which makes him believe everyone at the first word spoken, open his kind heart to every plausible flatterer and let others sway him as they like, so that he is led by whimsical ideas and ill-considered and unpractical projects to sacrifice his own name and interests, and even the interests and claims of his aged and honourable parents to those of strangers. This letter, I say, depressed me exceedingly, the more so as I was cherishing the reasonable hope that certain circumstances which you had to face already, as well as my own reminders, both spoken and written, could not have failed to convince you that not only for the sake of your happiness but in order that you may be able to gain a livelihood and attain at length the desired goal in a world of men in varying degrees good and bad, fortunate and unfortunate, it was imperative for you to guard your warm heart by the strictest reserve, undertake nothing without full consideration and never let yourself be carried away by enthusiastic notions and blind fancies.

My dear Son, I implore you to read this letter carefully—and take time to reflect upon it. Merciful God! those happy moments are gone when, as child and boy, you never went to bed without standing on a chair and singing to me *Oragna Figata Fa*, and ending by kissing me again and again on the tip of my nose and telling me that when I grew old you would put me in a glass case and protect me from every breath of air, so that you might always have me with you and honour me.

75

Listen to me, therefore, in patience. You are fully acquainted with my difficulties in Salzburg—you know my wretched income, why I kept my promise to let you go away, and all my various troubles. The purpose of your journey was two-fold—either to get a good permanent appointment or, if this should fail, to go off to some big city where large sums of money could be earned. Both plans were designed to assist your parents and to help on your dear sister, but above all to build up your own name and reputation in the world. The latter was partly accomplished in your childhood and boyhood; and it now depends on you alone to raise yourself gradually to a position of eminence such as no musician has ever attained.

You owe that to the extraordinary talents which you have received from a beneficent God; and now it depends solely on your good sense whether you die as an ordinary musician, utterly forgotten by the world, or as a famous *Kapellmeister*, of whom posterity will read —whether, captured by some woman, you die bedded on straw in an attic full of starving children, or whether, after a Christian life spent in contentment, honours and renown, you leave this world with your family well provided for and your name respected by all. . . .

You think all your ill-considered fancies as reasonable and practicable as if they were bound to be accomplished in the normal course of nature. You are thinking of taking her to Italy as a prima donna. Tell me, do you know of any prima donna who, without having first appeared many times in Germany, has walked on to the stage in Italy as a prima donna? . . . What impresario would not laugh, were one to recommend to him a girl of sixteen or seventeen, who has never yet appeared on a stage! . . . How can you allow yourself to be bewitched even for an hour by such a horrible idea, which must have been suggested by someone or other! Your letter reads like a romance. . . . Quite apart from your reputation—what of your old parents and your dear sister?

My son, you should regard me rather as your most sincere friend than as a severe father. Consider whether I have not always treated you kindly, served you as a servant his master, even provided you with all possible entertainment and helped you enjoy all honourable and seemly pleasures. . . . Hurt me now if you can be so cruel!

Write to me by the next post without fail. We kiss you both a million times and I remain your old honest father and husband.

MZT.[4]

Wolfgang replied with as much affection and detachment as ever, except that he chided his father for having made improper insinuations against a wellborn girl—and a cousin at that! Many of her friends in Mannheim, he said, considered that she had the finest voice in Europe. As for his father's other strictures, he implied that he forgave them, for "You only wrote it in a temper." In another letter to Leopold a few days later (March 7, 1778) he wrote: " 'Next God comes papa,' was my axiom when a child, and I still think the same." The proposed trip to Italy with the girl was indefinitely postponed.

[1] In Mannheim.
[2] *Letters of Mozart and His Family* (trans. and ed. by Emily Anderson), II, 571–73.
[3] *Ibid.*, 579, 581.
[4] *Ibid.*, 700–709.

☞ *Run from the Temptations of Cambridge College Orgies*

THE ancestors of the Reverend Henry Venn (1724–97) had been clergymen of the Church of England in an uninterrupted line from the time of the Reformation. He himself was vicar of Yelling in Huntingdonshire and the author of popular primers of virtue entitled *The Duty of a Parish Priest* (1760) and *The Complete Duty of Man* (1763). Although he sent his son, John Venn (1759–1813), to Sidney Sussex College at Cambridge, he feared the sins and temptations to which the boy would be exposed. Toward the end of the academic year the vicar learned that it was the "custom in several of the colleges at Cambridge, to allow an annual feast among the young men at the time of conferring the degree of Bachelor of Arts, and such occasions too often became scenes of intemperance." The vicar promptly addressed his son:

YELLING, Jan. 17, 1778
Very solicitous, my dear son, for your welfare, I cannot put out of my mind the danger you must be exposed to next week, at the Bache-

lors' entertainment. I regard the danger as the greater, because you do not seem apprehensive of it; nor to have, as I could wish, a just conception that such meetings are, almost without exception, abused, to intemperance and riot,—which I do not think can be prevented; consequently, they should be avoided, if possible. Now, were you to come over for three or four days, I do not see that any objection could be made; and you would be thus out of the way of temptation. But if you stay, and do go to the meeting, how much need have you to beg earnestly that you may be Kept!—for be assured, that every one who has been condemned by your exact conduct will be glad to see you yield; and exert their utmost to overcome you, that you may no more be able to frown on vice. I remember dear Mr. Adam of Wintringham (observing how little we have to be proud of) said most truly that half of our virtue was owing to our being out of the way of temptation. The Oracles of God affirm the same thing. The command in them is peremptory: "Go out from the presence of a man, as soon as thou perceivest the words of wisdom are not in him." ... May the Lord, therefore, bring a gracious fear always upon your mind, of entering at all into the place where scoffers sit, and their tongue speaketh against the Most High!

But Providence happily intervened, and on January 30 the vicar again wrote to his son:

How thankful was I, my dear son, that the feast was absolutely abolished, and your dangers thus absolutely prevented! What an heathenish way of congratulating each other on taking their degrees, to be intemperate, and exceed the limits of becoming mirth! How unavoidable the contempt of the Clergy, amongst the gentlemen who, remembering them at college, even till the time they were ordained, saw nothing in them that would rebuke vice, and lead the mind to fear and love the holy laws of our adorable Maker and Redeemer.[1]

Young John's virtue apparently survived the temptations of Cambridge, for he in his turn took orders and became the righteous but not very distinguished vicar of Clapham. His own son, the Reverend Henry Venn, not only continued for another generation the ecclesiastical record of the Venn family, but in 1834 wrote the admiring biography of his grandfather which included the description of the Cambridge orgies quoted above.

[1] Henry Venn, *Life of the Rev. Henry Venn*, 245–47.

☞ *One Whig Statesman Applies
His Liberal Principles at Home*

WILLIAM PETTY (1737–1805), Earl of Shelburne and after 1784 first Marquis of Lansdowne, was for a generation a leading states-man, a virulent critic of the North ministry's conduct of the war with America, and later as prime minister the chief formulator of the peace terms adopted after his fall. His unbending incapacity to work with others and some of his political maneuvres make his character difficult to assess, and history has perhaps given him less credit than he deserved. In this letter to his son, John Henry Petty (1765–1863), on his fif-teenth birthday, there is nothing but affectionate wisdom. John Henry later succeeded his father as the second Marquis of Lansdowne, and was chancellor of the Exchequer at twenty-six.

BOWOOD, 2 Decr. 1780

MY DEAREST MANNA:

I am excessively happy to hear so good an account of you from all hands—As to your coming here, you may be assur'd that you cannot wish it more than I do. I only wish you to consider that you are now *Fifteen*, and that in *Six* years more at furthest, you will have many duties to discharge, that in order to discharge them, you will have many Books to read, many Men to study, some countries as well as Cornwall to travel thro'; After this I leave it to you and Mr. Jervis to consider of the time & let me know, always remembering, that I mean to keep my Word in my former letter, & that I always leave it to *you* to be the Interpreter of that Word. I only honestly wish for many reasons that you may get just as much of the Academy, as you properly can.

79

Lady Shelburne and I desire to be most kindly remembered to Mr. Jervis, and you know that we are both

Tenderly Yrs.
SHELBURNE[1]

[1] Shelburne Papers, William L. Clements Library, University of Michigan.

☞ *"Cease to Think Your Honour Every Minute Concerned"*

JOHN STUART (1713–92), first Earl of Bute, was a Scot of charm and culture, wealthy through his marriage with the daughter of Lady Mary Wortley Montagu, who brought him the coal fortune of her father. During the latter years of George II, Bute became the idol and chief adviser of the Prince of Wales, who, shortly after his accession as George III, made Bute his first minister. But as a statesman Bute's power was brief; Whig canards made him highly unpopular and forced his complete retirement from active politics. His three sons were all ambitious and intolerant, and when one of them, young Lord Mountstewart, demanded without justification that he be made lord lieutenant of a county in Wales and was refused by Lord North, he remarked that he would have knocked Lord North down had the conversation not taken place in the halls of Parliament. The third son, Charles Stuart (1753–1801), embarked on a military career, and in 1780 complained to his father that his military opportunities were being circumscribed by the animosity of the North ministry. Bute replied in a chastening letter.

[LUTON, January, 1780]

I approved of your offering yourself for any service, as well as the manner in which I understand you did it; I thought you showed your ardour; but pray consider the present situation. Is there any one service you could point out for activity here at home? Certainly not, and can you be surprised that they should be silent about your proposal to attend a Siege that they, knowing the Fleet they have sent, will soon put an end to?

And this you look upon as an insult: I think nothing of it; that

80

they gave you a negative about Gibraltar is by no means a proof that you are not to be employed elsewhere.

I protest in this situation of things, I don't comprehend your meaning, when you ask for my advice. Tho' indeed one thing calls for advice, seriously, my dear Charles, and that is that you should cease to think your honour every minute concerned because this or that desire is not complied with; for this will not only affect your looks, words and actions, subversive of the capital point you ought to have in mind, which is that of gaining another step in Rank before the War ends.

This is of the utmost consequence to your whole future military life, and to obtain this I cannot see your honour in the least affected, tho' you should avoid shewing your dislike or resentment on being disappointed in something you may ask.

You cannot have an idea of giving up your profession, after having on so many occasions distinguished yourself, and yet I am sensible there is no line one can follow in which one will not meet disagreeable things.[1]

Young Charles, who ultimately became the third Earl of Bute, presumably learned his lesson, for he became a lieutenant general and in 1798 defeated the Spanish and took Minorca.

[1] E. Stuart-Wortley, *A Prime Minister to His Son*, 146.

☞ *Marriage à la Mode*

HENRY HERBERT (1734–94), tenth Earl of Pembroke, was in his freedom from social and linguistic inhibitions, one of the most refreshing of Georgian characters. In his youth he openly deserted his highly born wife and lived several years on the Continent with another woman. In time he returned to Lady Pembroke and accepted his responsibilities more soberly, though never without a devastating freedom of speech. He stood well at the court of George III until, about the time these letters were written, he broke with the King over the ministers and their American policy, and was temporarily removed from his high court offices. Thereafter he devoted himself chiefly to the improvement of his handsome estate of Wilton and the advancement of the interests of his family. Like his near-contemporary the first Earl of Bristol, already quoted, he was eager that his son marry an heiress. That son, George Augustus Herbert (1759–1827), had spent some years on the Continent, and his reluctance to settle down increasingly troubled his affectionate father. In the end George achieved a career his father would have approved, for he became a lieutenant general in 1802 and a full general in 1812 and also spent some £200,-000 in improvements at Wilton.

WILTON HOUSE, Fryday, 24 August, 1781

. . . I wish you would draw, not your sword, but your precious member, by which the Austrian family have thrived so renownedly. I really think that you might do it to a very great purpose, if you should be so inclined, & will seriously set about it immediately, for not a moment should be lost, and all shyness be banished; so many, of course, will be the Candidates on starting, which is to take place now, this winter. *Vous m'entendez bien*. Nothing, I am sure, is yet thought of, and I could put you on the road. If you should happen to like it, & can succeed, it would be *à tous égards*, a vast thing for the family . . . that would set you upon the highest pinnacle you conceive. . . .[1]

WILTON HOUSE, 20 Sep., 1781

. . . I have heard, & believe her good tempered, & all you said & wish. Upon honour, I have always heard so; and if she is not so, I will be the first to advise you against it. You can know nothing of her but through yourself, by getting acquainted with her, & that you may easily do *sans vous compromette du tout*, as I told Floyd; but if you wait for the information of others, and lay by for it, she will certainly be snapped up before you know anything about the matter. I really believe they have thoughts about you. Ralph can do nothing but perhaps give you an opportunity of seeing her; for he is hardly deep enough to be entrusted with a negotiation. Possibly by making Weston your way to town, you may see her. Pray try; if that fails, be bold in town. Speak, attack, *spada in mano pronta a ferir!* Believe me, I would rather have you marry a beggar & be happy than to see

82

you sacrificed for the Bank of England; but this, I own, by *all* I have heard, would, I verily believe, answer *all* ends. . . .[2]

Twelve days later the Earl renewed his project by indirection. In a characteristic letter from Wilton House dated October 2, 1781, he dealt first with other subjects, including the problems of rents and management at Wilton, the proper care of horses, and the sins of Lord North and his government, and then enclosed for his son a newspaper clipping, with only three words appended in his own hand: "Smithfield for ever." The press cutting read: "If the present Mrs. Child should live, and, as may be expected, the family have no additional issue, Miss Child will of course be the richest heiress in the British Dominions. Next to Miss Child, the other principal unmarried females of great wealth, are the Countess of Sutherland, Miss Banks, and Miss Curven of Cumberland"[3]

A week later the Earl renewed the attack more openly:

WILT. HOUSE, Wednesday, Oct. 10th, 1781

I have nothing to say about *l'Enfant*, but that [if] it not be too late I am for your just getting acquainted at the first opportunity, to see at least whether there is anything very agreeable or disagreeable, & so make inquiries in consequence or not, according as. . . .[4]

WILTON HOUSE, 13 Oct., 1781

I have questioned Ralph Heldon, now here, *sans faire semblant de rien,* & find that either you have grossly mistaken him, or that he has grossly misexpressed himself. He has often told me he was well in that family, & as frequently expressed a wish that you was legimately [*sic*] in it; upon which I said I wished he would *tâter le terrain.* He did so, & perhaps, probably indeed, awkwardly. The parents' fears are such, that whenever they see a name in the news papers about their girl, they cut out the article, before the print appears at breakfast, & they make it a rule to discourage all conversation upon the subject, but they declare themselves desirous that she should *know* proper people, & *chuse* for herself. She has declared, I have been assured, against York herself, & has said she has no partiality for Ld. Westmoreland. All others who have been mentioned are treated as without any foundation, & I verily believe are so. By what I heard, which I told you, I firmly think it is expected that you should produce yourself, & make yourself known; when you, she or they may cut, if it does not suit, without ceremony or bustle; but at any rate, to come to that, the acquaintance must be made, & most certainly time and every circumstance presses very much. No opportunity is to be lost, or can there be anything like pushing, or forwardness, for you to be at a friend's and relation's, as Heldon is; & in the neighborhood of Blenheim into the bargain; for everybody does not know what a strange, shy fellow His Grace of M[arlborough] is.[5]

Whether from lack of his own ardor or for other reasons, Lord Herbert's suit did not flourish, for in 1782 Miss Sarah Jane Child, the heiress in question, married the sixteenth Earl of Westmoreland. But the Earl of Pembroke did not abandon his quest, and three years later, when his son was twenty-six, he wrote to him from Rome:

ROME, 16 February, 1785

. . . Why not a foreigner? A cross in all breeds is generally supposed expedient; if you do not approve my last recommendation, give me leave to mention to you the daughter of His Britan: Majesty, Her Royal Highness the Dutchess of Albany, at Florence.[6]

Apparently Lord Herbert again replied unfavorably, but in the meantime, in collusion with his mother, Lady Pembroke, he was privately paying court to another of England's great heiresses, Lady Sutherland. The Earl got wind that something was under way and wrote to his son:

FLORENCE, 10 May, 1785

. . . Do you think of marrying, or rather have you thought of any particular person, on whom you propose to make a Grand Papa of me? By a letter I have read from Lady P. I suspect it; and if so, I cannot help adding that I shall be somewhat mortified at your not having immediately made me a confidential friend in the matter. In respect to what I can do, & you wish, you will never meet with difficulties on my side, be assured: but let me remind you that our family circumstances want a good fortune, & *que vous êtes d'un caliber* in every respect to expect it. . . .[7]

84

Lord Herbert once again proved a laggard in the race, for on September 4 the Countess of Sutherland was married to Viscount Trentham, and the Earl of Pembroke wrote to Lord Herbert:

> FLORENCE, 20 Nov. 1785
>
> ... Is it true, pray tell me, *entre amis,* that you was hot after Ly. Sutherland? The news papers have said so, & I have had it hinted by letters on a side wind kind of way. Why did you not mention it to me?[8]

But his sense of injury at having been ignored did not keep the Earl from further efforts.

> ROMA, 11th Jany., 1786
>
> ... Though you missed your aim at Lady S, I hope you will try again, for I have a passion for Grandchildren, & a handsome sensible and opulent *young* daughter in law. *Rien que ça,* & the sooner the better. . . .[9]

> LISBON, 28 July, 1786
>
> ... On all sides, except from your's, I hear of marriages; have you no thoughts of taking a leap? I wish you would, & *le temps se passe*. . . .[10]

Lord Herbert apparently did not confide to his father that in September of that year he proposed to his cousin, Lady Caroline Spencer, and was refused. But back in Paris the Earl unearthed another lucrative possibility and reported it to the questing lover:

> PARIS, 1 Jany., 1787
>
> ... If your objections to a foreign wife have ceased, I really believe I know of one, not in Paris, tho' in France, whom you would like vastly; might probably come at, & who would be unexceptionable in every respect, but let that rest till we meet.[11]

The poor Earl was trying to be tactful, but Lord Herbert's reply was a brusque denial of any interest in a foreign wife, since her foreign relatives were certain to be nuisances and perhaps an impediment to his career. This time, certainly with his mother's encouragement, Lord Herbert was pursuing a lady of his own choice. The first news the Earl had of it was a letter from his son on February 27, 1787. Lord Herbert began by asking assurances of an increase of one thousand pounds a year if he married, and then announced, briefly and without much filial warmth, that he was engaged to marry his first cousin, Elizabeth Beauclerc. The Earl's reply, though assuring his son of the increase in allowance and of his acceptance of the proposed marriage, did not attempt to conceal his hurt feelings and disappointment. He concluded: "I could have wished you had chosen somebody with some fortune. You know how very much the situation of our affairs stand in need of at least thirty thousand pounds." Could not Lord Herbert, he inquired, have found an acceptable wife who was "at least a thirty-thousand-pounder?"

1 *Pembroke Papers* (ed. by Lord Herbert), II, 141.
2 *Ibid.*, 154.
3 *Ibid.*, 159.
4 *Ibid.*, 161.
5 *Ibid.*, 163, 164.
6 *Ibid.*, 265. This was the daughter of the Young Pretender and Clementine Walkinshaw, then aged twenty-eight; she died unmarried four years later.
7 *Pembroke Papers*, II, 273.
8 *Ibid.*, 289, 290.
9 *Ibid.*, 298.
10 *Ibid.*, 307.
11 *Ibid.*, 323.

☞ *A Founding Father Deplores the Republic's Leadership*

CHARLES CARROLL of Carrollton (1737–1832) outlived all the other signers of the Declaration of Independence. He became a senator from Maryland, opposed the War of 1812, and died at ninety-five one of the wealthiest men in the nation he had helped to found. But he was not happy about the direction and the leaders it was following. In 1801 he wrote as much to his son, Charles Carroll of Homewood, whose career was less notable.

[ANNAPOLIS,] 8th February [1801]
... Neither Jefferson nor Burr can make so bad a president as Adams, had he been re-elected; it is fortunate indeed for this country

86

that he was not. I hope Burr will be chosen by the House of Representatives. I had some hopes, before I read Jefferson's letter published in the *Federal Gazette* of last Friday, that he would, if elected, administer the government wisely, and thus if not extinguishing party at least moderate its excesses; but it is impossible, if the sentiments disclosed in that letter are his real sentiments, that he can act with wisdom. The man who entertains such ideas is totally unfit to govern this or any other country. If he does not think as he writes, he is a hypocrit, and his pitiful cant is the step ladder to his ambition. Burr, I suspect, is not less a hypocrit than Jefferson; but he is a firm, steady man, and possessed, it is said, of great energy and decision; the other poor creature will be afraid of using his constitutional powers in defense of the people, lest he may offend those ignorant and suspicious sovereigns. Thus will the powers of the general government, at least the executive part of it, be benumbed and gradually usurped by the larger States and so will terminate the Union, if Jefferson should continue President for eight years.[1]

[1] Kate Mason Rowland, *The Life of Charles Carroll of Carrollton, 1737–1832,* II, 248.

☞ *"How Do You Bear the Long Days in the House?"*

JOHN CAMPBELL (1723–1806), fifth Duke of Argyll, loved his highland moors, west coast lochs, and brisk Scottish air more than London pavements, fogs, and smart society. But his son, John Douglas Edward Henry Campbell (1777–1848), with a career to make, must perforce endure the ways of city, court, and Sassenach by serving his regiment, representing Argyllshire in Parliament (1799–1822), and ingratiating himself in the society of London. That son would in time become a field marshal and in 1839 succeed his elder brother, George (1768–1839), as the seventh Duke of Argyll. But that was a long way before him in those youthful days in London, where his father's letter was a breath of the Highlands, with its talk of roebucks, salmon, military marches, and maps of Inverary. Such maps were worth encouraging a son to pick locks for, especially if the locks were, after all, one's own.

INVERARY, March 31st, 1801

MY DEAREST JOHNNY:

Your letters are always welcome, such as apply to me about Regimental Business less so than any. I cannot possibly comply with your request about Hopburne. I never have nor will I now overrule General Lister's opinion in such matters. I most heartily wish you could with propriety come away. How do you bear the long days in the house? I hope you attend closely, since you write me that you are perfectly well; it will give you the better pretensions to come away. I do not doubt your being tired of the Amusements of London, but you must not quite yet be tired of the Business of it. I desire you would by no means neglect going to the Queen's drawing room and to the Levy as soon as there is any. Tell George the same thing, and that I entreat and insist upon it, that he should not neglect it.

The books at Argyll House I fear much will be spoiled by damp; you must examine them carefully. I cannot send you the key, as it is locked up at Edinr., but you may pick the lock or get in at the window. If there still remains any farming or Gardening books, send them, or any Books which George thinks can be spared from London. Plans and maps relating to this place of Rosneath search for carefully and send, particularly one of the town of Inverary nailed up against the wall. Don't shilly shally and loiter about this, but set about it directly.

Send me the following Musick—*Non Nobis Domine,* in all the Parts as performed lately at the Oratorio. My favorite March for the Guards, much admired ten or twelve years ago, tho' perhaps scarcely known now. George knows what I mean.

I charge you strictly to visit frequently all your relations and Report to me the state of their health. . . . The Hills swarm with Roebucks and black Cocks. Richy began yesterday to whip the River, but without success. We have had very bad weather for eight or ten days, constant snow on the hills, but little or none on the downs; at present and for three or four days past remarkably fine. Best love to George. Influenza is at Edinr. and Glasgow and Campbelltown but scarcely a slight cold in this family during the whole winter, consisting of near 40 persons. Farewell, my dearest boy,

Most affectionately Yours,
ARGYLL[1]

[1] John . . . Campbell, ninth Duke of Argyll (ed.), *Intimate Society Letters of the Eighteenth Century*, II, 446–47.

☞ *Napoleon's Despotism Is a Fine Lesson for Intemperate Reformers*

WHEN Henry Temple (1739–1802), second Viscount Palmerston, after thirty-seven years in Parliament, wrote his last letter to his son, Henry John Temple (1784–1865), he did not know he was addressing a future prime minister (1855–58 and 1859–65). But he had great hopes for the promising young man, and thought that recent events in France should impress him with the danger of "violent and hasty revolutions." The Count Rumford he quoted was Benjamin Thompson, a precocious New Hampshire youth who turned against the American cause, ingratiated himself in London and Germany, and became Count Rumford and a member of the Royal Society.

Jan. 6, 1802

I should have written to you before had I had anything particular to say, but you have so many correspondents here that you are informed of all our transactions in the greatest detail and with the utmost exactness; and you leave me little opportunity of enlarging upon the usual topics of a father's lectures, which are reproofs for the past and good advice for the future. The first you take care never to deserve, and the latter you stand so little in need of that instead of holding out to you, as is often done, the example of some other person as a rule for your conduct, I am perfectly satisfied with entreating you to persevere as you have begun in a line so well-calculated to make you happy, respected and beloved.

Your good talents and your application have smoothed to you those difficulties which are often unsurmountable to those who are deficient in those qualities. As to what remains before you, your love of knowledge, a just disdain of being insignificant and an honest pride not to disappoint the general good opinion and expectation of the world will, I trust, induce you never to relax in your efforts to secure those attainments of which you will feel the advantage to the latest period of your life. . . .

Count Rumford thinks Buonaparte a very extraordinary character, full of energy and constant application, reserved and cold in his manner, forming no friendships, placing little confidence in and entering into no amusement or free society. . . . Nothing can be more despotic than Buonaparte's authority is or than all the quiet people wish it to be; seeing in it their only security against all the horrors and all the absurdities to which they were so long exposed. This is a fine lesson for intemperate reformers, and proves to all who wanted such proof that violent and hasty revolutions necessarily lead to a state of things so disastrous and an anarchy so dreadful and complicated, as to admit of no remedy but that of having recourse for protection (which is the principal object of real liberty) to a despotism far more absolute and complete than that which it was thought worth risking all those mischiefs to overturn. . . .

It is a melancholy consideration for those who have been honestly treading this reversable circle to find themselves come round at last to a point full as remote from liberty as that from which they set out. . . .[1]

[1] Brian Connell, *Portrait of a Whig Peer*, 453–56.

☞ *"Do Not Disappoint My Expectations"*

PROMINENT in Philadelphia as a patriot during the Revolution, Dr. Benjamin Rush (1745–1813) was for half a century the best-known physician in America. Here are two letters which he addressed to his son James Rush (1786–1869), the seventh of his thirteen children, then a student at Princeton and committed to a career in medicine. After graduating from Princeton in 1805, James took his medical degree at the University of Pennsylvania, where his father was a leader; he studied further in Edinburgh, and under his father's eye began the practice of medicine in 1811. He married an heiress and thereafter devoted himself to social as well as scientific interests. He was one of the first medical men to take an interest in psychology and published a two-volume *Analysis of the Human Intellect*.

PHILADELPHIA, May 25, 1802

MY DEAR SON,

Your letter which we received on Wednesday morning last gave great pleasure to all the family. I examined it critically and do not recollect to have met with but one word improperly spelled—and none improperly written. Continue to cultivate a taste for correctness in everything that comes from your pen. A man's future has sometimes been made by his letters' being seen by persons of judgment, and on the contrary many men have lost their characters for good sense and education from the same cause. Never write in a hurry. Even a common note upon the most common business should be written as if it were one day to be read in court or published in a newspaper.

I was much pleased to find that you begin to appreciate time. Recollect, my dear boy, your age and the years you have lost. Improve every moment you can spare from your recitations in reading useful books. Your uncle's library I presume will always be open to you, where you will find history, poetry and probably other books suited to your age. The last King of Prussia but one used to say, "A soldier should have no idle time." The same thing may be said of all schoolboys. Their common plays and amusements I believe instead of relaxing, often enervate their minds and give them a distaste to study. I do not advise you against such exercises as are necessary to health, but simply to avoid sharing in what are commonly called "plays." The celebrated Mr. Madison, when a student at the Jersey College,[1] never took any part in them. His only relaxation from study consisted in walking and conversation. Such was the character he acquired while at college, that Dr. Witherspoon said of him to Mr. Jefferson (from whom I received the anecdote) that during the whole time he was under his tuition he never knew him to do or say an improper thing.

Remember the profession for which you are destined. Without an extensive and correct education you cannot expect to succeed in it.

Do not, my dear son, disappoint my expectations and wishes of be-queathing my patients to an enlightened and philosophical physician. If you can discover a relish for knowledge, your wishes shall be grati-fied to the utmost of my power in your education after you leave col-lege. You shall visit Europe, if my life be spared, and draw from foreign universities all that you require to enable you to settle with advantage in Philadelphia. Think of these things and act up to them. But above all, preserve a conscience void of offense toward God and man. All true wisdom begins in true religion. Adieu! All the family join in love to you, my dear son, your affectionate father

BENJN: RUSH[2]

But two years later the young Princetonian's enlightenment was still incomplete:

PHILADELPHIA, March 27, 1804

MY DEAR SON:

The delay of your parents to answer your last letter was occasioned by the treatment they have received from you ever since your last return to Princeton, *manifested* in the careless manner in which your letters to them have been written. Your last was scarcely legible, and in point of composition such as we thought it very improper for a junior student in the College at Princeton and a young man of 18 years of age. From a sense of duty I shall continue my usual kind-ness to you. I have therefore enclosed you the money you have re-quested (25 dollars) from your distressed and offended father

BENJ: RUSH[3]

[1] The College of New Jersey became Princeton University.
[2] *Letters of Benjamin Rush* (ed. by L. H. Butterfield), II, 849.
[3] *Ibid.*, 879.

☞ *"The A.B.C. of Goodness
Is to Be Dutiful and Affectionate
to Parents"*

THE poetic imagination of Samuel Taylor Coleridge (1772–1834) could rise above reality to fabricate the palace of Kubla Khan and the painted sea of the Ancient Mariner, but as a father his exhortations differed only in their superior eloquence from those of many another parent, and seem a little cloying to men as well as boys of our own times. This letter was written to his younger son, Derwent Coleridge (1800–83), when the boy was seven years old.

ASHBY DE LA ZOUCH, COLEORTON,
Saturday night, Feb. 7, 1807.

MY DEAR DERWENT,

It will be many times the number of years, you have already lived, before you can know and feel thoroughly, how very much your dear Father wishes and longs to have you on his knees, and in his arms. Your Brother, Hartley, too whirls about, and wrings his hands at the thought of meeting you again: he counts the days and hours, and makes sums of arithmetic of the time, when he is again to play with you, and your sweet squirrel of a Sister. He dreams of you, and has more than once hugged me between waking and sleeping, fancying it to be you or Sara: and he talks of you before his eyes are fully open in the morning, and while he is closing them at night. And this is very right: for nothing can be more pleasing to God Almighty and to all good people, than that Brothers and Sisters should love each other, and try to make each other happy; but it is impossible to be happy without being good, and the beginning and the A.B.C. of goodness is to be dutiful and affectionate to their Parents; to be obedient to them, when they are present, and to pray for them [and to write] frequent letters from a thankful and loving heart when both or either of them chance to be absent. For you are a big Thought, and take up a great deal of room in your Father's Heart: and his eyes are often full of tears thro' his Love of you, and his Forehead wrinkled from the labor of his Brain, planning to make you good, and wise and happy. And your *Mother* has fed and cloathed and taught you, day after day, all your life; and has passed many sleepless nights, watching and lulling you, when you were sick and helpless, and she gave *you* nourishment out of her own Breasts for so long a time, that the moon was at its least and its greatest sixteen times before you lived entirely on any other food, than what came out of her body, and she brought you into the world with shocking Pains, which she suffered

93

for you, and before you were born for eight months together every drop of blood in your body, first beat in *her* Pulses and throbbed in *her* Heart. So it must needs be a horribly wicked thing ever to forget, or wilfully to vex a Father or a Mother, especially a Mother. God is above all: and only good and dutiful children can say their Lord's Prayer, and say to God, *"our Father,"* without being wicked even in their Prayers. But after God's name, the name of Mother is the sweetest and most holy. The next good thing and that without which you cannot either honor any person, or be esteemed by anyone, is *always to tell the truth.* For God gave you a tongue to tell the Truth, and to tell a Lie with it is as silly, as to try to walk on your Head instead of your Feet; besides it is such a base, hateful, and wicked thing, that when good men describe all wickedness put together in one wicked mind, they call it the Devil, which is Greek for *malicious Liar*: and the Bible names him a *Liar* from the beginning, and the Father of *Lies*. Never, never, tell a Lie—even tho' you should escape a whipping by it; for the pain of a whipping does not last above a few minutes, and the Thought of having told a Lie would make you miserable for days—unless, indeed, you are hardened in wickedness and then you must be miserable for ever—

But you are a dear Boy, and will scorn such a vile thing: and whenever you happen to do anything amiss, which *will* happen now and then, you will say to yourself "Well whatever comes of it, I will *tell the Truth,* both for its own sake, and because my dear Father [spoke] and wrote so to me about it."

I am greatly delighted that you are desirous to go on with your Greek; and shall finish this letter with a short Lesson of Greek. But more cannot be done till we meet, when we will begin anew, and, I trust, not to leave off, till you are a good scholar. And now go, and give a loving kiss to your little sister and tell her, that Papa sent it to her: and will give hundreds in a little time: for I am, my dear Child,

Your affectionate Father

S. T. COLERIDGE

P. S. I find that I cannot write in this space what I wished—therefore I will send you, dear child! a whole sheet of Greek Lessons in a few days. . . .[1]

94

Whether Derwent was uplifted by such letters or merely endured them, he took his degree at Cambridge and was ordained in 1825. He spent much of his later life as headmaster of Helston Grammar School in Cornwall (where Charles Kingsley was one of his students) and as rector of Hanwell. He also published religious tracts and theological pamphlets and a memoir of his elder brother, Hartley Coleridge (1796–1849), a prolific composer of verse and historical biography.

[1] *Unpublished Letters of Samuel Taylor Coleridge* (ed. by E. L. Griggs), I, 366ff.

☞ *The Sorrows of Werther Become the Adages of Paternity*

JOHANN WOLFGANG VON GOETHE (1749–1832), the great German poet and playwright, reacted in his youth against the ambitious pressures of his father and determined never to treat his own son in the same way, but could not resist offering some of the customary cautions to his illegitimate son August when the youth was nineteen and at the university.

KARLSBAD, August 17, 1808

As Michaelmas approaches, do write me your own view of your studies during the past semester; in what part of them you believe to have made progress, which you intend to take up during the coming winter. At the same time give me an accounting of your finances and an idea of your budget for the coming six months. I suppose I shall have to give you an extra allowance for travel and other unusual expenditures. . . .

Write [your mother] soon, unless you have already done so, and don't scribble so illegibly. The day is long enough. If you take one-third more time to write a letter, your correspondent will read it with pleasure, instead of having to take the trouble to practice the art of deciphering. . . .[1]

When August was twenty-seven and on the way to a respectable career of his own, Goethe wrote him a letter entirely concerned with

95

warnings against underwriting loans for anyone, and quoted his own father's precepts with approval:

[September 19, 1816]

When my good father started me out in life he gave me, among other examples of good counsel, one which had the force of a command, that never in my life was I to assume a responsibility of this character. He asked me not to let this warning die with him. . . . Such was the conviction of my father, and it has remained my own.[2]

Yet fourteen years later, when August was forty-one and an established citizen, the poet wrote him with unconscious humor:

. . . Any other remark would imitate the rhetoric of Polonius, a part I have never undertaken to play.[3]

[1] Ludwig Lewishon, *Goethe: The Story of a Man.*
[2] *Ibid.*
[3] *Ibid.*, I, 8.

☞ *A Great Inventor Is Ordered to "Form No Plans"*

THE Reverend Jedidiah Morse (1761–1826) was called "the father of American geography," but, as his letter shows, he was first of all a Congregational minister. He was also the father of Samuel Finley Breese Morse (1791–1892), who became the inventor of the telegraph. In the year Samuel was to graduate from Yale, he had acquired a local reputation for the miniatures in ivory he had made for amusement and had written his father that he wanted to become an artist.

CHARLESTOWN, July 26, 1810

DEAR FINLEY,—

I received your letter of the 22nd today by mail.

On the subject of your future pursuits we will converse when I see you and when you get home. It will be best for you to form no plans. Your mama and I have been thinking and planning for you.

96

I shall disclose to you our plan when I see you. Till then suspend your mind. . . .

It gives me great pleasure to have you speak so well of your brothers. Others do the same and we hear well of you also. It is a great comfort to us that our sons are all likely to do so well and are in good reputation among their acquaintances. Could we have reason to believe you were all pious and had chosen the "good part" our joy concerning you all would be full. I hope the Lord in due time will grant us this pleasure.

"Seek the Lord" my dear Son, "while he may yet be found."

Your affectionate father,

J. Morse[1]

[1] *Samuel F. B. Morse: His Letters and Journals* (ed. by Edward Lind Morse), I, 22.

☞ *"Abandon . . . Your Wicked Opinions"*

In March, 1811, Percy Bysshe Shelley (1792–1822) and his friend Thomas Jefferson Hogg were expelled from University College, Oxford, for declining to disavow authorship of a publication entitled *The Necessity of Atheism,* and for "contumacy in refusing to answer certain questions put them." Shelley, then nineteen, informed his father of this event in an affectionate but unrepentant letter. Sir Timothy Shelley came from a proud and ancient family, whose honor he may have cherished all the more because he had done more to preserve it conventionally than to enhance it adventurously. Had Percy been expelled from Oxford for the aristocratic peccadillos of gambling, seduction, or drunkenness, Sir Timothy would have been hurt and conventionally angry, but to have a son dismissed for writing a pamphlet which, reportedly, struck at the very roots of the establishment of church and state which the Shelley family had for generations ardently defended, was a blow almost too shocking to understand or endure. Not even the finest poetry that young Shelley later wrote could redeem in the eyes of his father that attack on the very roots of his society. He replied to Percy's report:

[April 5, 1811]

MY DEAR BOY:

I am unwilling to receive and act on the information you gave me on Sunday, as the ultimate determination of your mind.

The disgrace which hangs over you is most serious, and though I have felt as a father, and sympathized in the misfortune which your criminal opinions and improper acts have begot: yet you must know that I have a duty to perform to my own character, as well as to your younger brothers and sisters. Above all, my feelings as a Christian require from me a decided and firm conduct towards you.

If you shall require aid or assistance from me—or any protection—you must please yourself to me:

1st To go immediately to Field Place and to abstain from all communications with Mr. Hogg, for some considerable time.

2nd That you shall place yourself under the care and society of such gentleman as I shall appoint, and attend his instructions and directions he shall give.

These terms are so necessary to your well-being, and to the value, which I cannot but entertain, that you may abandon your errors and present unjustifiable and wicked opinions, that I am resolved to withdraw myself from you, and leave you to the punishment and misery that belongs to the wicked pursuit of an opinion so diabolical and wicked, as that which you have dared to declare, if you shall not accept the proposals. I shall go home on Thursday.—I am your affectionate and most afflicted Father.[1]

[1] Roger Ingpen, *Shelley in England,* 217.

☞ *"You Will Pass for More Than You Are Worth"*

JOHN LOWELL (1769–1840), bearer of one of the most distinguished names in Boston, had a large and lucrative law practice and was a founder and leader of Boston philanthropies and a member of the Harvard Corporation (1810–22), but he was also a cattle breeder and a botanist, and wanted to be known only as "the Norfolk farmer."

98

John Lowell to John Amory Lowell

When his son John Amory Lowell, who was to become a noted jurist and the grandfather of Harvard's famous president A. Lawrence Lowell, was entering Harvard College, his father gave him advice that blended Boston brahminism with Yankee plain speaking.

Roxbury, September 9, 1811

My dear Son:

Notwithstanding the time and labour which I have personally bestowed upon your education during the past few years, and although it might be expected, that I should consider an exemption from such incessantly repeated toils, a great relief, yet I can assure you, that the moment of surrendering these painful rights and of ceasing to perform these duties as a father, is to me the most anxious, and I may almost say, the most distressing of my life. We are about to vary in a very important manner the relation in which we have hitherto stood to each other. I am soon to lose forever a child, and you a father, so far as regards that parental discipline upon which the future character more than anything else, depends. Amidst the pains of this separation, I feel some consolation, that I have contributed to form or rather to preserve a heart pure, and affectionate, and I have been delighted to perceive, that through all the occasional but necessary strictness and sometimes severity, which an irritable sensibility to your welfare has obliged me to exercise, I have not in the smallest degree enfeebled that filial affection, which, is sometimes justly honoured with the name of Piety. . . .

Of the nature of your talents you have so frequently heard me speak, that you are well acquainted with my opinion of them. It is of the last importance, that you should be fully impressed with the natural infirmities of your understanding as well as any unfortunate propensities of your heart and disposition. . . .

It is peculiarly your misfortune that a certain readiness in acquiring a superficial knowledge of subjects has given you a reputation with many of your friends of possessing talents, with which both you and I know you are not favoured. The necessity is therefore greater, to exert yourself to support an opinion which you are conscious is too flattering. The most prominent trait in your mind is the rapidity with which you comprehend a subject and acquire some plausible knowledge of it,

99

unless this quality be equalled or exceeded by your feeble power of retaining what you have thus learned. . . . You have one other faculty of mind which in your present situation, and at your time of life, I consider a serious misfortune, and that is, the power of summoning all that you know upon any subject, and of displaying it to advantage. Hence it has often happened to you, and probably will always happen, that you will pass with those who do not know you intimately, for far more than you are worth. This will be a bribe to your indolence, and one of the greatest dangers which will beset you, because it may make you idle, and idleness will certainly lead you to vice in a place which offers so many temptations, or at least opportunities for it as the University does. . . .

Finally, remember what you owe to your ancestors. Let it not be said, that with advantages superior to any of them, you have been the first to tarnish a reputation which I hope and believe has been hitherto without a stain.

Your affectionate father,
J. Lowell[1]

[1] Letter in the Harvard University Archives, Hud. 811.51.

☞ *The Affectionate but Persistent*
Making of a Future Bishop

WILLIAM WILBERFORCE (1759–1833), Parliamentary leader in the abolition of the slave trade, exchanged more than six hundred letters with his third son, Samuel Wilberforce (1805–73), beginning when the boy was nine and the father fifty-five. Some boys would have reacted against such urgent indoctrination, but Samuel became Bishop of Oxford and of Winchester.

Sept. 13, 1814

I was shocked to hear that you are nine years old; I thought it was eight. You must take great pains to prove to me that you are nine not in years only, but in head and heart and mind. Above all, my dearest Samuel, I am anxious to see decisive marks of your having to undergo *the great change.* . . .[1]

June 5, 1817

Loving you as dearly as I do, it might seem strange to some thoughtless people that I am glad to hear you are unhappy. But as it is about your soul, and as I know that a short unhappiness of this kind often leads to lasting happiness and peace and joy, I cannot but rejoice. . . .[2]

May 2, 1818

How my heart bleeds at the idea of your being drawn into the paths of sin and bringing the grey hairs of your poor old father with sorrow to the grave—a most unlikely issue I do really hope; and, on the other hand, could you witness the glow of affection which is kindled by the prospect of your becoming the consolation of my declining years, you would want no more powerful motives to Christian obedience. . . .[3]

Sept. 17, 1819

My dear Boy, it is a great pleasure to me that you wish to know your faults. . . .[4]

BATH, Nov. 18, 1820

My dear Samuel, I am sorry to hear that your examination is, in part of it at least, disadvantageous to you. Does this not arise in part from your having stayed with us when your schoolfellows were at Maisemore? If so, the lesson is one which, if my dear boy digests it and bottles it up for future use, may be a most valuable one for the rest of his life. . . . Too much prosperity and self-indulgence (and staying at home may be said to be a young person's indulgence and prosperity) are good neither for men nor boys. . . . Our faults often bring some bad consequence long after they have been committed. . . .[5]

Feb. 20, 1822

The two chief questions you ask me relate to Repentance and to Predestination [Three pages of explanation of those topics follow.] I rejoice that it has pleased God to touch your heart. May I live, if it please God, to see you an honour to your family and a blessing to your fellow creatures. . . .[6]

March 17, 1822

... One of my chief motives now for paying visits is to cultivate the friendship of worthy people who, I trust, will be kind to my dearest children when I am no more. I hope you and the rest will never act so as to be unworthy of the connections I have formed. ...[7]

YOXHALL LODGE, Nov. 30, 1823

I enclose you the halves of bank notes; the remaining halves shall follow. Always, I repeat it, my dear son, open your heart to me without reserve on this as on any other subject. There is a vile and base sentiment current among men of the world, that if you wish to preserve a friend, you must guard against having any pecuniary transactions with him; but it is a caution altogether unworthy of a Christian bosom. It is bottomed on the supposed superior value of money to every other object, and on a very low estimate of human friendship. I hope I do not undervalue money, but I prize time at a far higher rate, and I have no fear that any money transactions can ever lessen the mutual confidence and affection which subsists between us. ...

... it affects me deeply to be now corresponding with four sons, one of them a husband and a father, and two of them at college. So life passes away. May you, my dearest son, be ever aware of the rapid flight of time, and of the uncertainty of life, that whenever the summons shall be issued, you may be found ready. Farewell!

Ever your affectionate Father,

W. WILBERFORCE[8]

[1] Religious conviction. *Private Papers of William Wilberforce* (ed. by A. M. Wilberforce), 176–77.

[2] *Ibid.*, 178.

[3] *Ibid.*, 180.

[4] *Ibid.*, 183.

[5] *Ibid.*, 187, 191.

[6] *Ibid.*, 195, 197.

[7] *Ibid.*, 202.

[8] Robert Isaac and Samuel Wilberforce, *The Life of William Wilberforce*, V, 208–209.

☞ *Most History is Falsehood,*
but Necessary to a Gentleman

BENJAMIN HENRY LATROBE (1764–1820) was engineer-architect of the Capitol in Washington and of various projects for the proper use and control of America's great rivers. It was while he was planning flood control of the Mississippi that he wrote this letter to his son, John H. B. Latrobe (1803–91), at West Point, later a lawyer for several railroad companies, inventor, public servant, and philanthropist.

NEW ORLEANS, May 4th, 1819

MY DEAR SON:

At the table at which I am sitting to write to you, and to congratulate myself on occasion of his birthday that I have a son such as you, I presume that my head is at least four feet below the present level of the water in the Mississippi, while yours is raised two or three hundred feet above the tide. You will be pleased to observe that I am congratulating myself in the first instance, but also most sincerely congratulate you that you are now sixteen and have hitherto given nothing but pleasure and satisfaction to your parents. May God preserve you, my dear boy, what you now are, an honest, upright and generous being, conscious of the errors of his own heart and head, and indulgent to those of his fellow beings, never looking for his own gratifications in the injury done to others, but always making self subordinate to humanity, to friendship and to justice. . . .

I am glad that you have taken seriously to the study of history. Gibbon's work will explain my motives for detesting dogmatic theology. But all history is a thing of misrepresentations, or absolute falsehoods, excepting in respect to great leading facts and events. Nothing, however, is so necessary to be known by a gentleman. Otherwise, a man may be apt to act one of the characters of your sporting clerk on the stage of real life. . . .

You see how old Daddies will preach.

Your truly affectionate father and friend,

B. HENRY LATROBE[1]

---

[1] J. E. Semmes, *John H. B. Latrobe and His Times*, 88.

☞ *The Affectionate Guidance of Budding Musical Genius*

GENIUS, especially in the arts, has seldom accepted with docility the opposition or cautions of parents. Genius is egocentric; fathers are often narrowly conventional or have other ambitions for their sons, and in many cases it is not easy to decide which is the more to blame for the resultant dissensions. But the relationship between Mendelssohn and his father was of a different and far happier kind. Abraham Mendelssohn-Bartholdy (1776–1835) made no pretension to talents or wisdom beyond those developed by his successful business, but he could appreciate what he could never wholly understand or share. Perhaps in this case, though not in comparable ones, the limitations imposed on Jewish families by German society made the inner life of the Mendelssohn family all the more gentle, loyal, and sympathetic. This letter was addressed not only to the future great musician Jacob Ludwig Felix Mendelssohn-Bartholdy (1809–47), then ten years of age, but to the younger children, Rebecca and Paul.

PARIS, July 2, 1819

First to you, dear Paul! I have been very well satisfied with your last two letters, and thank you for them. I wish you would not press so much on your pen. Get Mr. Gross to cut some for you, and then Uncle Joseph will cut them in the same way; keep your fingers loose, and sit upright. I have not at once answered your question regarding your marriage to Mieke,[1] because I wanted to consider the matter. Now I think we will wait till I come home, so that I may see Mieke first. If I find her properly washed and you are a good boy for a fortnight, we can speak about it.

You, my dear Felix, must state exactly what kind of music paper you wish to have; ruled or not ruled, and if the former you must say distinctly how it is to be ruled. When I went into a shop the other day to buy some, I found that I did not know myself what I wanted to have. Read over your letter before you send it off, and ascertain whether, if addressed to yourself, you could fully understand the commission contained in it.

You, dear Rebecca, have not written to me for a long time, and

104

shall not have a letter from me. You must be content with a kiss or a fillip—on paper. By-the-by, your last letter was a downright scrawl; I dare say the farm quills are to blame for it.

I beg to remind mother of the drilling-master for all of you. I think a good one might be found at Neufchâtel. Felix must diligently practice swimming, *but only in the swimming pool.* I hope the prohibition of gymnastics will not extend to our innocent place.

Your father and friend,
A.M.B.[2]

The happy relationship endured. Three weeks after the death of his father, Mendelssohn wrote of him: ". . . my Father was so good to me, so thoroughly my friend, that I was devoted to him with my whole soul, and during my long absence I scarcely ever passed an hour without thinking of him."

[1] The gardener's daughter, aged four. Paul was six.
[2] Walter Dahms, *Mendelssohn*, IV, 163.

☞ *"Do What I Request to Be Done"*

THERE is no convincing evidence that the great liberals of public life have been less authoritarian toward their children than great conservatives or merely average men. William Cobbett (1763–1835) goaded Parliament toward social reform and greater opportunity for the underprivileged. But when, in 1820, his son James Paul Cobbett was seventeen and alone in New York and Cobbett suddenly found himself made bankrupt by his debts, he sent firm orders to the youth he had always previously addressed as "My dear little James." The financial crisis passed; Cobbett returned to his crusades, and James settled in Manchester, practiced there at the bar, and once stood for Parliament as a radical.

LONDON, May 8, 1820

The time is now come, when you are to show by your actions that you have a real affection for your Mother and Sisters. It so happens that much will depend on you whether they are to be comfortable and respectable in future, or poor and forlorn. And the way for you to act is, cheerfully to do what I request to be done; not to set up your own will against mine; and to answer all my letters very punctually; not to think anything of little consequences because it may not hit your taste; but in all things to do my will to the utmost of your power. Pray be diligent and active and attentive, and your conduct will always be remembered by your affectionate Father,

WILLIAM COBBETT[1]

[1] Lewis Melville, *The Life and Letters of William Cobbett*, II, 138.

☞ *A Marriage Proposal under the Napoleonic Code*

GENERAL Comte Joseph Leopold Sigisbert Hugo (1774–1828) led a colorful life, both public and private. He was an early volunteer in the army of the French Republic and became a general under Napoleon. He displayed military skill as well as leonine courage in the Rhineland, Danube, and Italian campaigns, and later saved the French Army and the Emperor's brother Joseph Buonaparte in the retreat from Spain. After Waterloo the tide of his success ebbed, but he remained a vigorous gentleman and a kindly father. He saw, however, little of his son, Victor Marie Hugo (1802–85), for he had left the boy behind when he set up a separate home with his mistress in Blois.

Victor lived with his mother until he went to Paris to attempt a literary career. There he soon fell in love with Adèle Foucher, the daughter of family friends, but he was too impecunious to secure her parents' acquiescence to their marriage. Finally he gained something of a reputation and a few hundred francs from his writing, and believed that the parents Foucher would relent if his own father would urge their consent to the marriage. The old General wrote from Blois to Monsieur and Madame Foucher:

[BLOIS, 1822]

The military duties which engrossed me in my long career have prevented my having so thorough a knowledge of my children as you have. I know that Victor is exquisitely sensitive and has an excellent

106

heart, and I am fully persuaded that his other moral qualities in no way fall short of these. That heart, those good qualities, I venture to lay at the feet of your daughter. . . . Victor begs that I will demand from you in marriage the hand of this young lady whose happiness is bound up in his, and with whom he anticipates the greatest felicity.

Already, in order to do away with all preliminary difficulties, he has, with rare distinction, opened out for himself a brilliant career; he has in some measure secured a dowry in order to be able to offer your daughter a fitting establishment, reasonable hopes and excellent prospects. You know what he is, and what he possesses. Should brighter days ever dawn and the treaty of May 1814 be ratified,—if the mixed commission of sequestrations and indemnities should ever arrive at conclusions which would be adopted by the Government,— Victor would receive from his father the means of decently furnishing his house. As soon as I have received your answer, if it is what I hope it will be, I shall enclose the formal consent required by Article 76 in the Civil Code.[1]

> The proposal was accepted; the young pair were soon married, and gained prosperity by leaps and bounds. The marriage was on the whole a happy and successful one, though Victor in time gave evidence of having inherited his father's extramarital inclinations.

[1] *Victor Hugo: A Life* (believed to have been written by his wife, Adèle), II, 56.

☞ *The Dangers of Premature Travel*

HENRY WADSWORTH LONGFELLOW (1807–82) had not shown great promise as a poet when, at the age of sixteen and a student at Bowdoin College at Brunswick, Maine, he wrote to his father at their home in Portland asking permission to accept the offer of a seat in the sleigh of his classmate, Henry Weld, and thus spend a week in Boston during the college vacation. "I was never fifty miles from Portland in my life which I think is rather a sorrowful circumstance in the annals of my history." His father, Stephen Longfellow (1776–1849), graduate of Harvard and trustee of Bowdoin, distinguished lawyer, and congressman, replied:

[January 22, 1824]

Nothing affords me greater pleasure than to gratify the reasonable desires of my children, especially when they evince a disposition to promote the happiness of their parents, by diligent improvement of their time & talents, & uniform attention to those rules of morality which adorn the human character.

It is certainly desirable to know the world from observation as well as from books. A careful & accurate observation of men & manners is necessary to correct many erroneous impressions and impositions, to which the young & inexperienced are exposed in their first intercourse with the world. But there is danger on the other hand, that youth & inexperience by launching into the world too early, may imbibe many false & extravagant notions, that may prove injurious to them through life. To travel with advantage requires a maturity of understanding & an extensive knowledge of books. Youth is therefore the proper period for study, manhood for travelling, & intercourse with mankind. The ardor of youth is apt to place a false estimate on the novelties of the world, & is easily led astray by the achievements of pleasures, & enchanted by the visions of fancy, or the splendor of a deceitful world.

These are general observations, & not intended to have a particular bearing on your proposed visit to Boston, but designed to guard you against too ardent a desire to become a traveller early in life, which frequently injures rather than improves very young persons.

As the opportunity you mention will be a good one, if you are very desirous of availing yourself of it, I shall not object, if your mother thinks it best.[1]

[1] Lawrence Thompson, *Young Longfellow (1807–1843)*, 51ff.

☞ *A Poet Denies His Son
a Christmas Holiday*

ALTHOUGH for many years the popular poems and novels of Sir Walter Scott (1771–1832) brought him large royalties, he also spent largely and feared that the security of his children would have to depend on their own efforts. His second son and fourth child, Charles Scott (1805–41), was at Oxford, with an undergraduate's desire to make the most of every holiday, when Sir Walter wrote him a restraining letter. Charles was an obedient son; after Oxford he embarked on a diplomatic career, but died at the age of thirty-six at Teheran, where he had been an attaché at the British Embassy.

EDIN. 1st Dec. 1824

MY DEAR CHARLES,—

I write briefly at present to say that with every wish to yield to whatever suits your comfort I do not think it advisable that you should leave Oxford in the short Christmas vacation as you propose in a letter to Sophia. Nothing suffers so much by interruption as a course of study—it is in fact just stopping the stone while it is running down hill and giving yourself all the trouble of putting it again in motion after it has lost the impulse which it had acquired. I am aware that you propose to *read* in Wales but as the only object of your leaving college would be to find amusement I rather fear that to that amusement study is in much danger of being postponed. . . .

You will meet with many men and these by no means such as can be termed neither indolent or dissipated who will conceive their business at College well enough done if they can go creditably through the ordinary studies. This may do very well for men of independent fortune or who have a direct entree into some profitable branch of business or are assured from family connection of preferment in some profession. But *you* my dear Charles must be *distinguished,* it will not do to be moderate. I could have got you a good appointment in India where you might have had plenty of field sports and made money in due time. But on your affording me proofs when under Mr. Williams that you were both willing and able to acquire knowledge I was readily induced to change your destination. God knows if I have chosen for the best but this I am certain; that you like every youth of sufficiently quick talent have the matter much in your own power. Solitude and ennui you must endure as others before you, and there is the advantage in both that they make study a resource instead of a duty. The greatest scholars have always been formed in situations where there was least temptation to dissipation.

I do not mean that which is mischievous and criminal but the mere amusements, in themselves indifferent and even laudable, which withdraw the mind from serious study.

I beg you therefore to remain *inter silvas academi* although they are at the present season both lonely and leafless. We shall think of you with regret at Christmas but we will be comforted with thinking that you are collecting in your solitary chambers the means of making yourself an honour to us all and are paying an apprentice fee to knowledge and distinction.[1]

[1] *The Letters of Walter Scott* (ed. by H. J. C. Grierson and others), VIII, 441.

☞ *"You Have Hitherto Been a Spoiled Child"*

IF any man were capable of making an apparent letter to a son seem authentic when it was primarily a literary document, that man would perhaps have been Jonathan Swift, the author of *Gulliver's Travels*. But next to him, the choice might fall on William Hazlitt, critic, essayist, enthusiast over Shakespeare, and ardent seeker of truth in his own peculiar ways. Hazlitt (1778–1830) had several children, but only one survived early childhood, and that was his son William, who was born in 1811. Since the writing of this purported letter to a son cannot be confidently dated, we cannot tell whether it was really written to and for William when he went off to school, or whether William became merely the excuse for a literary essay. Its content suggests that it was authentic, or at least that the son provided the inspiration.

MY DEAR LITTLE FELLOW:

You are now going to settle at school, and may consider this as your first entrance into the world. As my health is so indifferent, and I may not be with you long, I wish to leave you some advice (the best I can) for your conduct in life, both that it may be of use to you, and as something to remember me by. I may at least be able to caution you against my own errors, if nothing else.

As we went along to your new place of destination, you often repeated that "You durst say they were a set of stupid, disagreeable people," meaning the people at the school. You were to blame in this. It is a good old rule to hope for the best. Always, my dear, believe things to be right, till you find them to the contrary; and even then, instead of irritating yourself against them, endeavor to put up with them as well as you can, if you cannot alter them. You said—"You were sure you should not like the school where you were going"—This was wrong. What you meant was that you did not like to leave home. But you could not tell whether you should like the school or not, till you had given it a trial. Otherwise, your saying that you should not like it was determining that you would not like it. Never anticipate evils; or, because you cannot have things exactly as you wish, make them out worse than they are, through mere spite and wilfulness.

You seemed at first to take no notice of your school-fellows, or rather to set yourself against them, because they were strangers to you. They knew as little of you as you did of them, so that this would have been a reason for their keeping aloof from you as well, which you would have felt as a hardship. Learn never to conceive a prejudice against others, because you know nothing of them. It is bad reasoning, and makes enemies of half the world. Do not think ill of them, till they behave ill to you; and then strive to avoid the faults which you see in them. This will disarm their hostility sooner than pique or resentment or complaint.

I thought you were disposed to criticize the dress of some of the boys as not so good as your own. Never despise any one for any thing that he cannot help—least of all, for his poverty. I would wish you to keep up appearances yourself as a defense against the idle sneers of the world, but I would not have you value yourself upon them. I hope you will be neither the dupe nor victim of vulgar prejudices. Instead of saying above—"Never despise any one for anything he cannot help"—I might have said,—"Never despise any one at all"; for contempt implies a triumph over and pleasure in the ill of another. It means that you are glad and congratulate yourself on their failings or misfortunes. The sense of inferiority in others, without this indirect appeal to our self-love, is a painful feeling, and not an exulting one.

You complain since, that the boys laugh at you and do not care about you, and that you are not treated as you were at home. My dear, that is one chief reason for your being sent to school, to inure you betimes to the unavoidable rubs and uncertain reception you may meet with in life. You cannot always be with me, and perhaps it is as well that you cannot. But you must not expect others to shew the same concern about you as I should. You have hitherto been a spoiled child, and have been used to have your own way a good deal, both in the house and among your play-fellows, with whom you are too fond of being a leader; but you have good-nature and good sense, and will get the better of this in time. You have now got among other boys, who are your equals, or bigger and stronger than yourself, and who have something else to attend to besides humouring your whims and fancies, and you feel this as a repulse or piece of injustice. But the first lesson to learn is that there are other people in the world besides yourself. There are a number of boys in the school where you are, whose amusements and pursuits (whatever they may be) are and ought to be of as much consequence to them as yours can be to you, and to which therefore you must give way in your turn. The more airs of childish self-importance you give yourself, you will only expose yourself to be the more thwarted and laughed at. True equality is the only true morality or true wisdom. Remember always that you are but one amongst others, and you can hardly mistake your place in society. In your father's house, you might do as you pleased: in the world, you will find competitors at every turn. You are not born a King's son to destroy or dictate to millions: you can only expect to share their fate, or settle your differences amicably with them. You already find it so at school: and I wish you to be reconciled to your situation as soon as and with as little pain as you can. . . .

Do not begin to quarrel with the world too soon: for, bad as it may be, it is the best we have to live in—here. If railing would have made it better, it would have been reformed long ago: but as this is not to be hoped for at present, the best way is to slide through it as contentedly and innocently as we may. The worst fault it has is want of charity: and calling *knave* and *fool* at every turn will not cure this failing. Consider (as a matter of vanity) that if there were not so many knaves and fools as we find, the wise and honest would not be those rare and shining characters that they are allowed to be. . . .

An inattention to our own person implies a disrespect to others, and may more often be traced no less to want of good nature than of good sense. The old maxim—*Desire to please and you will infallibly please*—explains the whole matter. . . . As to all worldly advantages, it is to the full of as much importance that your deportment should be erect and manly as your actions. . . .

You will find the business of life conducted on a much more varied and individual scale than you would expect. People will be concerned about a thousand things that you have no idea of, and will be utterly indifferent to what you feel the greatest interest in. You will find good and evil, folly and discretion more mingled, and the shades of character running more into each other than they do in the ethical charts. . . . It is the vice of scholars to suppose that there is no knowledge in the world but that of books. Do you avoid it, I conjure you; and thereby save yourself the pain and mortification that must otherwise ensue from finding out your mistake continually!! . . .

If you ever marry, I would wish you to marry the woman you like. Do not be guided by the recommendation of friends. . . . Chuse a mistress from among your equals. You will be able to understand her character better, and she will be more likely to understand yours. Those in an inferior station to yourself will doubt your good intentions, and misapprehend your plainest expressions. . . . As mistresses, they will have no sympathy with you; and as wives, you can have none with them. . . . No woman ever married into a family above herself that did not try to make all the mischief she could in it. . . .[1]

[1] *The Complete Works of William Hazlitt* (ed. by P. P. Howe), XVII, 86–100.

☞ *"All I Wish Is to Be Freed from You"*

LUDWIG VAN BEETHOVEN (1770–1827) had a brother Karl, who, according to the great composer, "had a bad wife." When Karl died in 1815, Beethoven took his eight-year-old nephew from the "bad wife" and brought up "like a nobleman," the boy "who is now to be my son." Beethoven's affection was highly emotional and possessive, and at the age of twelve young Karl ran away and joined his mother. Beethoven soon got the boy back, but it is doubtful that he ever forgave him. In any case, Karl repeatedly disappointed and angered him:

BADEN, May 31, 1825

. . . Enough of this! Spoiled as you may have been, it would do you no injury to pay some attention at least to simplicity and truth. I have suffered too much from your artifices, and it will be a hard matter for me to forget them. Even if I would always submit, without murmuring, like an ox to the yoke, if you should behave like this to others, you will never gain the good-will of any human creature. God knows all I wish is to be freed from you, from this base brother, and from these my worthless relations. May God hear my prayer! for I can never trust you more!

Your father—alas!
yet, fortunately, not your father[1]

In the nature and expressions of Beethoven's emotions, that letter might have been written by a passionate lover to an unfaithful mistress, and the likeness may be significant. It was written, however, just after Karl, at eighteen, had been expelled, apparently for laziness and deceit, from the University of Vienna. Alternating between wrath and affection, Beethoven gained the boy admission to the Polytechnic Institute, but there, too, he did poorly and was ethically incorrigible. Facing examinations he had not prepared for, he attempted, or pretended to attempt, suicide. Beethoven was reduced to frightened forgiveness:

BADEN [October 5?], 1825

MY DEAR SON,—

No more of this!—only come to my arms, you shall not hear one harsh word. For God's sake do not rush to destruction, you shall be received with as much affection as ever. As to what is to be thought of and done for the future, we will talk it over in a friendly manner together. Upon my word of honour, you shall hear no reproaches, which indeed can now do no good. You have nothing to expect from me but the most anxious and loving care and help. Only come, come to the heart of your father. Come at once on receipt of this!

BEETHOVEN[2]

Karl got into the army, but the army was as unenthusiastic as he about the results. He then entered the civil service, where he spent the rest of his career in obscure mediocrity.

[1] *Letters of Beethoven* (trans. and ed. by Emily Anderson), III, 1202; Alexander Wheelock Thayer, *The Life of Ludwig van Beethoven*, III, 254; *Beethoven's Letters* (trans. by J. S. Shedlock, ed. by A. C. Kalischer), 348.

[2] *Letters of Beethoven* (Anderson), III, 1258; Thayer, *Life*, III, 254; *Beethoven's Letters* (Shedlock and Kalischer), 356–57. The text of these letters is not identical with any one of the three translations cited, but is a carefully phrased version.

☞ *A Victorian Statesman Encourages His Son to Slaughter*

JOHN GEORGE LAMBTON (1792–1840), later ambassador to Russia, high commissioner to Canada, and first Earl of Durham, was the father of the "Master Lambton" of Sir Thomas Lawrence's famous portrait. At the age of eight "Master" Charles William Lambton (1818–31), whose health was precarious and who died five years later, gleefully wrote his father that he had shot a lark in the family park. The graphic enthusiasm of his father's reply may be excused by his pleasure in any sign of physical health in his invalid son.

HEATON PARK, Saturday night [1826]

MY DEAREST CHARLES,—

I am in a state of mingled astonishment and delight. Only think of your having killed a lark! *But* was it sitting, flying, or hopping? Do tell me all the particulars of so interesting an event. I hear from your mama that its head was nearly blown off. Did it sit still whilst you fired into its ear, or how was the murderous deed accomplished? I hope I shall find you so improved when I return that I shall get a dish of at least a dozen for dinner. By the way, I cannot say that your handwriting is improved.

Ever most affectionately,
D.[1]

[1] Stuart J. Reid, *Life and Letters of the First Earl of Durham, 1792–1840,* I, 188.

☞ *Learn from Europe, but Remain a Good Yankee*

THE prosperous old families of Boston never ceased to keep their contacts with the England of their origin. And like English aristocrats, they sometimes sent their sons to widen their education by travel on the Continent. But they often did so in the proud conviction that what Europe could teach a son was, though valuable, less good than what America could give him. Their concern was not that their sons would absorb too little of Old World ways and values, but too much. Amos Lawrence (1786–1832) had indeed a right to respect himself and his traditions. A wealthy banker of the inner social circle, he had led in developing the textile industry in New England, and one textile city bears his family name. He was also a generous philanthropist, and in his later years made a practice of giving away exactly five-sixths of his annual income. When he sent his son, William Lawrence, to Europe for a final polishing, he followed him with this letter. William returned safely to take his appropriate place as a Yankee and a Lawrence.

BOSTON, Nov. 11, 1828

I trust that you will have had favoring gales and a pleasant passage, and will be safely landed at Havre within twenty days after sailing. You will see things so different from what you have been accustomed to, that you may think the French are far before or behind us in the arts of life, and formation of society. But you must remember that what is best for one people may be the worst for another; and that it is true wisdom to study the character of the people among whom you are, before adopting their manners, habits, or feelings, and carrying them to other people.

I wish to see you, as long as you live, a well-bred, upright *Yankee*. Brother Jonathan should never forget his self-respect; nor should he be impertinent in claiming more for his country or himself than is his due; but on no account should he speak ungraciously of his country or its friends abroad, whatever may be said by others.

Lafayette in France is not what he is here; and, whatever may be said of him there, he is an ardent friend of the United States; and I will venture to say, if you introduce yourself to him as a grandson of one of his old Yankee officers, he will treat you with the kindness of a father. . . .[1]

[1] *Extracts from the Diary and Correspondence of the Late Amos Lawrence* (ed. by William R. Lawrence, M.D.), 83.

☞ *A Businessman Recommends His Son to a Public, Not a Clerical, Life*

SIR JOHN GLADSTONE (1764–1851) was a wealthy merchant of Liverpool and for many years a member of Parliament. His son, William Ewart Gladstone (1809–98), then twenty-one, wrote him a long letter in which, doubtless under the influence of the religious fervor at Oxford where he was then an undergraduate, he stated that he wished to make his career in the church. His father replied to the future prime minister:

LEAMINGTON, 10 May, 1830

MY BELOVED WILLIAM,—

I have read and given my best consideration to your letter, dated the 4th, which I only received yesterday. I did hope that you would have delayed making up your mind on a subject so important as your future pursuits in life must be to yourself and to us all, until you had completed those studies connected with the attainment of the honours or distinctions of which you were so justly ambitious, and on which your mind seemed so bent when we last communicated respecting them.

You know my opinion to be, that the field for actual usefulness to our fellow-creatures, where a disposition to exercise it actually exists, is more circumscribed and limited in the occupation and duties of a clergyman, whose sphere of action . . . is necessarily in a good degree confined to his parish, than in those professions or pursuits which lead to a more general knowledge, as well as a more general inter-course with mankind, such as the law, taking it as a basis and intro-duction to public life, to which I had looked forward for you, con-sidering you, as I do, peculiarly well qualified to be made thus emi-nently useful to others, with credit and satisfaction to yourself.

There is no doubt but as a clergyman, faithfully and conscientiously discharging the duties of that office to those whose spiritual interests are entrusted to your care, should you eventually be placed in that situation, that you may have both comfort and satisfaction, with few worldly responsibilities, but you will allow me to doubt whether the picture your perhaps too sanguine mind has drawn in your letter before me, would ever perhaps be practically realized.

Be this as it may, whenever your mind shall be finally made up on this most important subject, I shall trust to its being eventually for your good, whatever that determination may be. In the meantime I am certainly desirous that those studies with which you have been occupied in reading for your degree may be followed up, whether the shorter or the longer period may be necessary to prepare you for the results. You are young and have ample time before you. Let nothing be done rashly; be consistent with yourself, and avail your-self of all the advantages placed within your reach. If, when that ordeal has passed, you should continue to think as you now do, I shall not oppose your *then* preparing yourself for the church, but I do hope that your final determination will not until then be taken, and that whatever events may occur in the interval, you will give them such weight and consideration as they may appear to merit. . . .

Your mother is much as usual—with our mutual and affectionate love, I am ever your affectionate father

JOHN GLADSTONE[1]

[1] John Morley, *The Life of William Ewart Gladstone*, II, 600.

☞ "*Should You Ever Succeed
in Getting into Parliament . . .*"

IT is interesting that the two young men who would become rival Liberal and Tory prime ministers for Queen Victoria at almost the same time in their youth elected another career, and that both were urged by their fathers to embrace politics. Five years after Gladstone had informed his father that he wished to become a clergyman, Benjamin Disraeli (1804–81) was establishing himself as a writer, though his latest publication was concerned with government. Just before his thirty-first birthday in 1835 he published an essay of some two hundred pages entitled *A Vindication of the English Constitution*. His father Isaac D'Israeli (1766–1848), scion of a wealthy Jewish merchant family, literary researcher and author of *Curiosities of Literature*, wrote to Benjamin:

Dec. 23, 1835

Your vulgar birthday was, it seems, last Monday, but your noble political birth has occurred this week, and truly, like the fable of old, you have issued into existence armed in the full panoply of the highest wisdom. You have now a positive *name* and a *being* in the great political world, which you had not ten days ago. It is for you to preserve the wide reputation which I am positive is now secured. I never doubted your powers—they were not latent to me. With more management on your side they would have been acknowledged long ere now—universally. You never wanted for genius, but it was apt in its fullness to run over.

You have acquired what many a genius never could, *a perfect style,* and that's a pickle which will preserve even matter less valuable than what you, I doubt not, will always afford the world. You have rejected the curt and flashy diction which betrayed perpetual effort. . . . All that now remains for you to do is to register "a vow in heaven" that you will never write anything inferior to what you have now written, and never to write but on a subject which may call forth all your energies.

Should you ever succeed in getting into Parliament I will know that your moral intrepidity and your rapid combinations of ideas will throw out many "a Vindication" in the brilliance and irresistible force of your effusions. No man thinks more deeply, while he delights even common eyes by the beauties of his surface. . . .

Take care of your health—that is the only weak part which I fear about you— . . .[1]

[1] W. F. Monypenny and G. E. Buckle, *The Life of Benjamin Disraeli, Earl of Beaconsfield,* I, 310.

☞ *Old Hickory Shows His Softer Side*

ANDREW JACKSON (1767–1845) had no son, but adopted his nephew, Andrew Jackson, Jr. It was while Old Hickory was seventh President of the United States (1829–37) and deep in the reorganization of his cabinet and his struggle with the Bank of the United States that young Andrew wrote to him from Philadelphia that he had become engaged to marry Miss Sarah Yorke, a Quaker orphan whom the President had never seen. Old Hickory replied:

[WASHINGTON,] October 27, 1831

MY SON . . .

. . . the sooner this engagement is consummated the better. You say that Sarah possesses every quality necessary to make you happy. . . . You will please communicate to her that you have my full and free consent that you be united in the holy bonds of matrimony; that I shall receive her as a daughter, and cherish her as my child. . . . Present me affectionately to Sarah, for although unknown to me, your attachment has created in my bosom a parental regard for her. That, I have no doubt, will increase on our acquaintance. I am

Your affectionate father[1]

The parental regard of the old warhorse for Sarah did indeed increase on acquaintance. Within a few months he loved her more than any other woman since the death of his wife, Rachel. Young Andrew proved a disappointment, but Jackson wrote of Sarah in his will, "She has been more than a daughter to me."

[1] *Correspondence of Andrew Jackson* (ed. by J. S. Bassett), IV, 365.

☞ *On Giving up the Law for the Church*

WHEN James Robert Hope (1812–73) was an undergraduate at Christ Church, Oxford, he struck up a friendship with his fellow-student William Ewart Gladstone, who had inclinations to take orders in the Church of England. Hope planned to make his own career in the law, but he accepted first a flattering fellowship at Merton College. Oxford was at that time the center of a new and intense religious movement, and under its influence and perhaps that of Gladstone, Hope wrote to his father that he was eager to take holy orders. General the Honorable Sir Alexander Hope (1769–1837), member of Parliament and governor of Sandhurst military college, replied to his third son:

LUFFNESS [NORTH BRITAIN,] September 1, 1834

MY DEAR JAMES,—

I have been deeply interested and affected by your letter of the 28th ultimo. The single-heartedness with which you unfold to me the working of your mind with regard to the Church becoming your profession, shows a self-determination and honesty of intention which, in my opinion, and I believe also in the eye of God, fits you even now for undertaking the sacred duties of one of His servants.

The dreams of ambition and the temptations of the world, and the suggestions of indolence, though modified by the circumstances of each individual, are common to all men; and I may say that he is most likely to pass a happy life, and one profitable to salvation, whose mind *soonest detects, to its own conviction,* the emptiness of such speculations—which in their prosperous state have terminated in disappointment, whilst in most instances they never reach the maturity requisite for a trial. Such is the result of my experience in witnessing the career of men endowed beyond others with superior minds, whose life was a fever, and whose death was not prepared for *in the way which I feel* to be of vital importance to us all.

Beyond these reflections, I consider that we are in this world to do good, and, above all, that species of service which under the extended view of charity comprehends an universal benevolence, in constant activity, to soothe the afflicted and alleviate human suffer-ings—whether they proceed from bodily or mental causes; and when to the exercise of these Christian virtues is added the nobler exercise of eloquence to turn men to God, I deliberately give you a Father's opinion that the Church is the highest Profession that you can em-brace—and *in your case* the one under God's blessing most likely to conduce to the health and happiness of your life, as also to produce your talents and education in a sphere of the most extensive utility.

The decision now rests with you, and may God bless the course you may prefer, whatever that may be!

Yours affectionately,
ALEXANDER HOPE[1]

James decided, after all, to become a barrister, and soon developed a large and lucrative practice. But his interest in religion continued, and in time he became a chief adviser to John Newman, and himself joined the Roman Catholic Church, with Manning, in 1857. His father was not living then, but might not have taken kindly to his son's Catholicism. James remained a distinguished lay citizen, and on acquiring Abbotsford, the former home of Sir Walter Scott, changed his name to Hope-Scott.

[1] *Memoirs of J. R. Hope-Scott* (ed. by R. Ormsby), I, 69.

☞ *A Champion of Colonial Freedom* *Denies It to His Slaves*

JOSEPH GRAHAM (1759–1836) of North Carolina, captain of mounted infantry in the Revolution, was severely wounded when commanding the defense of Charlotte against Tarleton and Corn-wallis, but recovered to represent his state at the Constitutional Conven-tion in 1783, to be prominent in state politics and education and a ruling elder of the Presbyterian church. When he died at the age of seventy-seven, the *Charlotte Journal* eulogized him as "a bright pat-tern of those virtues which are essential to the purity and peace of society." But the gift he made two years earlier showed the limitations of that "bright pattern," for he was more generous to his son than to his slaves.

Know all men by these presents that I. Joseph Graham, of the County Lincoln, North Carolina, for and in consideration of the natural love and affection, which I have and do bear, to my son, James Graham, of the County of Rutherford, in the State aforesaid, and for divers other good causes and considerations, do give, grant, confirm and deliver to my said son, James Graham, the following negro slaves, Towit,—Carter, aged 44 years & valued at $500., Harvey, aged 9 years, & valued at $375., Sam aged 8 years & valued at $300., and Mary aged 15 years & valued at $200. To Have and to Hold all the aforesaid negro slaves and their future increase to the said James Graham, his Executors, administrators and assigns forever.

In testimony whereof I have hereto set my hand & seal this 23 day of September, A.D. 1834.

Test.—ALF'D GRAHAM
Ack'd—(Seal)—J. GRAHAM[1]

James left no mark on the annals of time, though Joseph's eleventh child, William Alexander Graham (1804–1875), who was not blessed by a similar gift, became congressman, senator, and governor of North Carolina, secretary of the navy, and a candidate for the vice-presidency with General Winfield Scott; a county in North Carolina was named for him.

[1] *Papers of William A. Graham*, I, 325.

A Father Consoles His Sick Child with the Prospect of an Early Entry into Heaven

THE Reverend Edward Bickersteth (1786–1850) had as a young man abandoned the law and "worldly prosperity" for the church, and was for many years rector of Watton in Hertfordshire and secretary of the Church Missionary Society. He also composed more than seven hundred hymns and was recorded as a "bright example of the grace of Christ." When one of his small children fell seriously ill, the "bright example" wrote this consoling letter.

May 15, 1835

My dearest C,—

And so it pleases God still to keep my dear child a weak, sickly, feeble creature! And why? because He loves you not? So the world would think. But those who know the word of God, as your parents and friends do, say the very reverse—because He does love you, and desires to make you His own dear child, and to call you to His heavenly kingdom. Say then to Him: "O my loving Father, I leave myself entirely in Thy hands, to be ill, or to be well, as Thou, who art all wisdom, and all love, seest best." . . .[1]

> Four months later the child died, and Bickersteth wrote to a daughter, "How thankful we ought to be that this dear child, the companion of your infancy, is taken from this evil world, and admitted to the glorious company above."

[1] T. R. Birks, *Memoir of Edward Bickersteth*, II, 70, 71, 74.

☞ On the Practical Uses of Liberal Learning

Daniel Webster (1782–1852) could move a nation with his eloquence more easily than he could move a son to wisdom. In 1836 that son, Daniel Fletcher Webster (1813–62) was twenty-three, and impatient to make his fortune. But the fortune did not come, and the young man grew restless and full of large ideas. His father offered advice on the practical uses of learning.

Washington, January 15, 1836

Dear Fletcher,—

I am sorry for your disappointment about the aid-ship; but never mind, I believe you are as well without it; if you think not, I will see more about it, when I get home. I believe the military honors of our family terminated with my father. I once tried to be a captain, and failed, and I canvassed a whole regiment to make your uncle an adjutant, and failed also. We are destined not to be great in the field of battle. We are not the sons of "Bellona's bridegroom"; our battles are forensic; we draw no blood, but the blood of our clients.

Your notions of matters and things are quite right, as applicable

124

to your own condition. You must study practical things. You are in the situation of the *haud facile energunts,* and must try all you can to get your head above water. Why should you botanize, when you have not field enough to bear one flower? Why should you geologize who have no right on the earth, except a right to tread on it? This is all very well; I thought so, at your age, and therefore studied nothing but law and politics. I wish you to take the same course; yet still save a little time, have a few *horas subsecivas* in which to culti- vate liberal knowledge; it will turn to account, even practically. If, on a given occasion, a man can, gracefully, and without the air of a pedant, show a little more knowledge than the occasion requires, the world will give him credit for eminent attainments, It is an honest quackery. I have practiced it, and sometimes with success. . . .

We find connections and coincidences, helps and succors, where we did not expect to find them. I have never learned anything which I wish to forget; except how badly some people have behaved; and I every day find, on almost every subject, that I wish I had more knowl- edge than I possess, seeing that I could produce it, if not for use, yet for effect. . . .[1]

In 1841, Webster, then secretary of state in the administration of Harrison and Tyler, appointed Fletcher his chief clerk, and when Webster was absent, Fletcher acted virtually as secretary of state. In 1849, President Zachary Taylor appointed Fletcher surveyor of the Port of Boston with an excellent salary, and he married the daughter of Supreme Court Justice Story. He edited his father's letters, and in 1861 helped to recruit the Twelfth Massachusetts Infantry and was made its colonel. In 1862 he was killed at the second Battle of Bull Run.

[1] *The Private Correspondence of Daniel Webster* (ed. by Fletcher Webster), II, 40.

☞ "What He Builds Today He Destroys Again Tomorrow"

IF someone had told Heinrich Marx in 1837 that his son would write the book which, more than any other, would upset the established structure of society, inspire wars and revolutions, and divide the twentieth-century world into two antagonistic camps, he would not have believed it, for he had little confidence in his son's creative capacities. And if Heinrich had then been told the tenets that son would advance with such devastating results, he would not have approved them. For Heinrich Marx was a cultivated, prosperous lawyer and judge in the city of Trier in the Moselle valley, a Jew who had embraced Christianity, a citizen of high standing and a conservative. So was his wife, who later remarked, "If Karl, instead of writing a lot about Capital, made a lot of Capital, it would have been much better."

On November 10, 1837, when Karl Marx (1818–83) was nineteen, he wrote to his parents of his life and interests in the university, where his activities were as extravagant as his letters. He worked, he said, day and night; read Greek and Latin not required; composed three volumes of verse; and, in his own words, "attempted to evolve a philosophy of law . . . laid down a few metaphysical principles, in all about 300 sheets . . . and a dialogue on the Source and Inevitable Development of Philosophy . . . as a result of these various activities I passed many sleepless nights, engaged in many battles, and had to endure much mental and physical excitement." In his reply, his father criticized his aimless and discursive studies, his "breeding monstrosities," his unwise living habits and his failure to concentrate on the organized and proscribed studies of the university. He then compared him with his more sensible fellow students:

[1837]

Indeed these young men sleep quite peacefully except when they now and then devote the whole or part of a night to pleasure, whereas my clever and gifted son Karl passes wretched sleepless nights, wearying body and mind with cheerless study, forbearing all pleasures with the sole object of applying himself to abstruse studies: but what he builds today he destroys again tomorrow, and in the end he finds he has destroyed what he already had, without having gained anything from other people.

At last the body begins to ail and the mind gets confused, whilst these ordinary folks steal along in easy marches, and attain their goal if not better at least more comfortably than those who condemn youthful pleasures and undermine their health in order to snatch at the ghost of erudition, which they could probably have exorcized more successfully in an hour of speech in the society of competent men— with social enjoyment in the bargain.[1]

[1] "Karl Marx Papers," *Neue Zeit*, Vol. I, No. 1 (16th year).

☞ *"I Send Money to You That You May Have the Option of Declining to Use It"*

NEXT to Boston, the Berkshire Mountain area was in the last century the home of cultivated and prosperous Yankees. One of its more cultivated but less wealthy residents was Charles Sedgwick (1791–1856). His public career as county clerk was modest but respected, and he and his family represented Yankee ideals of the Emerson type. When his son, Charles Sedgwick, Jr. (born *ca.*1821), then about sixteen, was away at school, Sedgwick wrote to him:

LENOX, September 19, 1837

. . . I should have answered your letter before, but I have not before today been in possession of ten dollars, which I enclose to you with pleasure. You do not say what you want it for, but I send it to you that you may have the option of declining to use it. I consider it one of the greatest uses for money for a young person to have it, and yet from sense, judgment and principle, to resist those temptations to which the young generally yield. Perhaps you will think the sum rather too small to give dignity to this moral, but to tell you the truth it is half I have, and the residue I want today. I think I can safely promise to procure and forward for your use all that you express a deliberate wish to have. I do not mean to go half way with you in my confidence. My *reliance* is on your character, your generous and disinterested disposition, your confidence in my affection, your determination to do the right thing, knowing my circumstances, and that there is nothing I wish to conceal from you. It is, if not my greatest, certainly one of my greatest pleasures to believe your virtue is strong, that it is not dependent so much on the guardianship and vigilance of your friends as on your own clear apprehension of right and fixed principles.[1]

[1] *Letters of Charles Sedgwick* (ed. by his sister), 87.

☞ *Find Your Happiness in Diligence and Marriage*

MANY a statesman has found it easier to formulate the welfare of society than to bring it to his son. One of them was Henry Clay (1777–1852), congressman, senator, secretary of state, and almost President. He had five sons and six daughters, among them James B. Clay, who had moved westward to Missouri to make his fortune. But his letters to his father indicated he had found neither fortune nor happiness. Henry Clay made suggestions:

WASHINGTON, January 22, 1838

MY DEAR JAMES,—

I received your letter of the 1st inst. this day, and the perusal of it gave me much concern. I had previously received from you a letter complaining of your solitary condition, and stating that you were not happy. I answered it, but as you do not acknowledge the receipt of my answer, I suppose it had not reached you.

I desire most ardently, my dear son, your happiness, and that of every child I have. You know that I was not anxious for you to go to Missouri. The very circumstances which now exist, I anticipated. But you were confident, and I yielded. I have wished to see you happily married, under the hope that with a wife whom you loved, and the prospects of a family, you might be contented and happy. You tell me that you have not the means to go into society; but you have not informed me what means you allude to. I have been very desirous that you should go much more into society than you have done, and why should you not? Do you want clothes? The slightest intimation of your wishes to me on that subject would have commanded them. I have refused you nothing that you have asked me. I have been, I own, exceedingly anxious that you should avoid all dissipation, but with that restriction, I have not cared how much

128

society you enjoyed, or, rather, I have wished that you should see more of it.

In my former letter, I expressed a wish that you would attend diligently to your business, make yourself as happy as you can, and upon my return home, I would see if we could not make some arrangement by which you should return to Kentucky.

Of one thing you may be certain, that you will be happy no where without constant employment. That is the great secret of human happiness.

I should be very glad to have you near us. Have you another overseer? You have never informed me. If you have, I do not see why you might not, at any time leave home for some weeks, go to Ashland, or make a visit to see our military lands, or go to your uncle Porter.

Of one thing you may be assured, my dear son, that I not only feel the deepest interest in your welfare and happiness, but that I am always willing to do everything to promote it. I am the more concerned about you, because John has lately given me great pain, and I almost despair of him. When you reflect how much anxiety I have suffered on account of my sons, I am sure that you will be stimulated to persevere in a course of regularity and propriety. . . .[1]

Neither James nor Henry Clay's other sons rose to their father's prominence, though James was later appointed chargé d'affaires at Lisbon by President Zachary Taylor and also served briefly in Congress before he died in 1863.

[1] *The Private Correspondence of Henry Clay* (vol. IV of *The Works . . .*, ed. by Calvin Colton), 424.

☞ *"For God's Sake, Remember Your Younger Brothers"*

WHATEVER was the group misconduct at Harrow in 1839, the fear that his second son, Frederick, was involved greatly troubled Sir Robert Peel (1788–1850), who had already served once as prime minister (1834–35) and would soon do so again. A serious misdemeanor at Harrow might impair the boy's career and also his own. He wrote to Frederick, then sixteen:

WHITEHALL, January 28, 1839

MY DEAR FREDERICK,

I take it for granted you are wholly and entirely free from the disgrace which has been inflicted on your companions, and I do earnestly implore you for your own sake, for the sake of your character and future happiness, for the sake of your name and family, and above all, for the sake of example to your younger brothers, to have manliness and firmness enough to resist the influence of bad example and the temptation to do what is wrong.

Do not listen to the silly advice that only turns industry and honourable exertion into ridicule. It is only given by those who have no hope to distinguish themselves and who wish to drag even superior minds and talents to their own level.

For God's sake, remember your younger brothers. They will form themselves on the example of their elder ones, and it is incumbent on you to set a good one.

Write us immediately and comfort us. Tell us that you are fulfilling the promises you made us, and that you are resolved not to swerve from the path which will lead you to honour.

Your affectionate father,
ROBERT PEEL[1]

Young Frederick Peel (1823–1906) survived both the event and the exhortations. He served for more than twenty years as a member of Parliament and at various times as financial secretary to the Treasury, railway commissioner, undersecretary for the Colonies, and undersecretary for war, and ended as Sir Frederick Peel, K.C.M.G.

[1] *The Private Letters of Sir Robert Peel* (ed. by George Peel), 219.

☞ *A Future Poet Is Warned Against Mere Verse-Making*

PETER GEORGE PATMORE (1786–1855), an intimate friend of Charles Lamb and William Hazlitt, was editor of the *New Monthly*

Magazine and something of an author in his own right. His son Coventry Kersey Patmore (1823–96) was at sixteen a student in France, where his studies were somewhat diverted by a devotion to verse-writing and to a "Miranda" living in the Place Vendôme, who was really a Miss Gore and two years older than her admirer. Coventry Patmore later rose above light verse and wrote *The Angel in the House*.

LONDON, Oct. 31, 1839

MY DEAR COVENTRY,

... Touching poetry—if you have any of it in you it will be pretty sure to come out—whether you will or no—but do not *entice* it out—for of all the follies there is none so foolish in its results as the habit of mere *verse*-writing. There is no harm in the Charivari man's phrenological prognostic about your head. But if there is anything in it (in the prognostic I mean) or if you think there is anything in it—it is a reason the more for eschewing verse-making: for I verily believe there never yet was a *poetical* genius that was not cursed rather than blessed by the possession—unless it was Shakespeare.

Bye the bye, you never tell me what you do in Paris when you go there—whether you stay there all day—whether you *dine* (or merely call) at the "Place"—if not, *where* and *how* you dine, etc. Not that I am anxious about your proceedings at the "Place"—but (shall I say it) I am rather anxious. And this is not so much from what you say, as from what you do *not* say. Whenever Telemachus was *silent* to his mentor, there was always some cause for fear to both. Do not suppose that I (your mentor—if you will let me be so) have any fear that the "Place" should prove to you a Calypso's Island. But it may prove a more dangerous place—a Prospero's Island—without a Prospero to watch over the welfare of its inhabitants. You will tell me in reply that it is indeed a place

> *"full of sweet airs*
> *That give delight and hurt not"*

and that its Miranda *is* a Miranda—and what would I desire more? Yes—my dear little boy—but you are not a Ferdinand. But (again you reply) can evil come out of good? Yes—the greatest evils out of the greatest goods—always understanding the axiom of now—

131

middle of the 19th century. Still, be assured, no evil can come to you even out of evil, much less out of good, while you lay bare all your thoughts and feeling to *me*, and listen to mine in return, as those of one who would fain be to you a Mentor and a Ulysses in one.

I never preach to you, and never shall: though I am by no means sure that I may not some day or other—if you should happen to be cast away on an enchanted ilse like that of Calypso, and wish to take up your abode there—watch an opportunity of inveigling you to the top of a convenient cliff, and push you into the sea, jump in after you, at the imminent peril of both our precious lives: which is more than Mentor did for his Telemachus—for, being an immortal, he knew that there was no danger for either of them.[1]

[1] Basil Champneys, *Memoirs and Correspondence of Coventry Patmore*, I, 39–41.

☞ *Dumas Defends His Mistress to His Protesting Son*

HISTORY provides no parallel to Alexandre Dumas *père* (1802–70) and Alexandre Dumas *fils* (1824–95), for both were outstanding novelists. They were also unique in the volatility of their emotional relationship, which varied from bitter reproaches to deep affection and mutual admiration. When Alexandre the son was only sixteen he broke with his father in bitter protest against his father's long-term mistress, Ida Ferrier. The situation was not without irony, since the son was illegitimate. Dumas *père* reacted in a fashion which some readers have thought typically French.

[January, 1840]

It is not my fault, but yours, that the relationship between us is no longer that of father and son. You came to my house, where you were well received by everyone, and then, suddenly, acting upon whose advice I do not know, decided no longer to recognize the lady whom I regarded as my wife, as should have been obvious from the fact that I was living with her. From that day, since I had no intention of taking advice (even indirectly) from you, the situation of which you complain, began and has lasted, much to my sorrow, for six years.

It can cease whenever you wish. You have only to write a letter to Madame Ida, asking her to be to you what she is to your sister; you will then be always, and eternally, welcome. The happiest thing that could happen to you is that this liaison should continue, since, having had no child for six years, I am now certain that I shall never have any, so that you are now not only my eldest, but my only, son.

I have nothing else to tell you. All that I would have you consider is this, that, should I marry any woman other than Madame Ida, I might well have three or four children, whereas with her, I shall have none.

I trust that in all this you will consult your heart rather than your interests, though this time—contrary to what usually happens—the two are in agreement. I embrace you with all my heart.[1]

That disagreement was amicably settled in the end, but there were other dissensions equally emphatic, larded between periods of the closest and most intimate affection. Something more than a decade later, when the son as well as the father had become a literary figure in Paris, each professed to admire the other's writing more than his own. After the first night of a successful play by his son, Dumas *père* told his friend Villemissant, "He is my best work." When another friend remarked that the son's play was so good that his father must have had a share in it, Dumas *pere* replied, "Oh, but I had! The author is by me." On a New Year's Day in the 1850's, Dumas *père* wrote his son:

MY DEAR CHILD,—

One more year of loving you; one less year to love you in. That is the sad side.

Meanwhile, without totting up the time that remains, let us love each other as much as we can.

Your

January first   A. DUMAS[2]

[1] André Maurois, *The Titans: A Three-Generation Biography of the Dumas*, 151.
[2] H. A. Spurr, *The Life and Writings of Alexandre Dumas*, 146.

☞ *A Bishop of London Recommends*
Expedient Deference to Social Prejudice

THE several sons of Charles James Blomfield (1786–1857), bishop of London and translator of Aeschylus and the Greek lyric poets, had varied careers. One commanded a ship in the Mediterranean; another became president of the Architectural Association and consulting architect to the Bank of England; a third was a Fellow of All Souls College, Oxford, and author of a biography of his father. It was probably to the last of these, then at Oxford preparing for a career in the Church of England, that the Bishop wrote about 1840:

I do not absolutely condemn shooting, even in a clergyman, though I think it much better that he should not indulge in it; as I know, from inquiry and observations, that it gives great offense to many people. This being the case, I think it desirable that a young man intended for Holy Orders should not acquire a taste for it, which may sometimes be a temptation to him afterwards; and, generally speaking, it is better that the sons of clergymen should be very guarded in their pursuits and amusements, and especially the sons of Bishops, who are always watched with a jealous and often with an unfriendly eye.

Of course, the example of my own family will always be brought in answer to any reasoning I may employ in speaking to young men who are looking for admission into the ministry; and it is rather on account of your peculiar position as my son, than from anything absolutely wrong in the amusement itself, that I should request you to make this little sacrifice for my sake. I thank you, my dear F——, for writing to ask my opinion, the propriety of which, I am persuaded, you will see by and by, if you think it rather strict at present. But you will readily perceive a great difference between this and questions of dress, etc.—*that* principle, if just, might be extended to all the necessary business of life. Clergymen *dress* as other men do, but more soberly than other men are required to do, by reason of the nature of their calling. Here the question is—not whether they shall *shoot* as other men do, but whether sporting *at all* is suitable to their profession. If that be settled in the negative, it then becomes a question, whether those who are looking to be clergymen had better sport, or not, and, with the knowledge which I have of people in general, I am inclined to recommend that they should not.

The same objection does not apply to *fishing*, simply because it is *considered* to be a more quiet and peaceable amusement. In fact, if the thing in itself is admitted to be innocent, the question of doing it, or not, becomes very much one of expediency, with reference partly to our tastes and habits, and partly to the feelings and prejudices of other men.[1]

[1] Alfred Blomfield, *Memoir of Charles James Blomfield*, 355.

☞ *"A Man's Character Must Be Graduall," and Not Without Humility*

THOMAS WATSON BAGEHOT, banker in Somersetshire, was able to provide his promising son with the university education he himself lacked and admired. That son, Walter Bagehot (1826–77), future editor of *The Economist* and writer on politics, was doing well at Balliol College, Oxford. Although in his letters to his son Thomas Bagehot with implicit humility professed his own limitations of talent and education, he set standards of mind and character that even a young Balliol scholar could wisely admire and emulate.

HERDS HILL, 11th December, 1842, Sunday Morning
The education required in the present day must be laid on a wide foundation, and ample time given for raising the structure. A tree and its roots and branches is a better figure. The roots must be deep and firm if the trunk is to grow high and its branches spread safely, and all its parts must grow together. A man's character must be graduall: forming religiously, morally, and intellectually, which cannot be done, I think, but through the influence of time and the circumstances which accompany it. If one part of the character be forced too much, it will generally be at the expense of some strength in another, and I often think that we may trace some of the faults of young and old collegians to the too exclusive pursuits of collegiate

honours. In saying this, however, I know you will not think that I under-rate the exertions that must and ought to be made by them. Temperance is all I wish to inculcate and a wide view of the blessings of education founded in wisdom and virtue.

Every day do I feel how much I have lost in not having had such an education as I wish to give you, and you need not therefore fear that anything will be wanting on my part to secure you its advantages. I do not repine although I feel that there is a world beyond my ken, and that that world of knowledge and usefulness may bring with it more happiness than can be mine. But thankfulness and not mere contentment is the deep sentiment of my heart for the blessings of my lot, and as I have education enough for the immediate duties of my station, and for growing wiser and better for that world where light and truth and peace reign now and forever, I must be more anxious to make a right use of the talent I have, than disappointed that it is not larger.[1]

[1] E. I. Barrington, *Life of Walter Bagehot*, 96–97.

☞ Paternal Deference to Demanding Young Genius

ALTHOUGH John James Ruskin (1785–1864), "an entirely honest merchant," dealt chiefly in wines, his taste was said to have been "as exact in art as in sherries," and when his son, John Ruskin (1819–1900), showed precocity in artistic fields, his parents gave him every possible encouragement and support. Perhaps they were too sympathetic, for at the age of twenty-eight John was a very spoiled young man and thought his budding genius justified excessive sacrifices from his doting parents. Even then, his father assumed the blame for disappointing the son, then on a tour of Scotland.

[FOLKSTONE, Oct. 4, 1847]

I have already said that the tone of your later letters was so much more cheerful and confiding, and expressive of some, if not continued, at least frequent snatches of enjoyment, that they were most agreeable. Out of the cold and barren country your more healthy feelings were gleaming a little. The blues and purples and mountain shades and moist heather were making themselves seen and felt; and I guessed you were better at Macdonalds than at Leamington or Dunbar, from whence a few letters rather dulled my spirits, for they disclosed that, more than I had had an idea of, we had been, from defects perhaps on both sides, in a state of progression by antagonism, each discerning half the truth and supposing it to be the whole. I suppose we may have mutually defrauded each other's character of its right and merit.

In some of these letters I read more of the suffering and unpleasantness I had unwittingly in part inflicted on you in past hours. To my memory they are burdened with no greater share of troubles than attaches, I believe, to most families since the fall. I have, however, no fear of the future, for tho' I have no prospect of becoming greatly changed, a circumstance has made me reflect that I was exceedingly wrong and short-sighted in all interruptions occasioned to your pursuits. Mama says I am very exacting, and so I was about the Book-revising, but never more after it was done.

Whilst reading now this unlucky first volume for press, I had by me some loose proof sheets for second, and I have been so struck with the superiority of second volume, and so positively surprised at the work, that I became angry with myself for having by my impatience and obstinacy about the one thing in any way checked the flight or embarrassed the course of thoughts like these, and arrested such a mind in its progress in the track and through the means which to itself seemed best for arriving at its end. You will find me from conviction done with asking you to do anything not thought proper by yourself to do. I call this reading with profit and to the purpose.

Two points in your letters I only remember half-distressed me, and perhaps they were merely illustrative as used by you. You say we could not by a whole summer give you a tenth of the pleasure that to have left you a month in the Highlands in 1838 would have done, nor by buying Turner and Windus' gallery the pleasure that two Turners would have done in 1838, you having passed two or three years with a sick longing for Turner. I take blame to myself for not sending you to the Highlands in 1838 and not buying you a few more Turners; but the first I was not at all aware of, and the second I freely confess I have been restrained in from my very constitutional prudence. . . . I have, you know, my dearest John, two things to do: to indulge you and to leave you and Mama comfortably provided for. . . . but if you have any longings like 1842 I should be glad to know them, whilst I honour you for the delicacy of before suppressing the expressing them. . . .

On the subject noticed in one of your letters on our different regard for public opinion, this is a malady or weakness in me, arising from want of self-respect. The latter causes much of my ill-temper, and when from misunderstanding or want of information I was losing some of my respect for you my temper got doubly bad. We are all wanting in our relations towards the Supreme Being, the only source of peace and self-respect. . . .[1]

[1] *Works of John Ruskin* (ed. by E. T. Cook and Alexander Wedderburn), XXXVI, *xviii.*

☞ *The Emancipation of a Future King*

On the ninth of November, 1858, Robert Edward (1841–1910), Prince of Wales, later King Edward VII (1901–10), entered upon his eighteenth year. On the morning of that day a document, signed by both his parents, was delivered to him. A son of Queen Victoria (1819–1901) and Prince Albert (1819–61) could hardly have expected that his birthday letter would be without moral exhortations, or his new freedoms without oversight. It was reported that as he read the letter, "Dear Bertie" had tears in his eyes. Readers of the present generation, less used to the parental attitudes of the Victorians, may wonder whether the tears were those of gratitude or frustration. Certain it is that when finally free of parental restraints, "Bertie" reacted notably against the parental code.

Life is composed of duties, and in the due, punctual and cheerful performance of them the true Christian, true soldier and true gentleman is recognized.

You will in future have rooms allotted to your sole use in order

to give you an opportunity of learning how to occupy yourself un-
aided by others and to utilize your time in the best manner, viz: such
time as may not be otherwise occupied by lessons, by the different
tasks which will be given you by your director of studies, or reserved
for exercise and recreation. A new sphere of life will open for you,
in which you will have to be taught what to do and what not to do,
a subject requiring study more important than any in which you have
hitherto been engaged. For it is a subject of *study* and the most
difficult one of your life, how to become a good man and a thorough
gentleman. . . .

Your personal allowance will be increased; but it is expected that
you will carefully order your expenditure so as to remain strictly
within the bounds of the sum allowed to you, which will be amply
sufficient for your general requirements. . . .

You will try to emancipate yourself as much as possible from the
thraldom of abject dependence for your daily wants of life on your
servants. The more you can do for yourself, the greater will be your
independence and real comfort.

The Church Catechism has enumerated the duties which you owe
to God and your neighbor—let your rule of conduct be always in
strict conformity with those precepts, and remember that the first and
principal one of all, given us by our Lord and Saviour Himself, is
this: "that you should love your neighbor as yourself, and do unto
men as you would they should do unto you." . . .[1]

[1] Sir Sidney Lee, *King Edward VII: A Biography*, I, 52.

☞ *The Hero of Texas Deplores
Concealed Weapons—and Tobacco*

THE greatest name in Texas is still that of Sam Houston
(1793–1863), warrior, Indian fighter, creator of the Lone Star State,
congressman from 1823 to 1846, and then senator from the new state
of Texas from 1846 until secession in 1861. Houston opposed secession
on any terms, but was enough of a Southerner to bequeath to his eight
children his twelve Negro slaves on his death in 1863, just before Lin-

139

coln's Emancipation Proclamation. His son Sam joined a Texas Confederate regiment at the age of eighteen, was wounded and repeatedly reported killed, but survived the war and its difficult aftermath. Shortly before that cataclysm, when young Sam was sixteen, the old warhorse of a Senator wrote him rather surprising advice.

WASHINGTON, 18th Feby. 1859

DEAR SON,

In writing to you in my last letter, I did not admonish you not to carry concealed weapons.

I hope that you will never do it, and were I with you I could state my reasons, which I am sure you would approve, with your perceptions of propriety. And oh, my son, by all means keep from the use of tobacco. Don't smoke or chew. Besides the habit of its use it is an expense and trouble. I look to you as one on whom my mantle is to fall, and I wish to leave it to you, without a rent in it. It is natural that I should desire you to wear it worthily, aye nobly, and to give additional lustre to all that may descend to you! If you have a suitable opportunity, I wish you to pay more attention to Language, History, Geography and Grammar, than to Mathematics. If this can be done delicately, I wish it done, not otherwise. . . .

Affectionately thy Father,
SAM HOUSTON[1]

[1] *The Writings of Sam Houston* (ed. by Amelia W. Williams and Eugene C. Barker), VII, 300.

☞ *Study Your Lessons So That You Will Be Taken for a Gentleman*

IT was the poet in Alfred Tennyson (1809–92) who found in Cornwall the castles and scenery that inspired his idylls of the Arthurian knights, but the father in Tennyson who in the same short letter gave his son the customary paternal advice, with a slightly class-conscious tinge. His elder son, Hallam Tennyson (1852–1928), was about eight years old when he received this note.

TINTAGEL, Aug. 25th, 1860

MY DEAR HALLAM:

I was very glad to receive your little letter. Mind that you and Lionel do not quarrel and vex poor mama who has lots of work to do; and learn your lessons regularly; for gentlemen and ladies will not take you for a gentleman when you grow up if you are ignorant. Here are great black cliffs of slate-rock, and deep black caves, and the ruined castle of King Arthur, and I wish that you and Lionel and mama were here to see them. Give my love to Grandpa and to Lionel, and work well at your lessons. I shall be glad to find you know more every day.

Your loving papa,
A. TENNYSON[1]

Hallam succeeded his father as the second Lord Tennyson, served as governor general of Australia (1902–1904), published a two-volume life of his father (1897), edited sonnets by Charles Tennyson Turner (1880), and wrote casual verse of his own.

[1] Hallam Tennyson, *Alfred Lord Tennyson: A Memoir*, I, 461.

☞ *A General from Texas*
Resigns His Commission in 1861

ONE of the ablest generals in the Confederate Army, until his untimely death at the moment of victory in the bitter and bloody Battle of Shiloh against Grant in 1862, was Albert Sidney Johnston (1803–62). He was also, according to Southern historians, a man of "unimpeachable character," as the following letter to his son William Preston Johnston (1831–99), then in Louisville, Kentucky, indicates. When the Civil War was about to break out, General Johnston was in command of the United States Army of the Pacific, with headquarters in San Francisco.

SAN FRANCISCO, CALIFORNIA, April 9, 1861

MY DEAR SON:

Yesterday the newspapers of this city announced that Texas had completed all arrangements contemplated as necessary to separate her

destiny from the General Government, the final act being the taking
[of] the oath of allegiance to the new Confederacy by the Legislature
and the other State officers. I had hoped to the last that a reconciliation
would be, by some great statesmanlike move in the right direction,
effected, with such guarantees as would be satisfactory and re-estab-
lish the tranquility of the Southern mind and those fraternal relations
which alone make our confederate system possible. Whether these
acts could or could not be rightfully done under the Constitution
need no longer be discussed. The people have resolved, and so declared to the world, to establish a government for themselves. A great
fact thus presents itself, which must be dealt with not with techni-
calities, but in view of all the considerations and interests which affect
the future of two great sections of our country. To continue to hold
my commission after being apprized of the final action of my State,
to whose partiality in a great measure I owe my position, could find
no justification in my conscience; and I have, therefore, this day forwarded the resignation of my commission for the acceptance of the
President, which I hope may be promptly accepted. I have asked
that my successor be appointed and ordered to relieve me as soon as
practicable. . . .

My escutcheon is without a blur upon it and will never be tarnished.
I shall do my duty to the last, and when absolved take my course.
I must now look out for a livelihood for my poor family; how or
where to find it is not apparent, but with my courage all will not be
lost. Give my love to Hennie, Rosa, Mrs. Duncan and the children.

Your affectionate father,
A. S. JOHNSTON

P.S. You had, perhaps, better let the announcement of my resignation come from the department.[1]

William Preston Johnston (1831–99) graduated from Yale in
1852 and established himself in legal practice in Louisville. He became
a lieutenant colonel in the Confederate Army and an aide-de-camp of
President Jefferson Davis. After the war he returned to his law practice in Louisville, but in 1880 accepted the presidency of the University
of Louisiana (later, in 1884, called Tulane) and served until his death

nineteen years later. He also wrote the life of his father. He was "a typical gentleman of the old South; well-bred, courteous, kindly."

[1] William Preston Johnston, *The Life of Gen. Albert Sidney Johnston,* 270.

☞ *A Southerner Regrets Secession but Detests Democracy*

JONATHAN WORTH (1802–69), a descendant of Nantucket Quakers, somehow found his way to North Carolina, where he became a leading citizen before the Civil War. When that war came, he confessed his opinions to his son, David G. Worth, then "a prosperous merchant in Wilmington, North Carolina." But like many another Southerner he supported his state in decisions he did not approve, and during the war served as state treasurer. From 1866 to 1868 he was governor of North Carolina.

ASHEBORO [North Carolina,] May 15, 1861
I have been forced by surrounding facts to take sides, or rather front, with my section. I regard a prudent peace, even accompanied with the contemplated secession of the State, and her union with the Confederate States, as preferable to a civil war on a gigantic scale; but I have not a particle of confidence in the wisdom or the patriotism of the new rulers. to whom we submit. I leave the Union and the flag of Washington because I am subjected and forced to submit to my master—democracy, detesting it with more and more intensity as I become better acquainted with its leaders and its objects. I still believe that no respectable and stable government can ever be established in America, except on the plan of a Union, such as that we are now so wickedly and foolishly overthrowing. Even on the plan of a peaceful separation, North America will soon become Mexicanized. New York will next secede, the doctrine being once recognized. The great and populous Northwest, cut off from the Ocean, excepting by the assent of foreign states, will open a road to the great highway of Nations with the sword—but if the free States act on the plan they

now avow of preserving the Union by force of arms, no odds at what cost of life or treasure, the civil strife will soon beget the most diabolical purposes. The masses, already deluded with the notion that Slavery is the *cause*, when in fact it is now only the *pretext* with the leaders of both sections, will proclaim freedom to the slaves and arm them against us.

I think the South is committing suicide, but my lot is cast with the South and being unable to manage the ship, I intend to face the breakers manfully and go down with my companions.

These are my calm conclusions.

I have been deeply pained at the responsibilities of my position. I have become resigned from conscious impotence to do anything to impede the evils upon us, and have concluded to drift with the current, keeping a sharp lookout for some opportunity, by the aid of Divine Providence, to divert the ship of State from the gulf of ruin toward which we are bound.

What are your plans? Will you stay in Wilmington or return to the back country and make corn until the war is over?

Soon after the Fourth of July war will begin in earnest, if not sooner; or peace will be made. The former, in my opinion, is most probable. I do not think the North is making her military preparations as a mere bravado.

In the event of war can you continue your business with any prospect of success? If an invasion of this State is made, is not Wilmington likely to be one of the first places to be attacked? . . .[1]

[1] *The Correspondence of Jonathan Worth* (coll. and ed. by J. G. de Roulhac Hamilton), I, 144.

☞ *An Adams Criticizes Some Trends in American Democracy*

No American family has served its nation with more continuous distinction than the Adams family of Quincy and Boston. John Adams helped to found the Republic; he and his son John Quincy Adams were its presidents; their descendants have served it in public office and private character. One of them, Charles Francis Adams (1807–86), was, as minister to Great Britain during the Civil War, more instrumental than any other man in persuading England not to support the Confederate cause, as the public records and the distinguished account by his son Henry Adams make clear. Yet even while serving his country so well, Charles Francis Adams confided his disappointment in some of its trends to his eldest son, Charles Francis Adams, Jr. (1835–1915), then in the Union Army. That son, "inheriting a great tradition of public service . . . felt the obligations which it imposed." He ended the Civil War a brigadier general and became an expert on American railroads, a historian, and a civic leader. His own son, who bore his name, was a secretary of the navy.

LONDON, July 4, 1862

. . . This detestable war is not of our own choosing, and out of it must grow consequences important to the welfare of coming generations, not likely to issue from a continuance of peace. All this is true, and yet here in this lonely position of prominence among people selfish, jealous, and at heart hostile, it needs a good deal of fortitude to conjoin private solicitude with the unavoidable responsibilities of a critical public station. I had hoped that the progress of General McClellan would have spared us much of this trouble. But it is plain that he has much of the Fabian policy in his composition which threatens to draw the war into greater length. Of course we must be content to take a great deal on trust. Thus far the results have been all that we had a reasonable right to expect. Let us hope that the delay is not without its great purposes. My belief is unshaken that the end of this conflict is to topple down the edifice of slavery. Perhaps we are not yet ready to come up to that work, and the madness of the resistance is the instrument in the hands of Divine Providence to drive us to it. It may be so, I must hold my soul in patience, and pray for courage and resignation.

This is the 4th of July. Eighty-six years ago our ancestors staked themselves in a contest of a far more dangerous and desperate character. The only fault they committed was in omitting to make it more general and complete. Had they then consented to follow Thomas Jefferson to the full extent of his first draught of the Declaration, they would have added little to the seven years' severity of their struggle and would have entirely saved the present trials from their children. I trust we shall not fall into any similar mistake, and if we are tempted to do so, I trust the follies of our enemy will avert us from the consequence of our weakness. This is the consideration which makes me most tolerant of the continuance of the war. I am not a friend of the violent policy of the ultras who seem to me to have no guide but their own theories. This great movement must be left in a degree to develope itself, and human power must be applied solely to shape the consequences so far as possible to the best uses. . . .[1]

[1] W. C. Ford, *A Cycle of Adams Letters*, I, 161.

☞ *An Inciter of the Civil War Opposes Fighting in It*

No man more deliberately angered the men of the Southern states or more ardently incited the men of the North to belligerence than William Lloyd Garrison (1805–79), the "Great Liberator" who courageously devoted his life to condemning slavery. But when his son George T. Garrison, then twenty-seven, wished to take a commission in the Fifty-fifth Massachusetts Regiment (the second regiment comprised, except for its officers, of Negroes), his father, though professing not to impede his son's free decision, brought not only arguments but strong moral pressure to bear on him not to join.

BOSTON, June 11, 1863

Though I could have wished that you had been able understandingly and truly to adopt those principles of peace which are so sacred and divine to my soul, yet you will bear me witness that I have not laid a straw in your way to prevent your acting up to your own highest convictions of duty; for nothing would be gained, but much lost, to have you violate these. Still, I tenderly hope that you will once more seriously review the whole matter before making the irrevocable decision. . . .

In making up a final judgment, I wish you to look all the peculiar

146

trials and perils in the face that you, in common with all others connected with the colored regiment, will have to encounter. Personally,
as my son, you will incur some risks at the hands of the rebels that
others will not, if it is known that you are my son. My impression is,
that upon the colored regiments the Government means to rely to
do the most desperate fighting and occupy the post of imminent danger. Your chance of being broken down by sickness, wounded, maimed
or killed, in the course of such a prolonged campaign, is indeed very
great. True, this is not a consideration to weigh heavily against the
the love of liberty and the promptings of duty; but it makes me
tremble in regard to the effect that may be produced upon the health
and happiness of your mother, should any serious, especially fatal,
accident befall you. Her affection for you is intense, her anxiety beyond expression. . . .[1]

In February, 1865, Lieutenant George Garrison entered Charles-
ton, South Carolina, with his regiment, after the devastating effects
upon the South of General Sherman's march to Atlanta and the sea.
In April of that year he was joined and embraced there by an enthusiastic father, who had lost no time in getting south to share in the
triumph of the Union troops once the shooting had ended. Lieutenant
Garrison was given a prolonged furlough in order to accompany his
father north to Boston. After the war George returned to home and
family and lived for many more years in undistinguished rectitude.

[1] Wendell Phillips Garrison, *William Lloyd Garrison, 1805–1879: The Story
of His Life Told by His Children,* IV, 80.

☞ *"They Will Try to Blow Me Up
if They Can"*

THE capture of Mobile by Admiral David Glasgow Farragut (1801–70) was one of the most daring and dramatic exploits of
the Civil War. But though Farragut had the determined courage to
tell his captains to "Damn the torpedoes: Go ahead," he did not embark on the desperate battle without private fears and preparation for
his own death. On the eve of the battle he wrote to his son Loyall,
later his father's biographer.

OFF MOBILE, July 31st [1864]

MY DEAR SON:

I have been trying for some time to find a spare moment to drop you a line, but could not do so; but as this may be my last opportunity, I avail myself of it, as the boat is now off for New Orleans.

The monitors have all arrived, except the Tecumseh, and she is at Pensacola and I hope will be here in two days. The Confederates at Fort Morgan are making great preparations to receive us. That concerns me but little. I know Buchanan, and Page, who commands the fort, will do all in their power to destroy us, and we will reciprocate the compliment. I hope to give them a fair fight, if once I get inside. I expect nothing from them but that they will try to blow me up if they can. . . .

With such a mother, you could not fail to have proper sentiments of religion and virtue. I feel that I have done my duty by you both, as far as the weakness of my nature would allow. I have been devoted to you both, and when it pleases God to take me hence, I shall feel that I have done my duty. I am not conscious of ever having wronged any one, and have tried to do as much good as I could. Take care of your mother if I should go, and may God bless and preserve you both.

Your devoted father,
D. G. FARRAGUT[1]

But the Admiral was spared to offer further parental advice:

MOBILE BAY, October 13, 1864

MY DEAR SON:

In regard to your studies, bear in mind, that which is easily acquired does not stick so well by you as that which has required labor. I confess I don't know much about analytical geometry, and I might not have seen the use of steam, telegraphs and railroads, when I was as young as you are; but I do now fully comprehend the difficulties of keeping them all in order for working. So go along with your age, my boy, and remember also that one of the requisite studies for an officer is *man*. Where your analytical geometry will serve you once, a knowledge of men will serve you daily. As a commander, to get the right men in the right place is one of the questions of success or defeat.

Take another lesson from the affair to which you allude—about contending with the Government. Dr. Franklin said: "Always stoop your head a little, rather than run it against a beam." It is not necessary to do wrong to avoid a difficulty. To submit to the decisions of the Government is what we all have to do. The object of government is to decide these matters. It may sometimes do injustice, but an unwise decision will recoil on the officials that be, sooner or later. Therefore, my son, avoid difficulties with your superiors if possible, but never submit to indignity without becoming remonstrance. . . .[2]

[1] Loyall Farragut, *The Life of David Glasgow Farragut,* 404.
[2] *Ibid.,* 470.

☞ **"There Are Too Many Lees on the Committee"**

In the darkest days of the Confederacy, young William Henry Fitzhugh Lee (1837–91) was in charge of a brigade near Charlottesville, Virginia, where his younger brother, Robert E. Lee, Jr., was also on duty as a captain. To raise the spirits of their men, the officers organized a ball for the ladies of the area. It was to be a grand affair, and printed invitations were issued. Captain Lee, as a member of the committee of arrangements, forwarded an invitation to the General commanding the Army of Virginia, who happened to be his father, Robert E. Lee. (1807–70). The General replied:

[1864]

Tell Fitz I grieve over the hardships and sufferings of his men, in their late expedition. I should have preferred his waiting for more favorable weather. We have too grave subjects in hand to engage in such trivial amusements. I would rather his officers should entertain themselves in fattening their horses, healing their men, and recruiting their regiments. There are too many Lees on the committee. I like all to be present at battles, but can excuse them at balls. But the saying is, "Children will be children." I think he had better move his camp further from Charlottesville, and perhaps he will get more work and less play. He and I are too old for such assemblies. I want him to write me how his men are, his horses, and what I can do to fill up his ranks. . . .[1]

Fitzhugh Lee survived the reproof, the ball, and the war, to serve as a state senator in post bellum Virginia, and, from 1887 to 1891, as a member of Congress of the United States, against whose armies he had fought. Young Robert also took his part in state and national affairs, and was the author of an account of his father, from which the above letter is taken.

[1] Robert E. Lee, Jr., *Recollections and Letters of General Robert E. Lee*, 120.

☞ *A Boston Brahmin Warns His Son Against Advocating Emancipation*

EVEN as the Civil War reached its crisis in 1864, and even in Boston, the uncompromising advocates of emancipation were not popular in conservative high society. They seemed, like their vociferous leader William Lloyd Garrison, to be rabble rousers without judgment or perspective, confusing the even greater cause of preserving the Union. It was natural that William Gray Brooks, a substantial and cultivated businessman from a Boston best family, should urge caution, for the sake of his own future career, upon his son, Phillips Brooks (1835–93), then the twenty-nine-year old rector of the Church of the Holy Trinity in Philadelphia, and later to become an Episcopal bishop and a famous pulpit orator.

BOSTON, December 13, 1864

MY DEAR SON,

. . . We have seen the notices of your Thanksgiving sermon in the "Independent" and the "Anti-Slavery Standard." You seem to be in favor with the radicals of that stamp. Don't go too far. It will require all your best judgment to know just how far to go.

Remember you occupy a prominent position and your course will be watched. Don't make it too much "one idea," or you will split on the rock so many ministers have before you, of making your situation as a minister of the gospel a secondary matter. How thoroughly has Ward Beecher done this! Do you suppose his congregation go to hear him as a Christian minister? No, it is all for his allusions and quaint expressions upon his one idea, and they are followed up by *applause*. It is sad to see the house of God and the pulpit so debased, Cheever is another instance: how essentially he has lost his character as a Christian minister.

Are you not going too fast to advocate the entire freedom and equality of the negro, even to the right of suffrage, as I understand from those notices that you do? I cannot believe that it is best or advisable to introduce another foreign element into our elections; it certainly cannot raise the standards of our right of suffrage or the character of the candidates. Let us keep the ballot box as pure as we can. However you may argue the point of the races being intellectually equal, yet politically to my mind there is no question. I hope I shall never live to see it, and for the sake of my children I hope it will never be done. *Don't go too far.* How many good causes have been injured, nay ruined, by that. Go on in aid of the Freedmen as much as you may please, but such a measure as that is not to their aid in the present state of affairs. . . .

Yours affectionately,
FATHER[1]

[1] A. V. G. Allen, *Life and Letters of Phillips Brooks*, I, 552.

☞ *"O Gerard My Darling Boy Are You Indeed Gone from Me?"*

THE religious movement that began in Oxford in the 1860's brought emotional strength and spiritual depth to the Church of England and several important converts to the Church of Rome. It also brought deep distress to a few devoted, prosperous, and conservative fathers. Manley Hopkins, whose son, Gerard Manley Hopkins (1844–89), was then an undergraduate at Balliol College, replied thus to a letter from the young man saying that after religious discussions and soul searching he was joining the Roman Catholic church.

151

18 Oct., 1866

There are one or two things I should like to say to you though you will perhaps not regard them. At least the tone of your letter is so hard and cold, it gives me little encouragement—nevertheless I shall put them down, that they may explain our views a little.

You say that when you were first assailed by doubts as to the position of the English church, you told Mr. Liddon of it, and that he advised you, your own judgment agreeing thereto, to repel the thoughts. When you were on the Wye with Addis (the time was less than a week) and after a sermon of Mr. Lane's, these thoughts returned—and either then or at Horsham immediately afterwards, the idea of joining the Church of Rome occurred to you. You no longer repelled the thought but cherished it. In fact, you decided at once and without hesitation—without asking any advice whatsoever.

That although you waited to announce your decision it was taken, is clear, first, from your carefully avoiding to ask advice or mention your state of mind to anyone that might have taken a different view. You did not seek Mr. Liddon or Dr. Pusey—you did not wish to be urged to pause. But you did seek out Dr. Newman. It was of course from the nature of the case that he should advise you to stay where you were. You wanted of him, not advice but encouragement. Even he I think must have considered you rash, since he said it would be better to have done with Oxford first.

Secondly, from that time you discountinued attendance upon the Holy Sacrament. To us it seems that finding yourself by no act of your own, but by the providence of God, in the English Church, you were bound so long as you remained in her, and until you were perfectly satisfied that you were wrong in remaining, to avail yourself of such means of grace as she could offer you. You have received while in her grace to fulfil many duties, to lead a pure life. Should not your course have been to frequent her altar, praying for light, so long as you had not openly left her? When you were without sacramental grace could you be so likely to be rightly guided?

One thing more—Have you not dealt hardly, may I not say unfairly, by us in leaving us in absolute ignorance of all till your decision was finally taken? Were you not on the point of being received into the Church of Rome without even warning us? and were you not saved from what would have been a cruel insult to us, not by your own good feeling, but by Edward Bond's entreaties? If then you were wrong in this, and as we think in other points, are we not justified in asking you to pause? Can you really put aside all our claims upon you by saying that it rests with us to think as you do?—You say years would not be sufficient to go into the question by study—therefore you will not study at all, but decide without any deliberation. Is not that almost absurd?

I shall not touch on this morning's letter, further than to say that the manner in which you seem to repel and throw us off cuts us to the heart. All we ask of you is for your own sake to take so momentous a step with caution and hesitation; have we not a right to do this? Might not our love and our sorrow entitle us to ask it?—and you answer by saying that as we might be Romanists if we pleased the estrangement is not of your doing. O Gerard my darling boy are you indeed gone from me?[1]

> When Gerard received that letter, he wrote to Newman that his reply from his father was "terrible," and that he could not bring himself to read it a second time. "Pray for them!" he begged Newman, who was also a convert to Rome. His parents, Gerard reported, would have him wait, but "of course it is impossible." He promptly joined the Church of Rome and remained its ardent devotee throughout his life. His poetry, highly religious in content and feeling, has over the past half-century been increasingly recognized and valued by a widening though limited circle.

[1] *Further Letters of Gerard Manley Hopkins* (ed. by C. C. Abbott), 95–97.

☞ *A Naturalist Lectures His Son on Taste in Poetry*

SIR EDMUND WILLIAM GOSSE (1849–1928), poet and man of letters, was the only child of Philip Henry Gosse (1810–88), distinguished writer on biology and friend of Charles Kingsley. Both parents were devoted members of the Plymouth Brotherhood, and Edmund was brought up in an atmosphere of rigid piety, so that until he was seventeen his only knowledge of poetry and fiction was gained surreptitiously. He so resented that atmosphere, and particularly his father's lack of sympathy, that in later life he wrote a book so critical of his father that many readers thought him unpardonably lacking in family loyalty. When he was seventeen, Edmund wrote from school asking his father to finance the publication of his poem, and Phillip Gosse replied:

[MARYCHURCH, DEVONSHIRE, late 1867]

. . . But you have not yet submitted a single word of your Poems to my examination. . . . There is one test indeed. . . . You praised in strong terms a poem[1] which since you have sent for Mama's perusal. We value the love which prompted your sending it; but was it also sent to indicate to us the standard of poetic excellence to which you aspire? I hope not indeed! . . . but I will ask you: How can you be captivated with this turgid rant? When the brass band in front of a puppet show in a village fair opens up, the open-mouthed bumpkins have all their attention given to the negro fellow that clangs together the two cymbals or brass plates, the more noise, the more music. Myers' clangor reminds me of this. Where are all the *thoughts* amidst this clash of words? They are like Falstaff's ha'p'orth of bread in the endless pints of sack. . . . My object is to show that the noblest in Poetry is ever the simplest; that our best poets know nothing of this craving after the uncouth, the intense, the obscure, the mystical. You will perhaps impatiently say that you know all this. I reply, I thought you *did* know it; now I doubt it. How else can you admire such a style as Myers'?

. . . The poor ass! He thinks he is very grand and he is only very muddy: he makes a terrible flapping of feathers and mistakes it for lofty soaring. You speak of an impatience with shams: do you not see that this style of writing is an utter sham? I have said nothing about the doctrine, tho' the Paul of Myers has no resemblance to the Paul of the N.T.: nor is his rant about Christ anything more than profane human interest.

And here again I am afraid for you. I am afraid lest you lose the things that you have learnt in the School of God. I am afraid lest you take up with this hollow, sickly, fashionable tone of mere human sentiment and mistake it for godliness.... I would feel stricken down by a horrible calamity in my hoar hairs, if my only son took his place in the ranks of the frothy, sentimental spouters of the day.... Spare me this agony, my darling child.[2]

[1] It was "St. Paul," by F. W. Myers.
[2] Hon. Evan Edward Charteris, *The Life and Letters of Sir Edmund Gosse*, 14ff.

☞ *Aristocratic Survival in the Post Bellum South*

BEFORE the Civil War, William Gilmour Simms (1806–70) was not only a prosperous South Carolina plantation owner with many slaves, but the literary light of his state, and had published much fiction and verse. His plantation was almost entirely destroyed by General Sherman's troops. Soon after the war ended, he went to New England in the hope of making enough money by writing and lecturing to support his family and slowly restore the plantation. His son, William Gilmour Simms, Jr. (1843–1912), known on the plantation as "Mass Billy," was a very athletic youth—a good rider, a fine swimmer, and an excellent shot—though his father pronounced him no intellectual genius. He became an officer in the Confederate Army and nearly lost his life in battle. After the war he began to train himself for his coming role as mainstay of the family, studying law while also trying to manage the devastated plantation, and it was then that his father sent him this letter from New England. The son served for many years as clerk of the court of Barnwell County, and "His scholarly tastes, his delightful conversational powers and his fine integrity are remembered in South Carolina today."

WEST ROXBURY, NEAR BOSTON, Midnight—Sept. 14, 1868.
DEAR SON:
I am, at 3 A.M., writing to you from the table of my friend, Austin. All the house is asleep. But I find I cannot sleep again tonight, and sitting here, wearily alone, my heart and thoughts turn homeward

with longing anxieties. . . . Were you all in comfort, I should probably feel and fear nothing. I have survived myself, and I now live wholly in, & perhaps through, my children. . . . I shall be busied daily beating about among the publishers, seeking money and employment for the future. . . .

In the winter, God having spared us all, we will confer about the future. My wish is that you should break ground in your profession, and, in the spring, if this be possible to our means, take a month or six weeks in the North, and learn what you can of the improved instruments and agencies of agriculture. . . . Meanwhile, secure all, watch all, lock up all, be vigilant, circumspect, never from home at night, and get rid as fast as you can of all the drones, rogues & idlers. Be rigid in respect to letting lands, so that you shall have none about you not capable of doing for themselves. Such only is the class who will be able to compensate you.

Let me entreat & counsel you and Donald forbear all public meetings, all gatherings and assemblages, to which you are not directly called by the elections; & then stay only till your votes are delivered, & return promptly home. Avoid all collisions with every body, all petty strife, & treat with contempt all small provocations from worthless people. You are not to waste yourself upon the vile and vulgar. . . .

Ever affectionately, Your Father,

W. GILMOUR SIMMS[1]

---

[1] *Letters of William Gilmour Simms* (coll. and ed. by Mary C. Simms Oliphant, Alfred Taylor Odell, and T. C. Duncan Eaves), I, 159.

Dickens' Farewell to an Emigrant Son

CHARLES DICKENS (1812-70) had ten children, some of them named after his friends among contemporary men of letters. As they reached manhood, several of his sons departed for far places in the Empire, then at its apogee. Walter Landor Dickens went to India with the army and died in Calcutta in 1863. Alfred Tennyson Dickens (b.1845) settled in Australia. In 1868, Dickens' youngest son, Edward Bulwer Lytton Dickens, aged sixteen, was about to set off for Australia, too. Dickens wrote a farewell letter to a son he was unlikely ever to see again.

September, 1868

I write this note today because your going away is so much upon my mind, and because I want you to have a few parting words from me, to think of now and then at quiet times. I need not tell you that I love you dearly, and am very, very sorry in my heart to part with you. But this life is half made up of parting, and these pains must be borne. It is my comfort and my sincere conviction that you are going to try the life for which you are best fitted. I think its freedom and wildness more suited to you than any experiment in a study or office would have been: and without that training, you could have followed no other suitable occupation.

What you have always wanted until now has been a set, steady, constant purpose. I therefore exhort you to persevere in a thorough determination to do whatever you have to do, as well as you can do it. I was not so old as you are now, when I first had to win my food, and to do it out of this determination; and I have never slackened in it since. Never take a mean advantage of anyone in a transaction, and never be hard upon people who are in your power. Try to do to others as you would have them do to you, and do not be discouraged if they fail sometimes. It is much better for you that they should fail in obeying the greatest rule laid down by our Saviour than that you should.

I put a New Testament among your books for the very same reasons, and with the very same hopes, that made me write an easy account of it for you, when you were a little child. Because it is the best book that ever was, or will be, known in the world; and because it teaches you the best lessons by which any human creature, who tries to be truthful and faithful to duty, can possibly be guided. As your brothers have gone away, one by one, I have written to each such words as I am now writing to you, and have entreated them all to guide themselves by this Book, putting aside the interpretations and inventions of man. You will remember that you have never at home been harassed about religious observances, or mere formalities. I have always been anxious not to weary my children with such things, before they are old enough to form opinions respecting them. You will therefore understand the better that I now most solemnly impress upon you the truth and beauty of the Christian Religion, as it came from Christ Himself, and the impossibility of your going far wrong if you humbly but heartily respect it. Only one more thing on this head. The more we are in earnest as to feeling it, the less we are disposed to hold forth about it. Never abandon the wholesome practice of saying your own private prayers, night and morning. I have never abandoned it myself, and I know the comfort of it. I hope you will always be able to say in after life that you had a kind father. You cannot show your affection for him so well, or make him so happy, as by doing your duty.[1]

[1] W. B. Scoones, *Four Centuries of English Letters*, 561, 562.

☞ *"Try to Follow the Example of Your Father"*

HEINRICH JOHANN LUDWIG SCHLIEMANN (1822–90) was born in Germany, made a fortune in Russia, became an American citizen, and spent his wealth on his archaeological discovery of the ancient city of Troy. Experts have disagreed on the significance of some of his findings and claims, but not on the fact that he was, in the words of his biographer Emil Ludwig, "a complete egoist," with a conceit rarely equaled and even more rarely so boldly flaunted. Schliemann was constantly in bitter conflict with his father and his wife, but set his heart on making his son worthy of his own greatness and insisted on the boy's complete mental and moral subordination to himself. His method failed, for the career of Serge Schliemann (b. 1855) has left no mark on history. When Serge was fifteen, he received this typical letter from his father.

[Paris, June 24, 1870]

I have received your good letters of May 24 and June 4, and am sad to learn that you aren't advancing. In this life one must progress continually if one isn't to become discouraged. Try to follow the example of your father who—in whatever situation—always proved what a man can accomplish by sheer energy. During the four years in Amsterdam, from 1842 to 1846, I truly performed wonders. I did what never has been done before, nor will ever be done again. Later when I was in business in St. Petersburg, I was the most successful and at the same time the most prudent dealer on the stock exchange. When I began to travel, I was a traveller par excellence. No St. Petersburg merchant has ever written a learned book, but I have written one that has been translated into four languages, and is universally admired. At the moment, as an archaeologist, I am the sensation of Europe and America because I have discovered the ancient city of Troy for which archaeologists of the entire world have searched in vain for the past two thousand years. . . .[1]

[1] Robert Payne, *The Gold of Troy*, 136–37.

☞ *A Physician Approves His Son's Spiritual Integrity*

DR. JAMES HINTON (1822–75) had won in China and Sierra Leone a fine reputation as a surgeon and medical researcher. But his scientific career was only one aspect of his life; indeed, his science and his faith waged bitter war within him. As a young man he fell deeply in love with Miss Haddon and she with him, but when he confessed to having lost his faith in Christianity, she felt she could not marry him. Then, during his long years overseas, when both suffered and prayed for a return of his faith, he gradually regained some of his religious conviction—at least enough to induce Miss Haddon, at long last, to marry him. From that time onward his extensive writings on medicine were interlarded or balanced with philosophical speculations. All of his inward struggle must have come back to him when his eldest son, at Rugby School, wrote of his own spiritual perturbations. Dr. Hinton replied:

18 SAVILLE Row, March 24, 1870

MY DEAR BOY,—

. . . I am glad you decided for yourself about the confirmation, and also I am glad that you decided not to be confirmed. It might have been in many respects good, but I think you did right not to consider the advantages it offered equivalent to its being connected with a mode of religious thought and action with which you had not perfect

159

sympathy; so that you could not throw yourself into it without reserve. I think, and I believe you will think with me in this always, that in all that we call religion, the very first and chief condition is, that we should be utterly and absolutely sincere, open, straightforward, and free from pretense, and should consider nothing an advantage that has to be purchased at the least shade of falsity. In other regions, as of material advantage, though falsehood must always be a crime and a mistake, yet at least some visible results may be for a time secured by it, it has some excuses if no reasons; but in religion the whole meaning and worth of which lies in honesty, purity, holiness, and devotion of the heart, the least shade of insincerity, or of endeavoring to secure *results,* is as absurd as it is hateful. If religion means anything, it must mean absolute truthfulness. We may dream we can serve our fellow-men by pretenses, but to think of serving God by make-believes, is to insult Him. But, indeed, I know you feel this much as I do, and I am sure that you will try as much as ever I could wish to make all your life transparent, and to banish all the false pretenses which fill our present life with evil.

If you wish to spend another term at Rugby, I think we must spare you; you will make a good use of it. We want you to come soon and live at home; because the opportunity won't last very long, and it is time now you began to share our life. We want you to do this so very much; but still distance does not prevent this, and that is the best sharing which best enables you to take up what we leave unfinished, and perfect what we do incompletely. I am sure it is a great age of the world for which you are preparing—an age in which the great question of the true significance of human life will, at least, begin to decide itself. I like to think of my sons and daughters having a part in that. It need not be great (as men call greatness) but it cannot be *little* if it is honest and faithful. This is one question men will have to answer. Is it our nature to take the best care of ourselves or to live in giving up? I know how your heart would answer this, and I think the time is coming when all men will give the same.

Your loving father,
JAMES HINTON[1]

---

[1] *Life and Letters of James Hinton* (ed. by Ellice Hopkins), 215.

Rev. Charles Kingsley to One of His Sons

☞ *On Placing a Bet on the Derby*

CHARLES KINGSLEY (1819–75), rector of Eversley and author of *Westward Ho!* and *The Water Babies,* was, like his fellow novelist Charles Dickens, fated to lose his sons to the lure of distant places. His son Maurice (1847–1911) went to New York when a young man and settled there. A younger son, Granville Arthur (b. 1857), later departed for distant Queensland. It was to one of these boys, away at school, that the rector wrote regarding a practice he strongly denounced from many a pulpit.

MY DEAREST BOY,

There is a matter which gave me great uneasiness when you mentioned it. You said you had put into some lottery for the Derby and had hedged to make it safe.

Now all this is bad, bad, nothing but bad. Of all the habits gambling is the one I hate most and have avoided most. Of all habits it grows most on eager minds. Success and loss alike make it grow. Of all habits, however much civilized man may give way to it, it is one of the most intrinsically *savage*. Historically it has been the peace excitement of the lowest brutes in human form for ages past. Morally it is unchivalrous and unchristian.

1. It gains money by the lowest and most unjust means, for it takes money out of your neighbor's pocket without giving him anything in return.

2. It tempts you to use what you fancy your superior knowledge of a horse's merits—or anything else—to your neighbor's harm.

If you know better than your neighbor, you are bound to give him your advice. Instead, you conceal your knowledge to win from his ignorance; hence come all sorts of concealments, dodges, deceits—I say the Devil is the only father of it. I'm sure, moreover, that B. would object seriously to anything like a lottery, betting, or gambling.

I hope you have not won. I should not be sorry for you to lose. If you have won I should not congratulate you. If you wish to please me, you will give back to its lawful owners the money you have won. If you are a loser in gross thereby, I will gladly reimburse your losses this time. As you had put in you could not in honour draw back till after the event. Now you can give back your money, saying you understand that Mr. B. and your father disapprove of such things, and so gain a very great moral influence.

Recollect always that the stock argument is worthless. It is this: "My friend would win from me if he could, *therefore* I have an equal right to win from him." Nonsense. The same argument would prove that I have a right to maim or kill a man if only I give him leave to maim or kill me if he can and will.

I have spoken my mind once and for all on a matter on which I have held the same views for more than twenty years, and trust in God you will not forget my words in after life. I have seen many a good fellow ruined by finding himself one day short of money, and trying to get a little by playing or betting—and then the Lord have mercy on his simple soul for simple it will not remain long.

Mind, I am not in the least *angry* with you. Betting is the way of the world. So are all the seven deadly sins under certain rules and pretty names, but to the Devil they lead if indulged in, in spite of the wise world and its ways.

Your loving,
PATER[1]

[1] *Charles Kingsley: His Letters and Memories of His Life* (ed. by his wife), II, 106.

☞ *Believe in God if You Can, but Follow Truth*

WHEN the poet and novelist George Meredith (1828–1909), left a widower, remarried, his nineteen-year-old son, Arthur Griffith Meredith (1853–1890), did not take happily to the new arrangement. A solution was reached by sending him to study for a while in Germany. Despite letters full of understanding and affection from his father, Arthur avoided returning, and remained for some ten years on the Continent. He died at the age of thirty-seven.

Box Hill, Dorking, Surrey, April 25, 1872

My dear Arthur,—

Strong friendships and inter-communications with foreigners will refresh your life in this island, and the Germans are solid. Stick to a people not at the mercy of their impulses, and besides a people with so fine a literature must be worthy of love.

Captain Maxse wrote to me the other day about an examination in the Foreign Office for the post of Chinese interpreter for you: if successful to go out to China with a salary of £200 per annum and learn the Chinese tongue of li-ro and fo-ki. I declined it: I hope I was right. I felt sure that it would be repugnant to you to spend your life in China, where the climate is hard, society horrid, life scarcely (to my thought) endurable. Perhaps you might have chosen Japan. But it would have been for very many years perpetual banishment. Let me hear what you think of it.

Study Cicero carefully. He is a fine moralist, a friend of scholars, a splendid trainer for a public life of any serious and exalted ambition.

What you say of our religion is what thoughtful men feel: and that you at the same time can recognize its moral value is a matter of rejoicing to me. The Christian teaching is sound and good; the ecclesiastical dogma is an instance of the poverty of humanity's mind hitherto, and has often in its hideous fangs and claws shown whence we draw our descent.—Don't think that the obscenities mentioned in the Bible do harm to children. The Bible is outspoken upon facts, and rightly. It is because the world is pruriently and stupidly shame-faced that it cannot come in contact with the Bible without convulsions. I agree with Frommen that the book should be read out, for Society is a wanton hypocrite, and I would accommodate her in nothing: though for the principle of Society I hold that men should be ready to lay down their lives.

Belief in the religion has done and does this good to the young; it floats them through the perilous sensual period when the animal appetites most need control and transmutation. If you have not the belief, set yourself to love virtue by understanding that it is your best guide both as to what is due to others and what is for your positive personal good. If your mind honestly rejects it, you must call on your mind to supply its place from your own resources. Otherwise you will have only half done your work, and that is always mischievous. Pray attend to my words on this subject.

You know how Socrates loved truth. Virtue and Truth are one. Look for the truth in everything and follow it, and you will then be living justly before God. Let nothing flout your sense of a Supreme Being, and be certain that your understanding wavers whenever you chance to doubt that he leads to good. We grow to good as surely as the plant grows to the light. The school has only to look through history for a scientific assurance of it. And do not lose the habit of praying to the unseen Divinity. Prayer for worldly goods is worse than fruitless, but prayer for strength of soul is that passion of the soul which catches the gift it seeks. . . .

Your loving father,
GEORGE MEREDITH[1]

Nine years later it became clear that Arthur's health was seriously failing, and his father made further efforts to heal the breach that lay between them:

BOX HILL, DORKING, SURREY, June 23, 1881

. . . We have long been estranged, my dear boy, and I awake from it with a shock that wrings me. The elder should be the first to break through such divisions, for he knows best the tenure and nature of life. But our last parting gave me the idea that you did not care for me; and further I am so driven by work that I do not contend with misapprehension of me, or with disregard, but have the habit of taking it all alike, as a cabhorse takes the whip. Part of me has become torpid. . . .

I shall hope to hear from you soon . . . We should all have had delight in welcoming you home, but your project is in every way advisable. . . . I will write you again next week. It will be a grief to me if I cannot meet you. . . .

Yours loving father,[2]

---

[1] *Letters of George Meredith* (coll. and ed. by his son), I, 236–38.
[2] *Ibid.*, 318–20.

Dr. Silas W. Mitchell to John Mitchell

☞ *"I Am Going to Marry"*

No man of his time was more popular and respected in Philadelphia society than Dr. Silas Weir Mitchell (1829-1914), neurologist, poet, and novelist under the pseudonym of Ik Marvel. Thirteen years after his first wife died leaving two small sons, he wrote to one of them, John Kearsley Mitchell (b. 1859), then sixteen and away at school:

Tuesday, April 13, 1875

PRIVATE

MY DEAR JACK:

I have just now received your last letter when about to write you on a matter in which we are both deeply interested and which probably will much surprise you. At first thought it will not please you, until you come to reflect on the sadness and loneliness of my life and to know as you hardly do yet what an endless sacrifice it has been to others. I want first to tell you what no one else knows, that I am going to marry Miss Mary Cadwallader. If, my dear boy, this gives you any sudden sense of hurt, don't hide it from me but write it out as friend to friend in honest trust. Your dear grandmother is fully satisfied. Not only that I am about to do what is wise, but that for you and Lany as well it is a wise step. For present and future as far as you are concerned there could be no better thing happen than my marriage, and when once the idea grows familiar to you to know that I am to have a fresh hold on life. . . . But over and above all, do be honest in writing to me of it, saying without reserve what you feel and letting me answer you as freely. As to my best and nearest friend, I write first to you. Drop me a line on receipt of this.

God keep you—

P. S. As yet this is between us—how I yearn to have seen you and talked myself out.[1]

John Mitchell followed his father into medicine and was long his assistant. In 1909 he was vice-president of the American Neurological Association. His brother, Langdon Elwyn Mitchell, became a poet and playwright.

[1] A. R. Burr, *Weir Mitchell*, 168-69.

☞ "I Am Old-fashioned Enough to Know What Is Right"

NICHOLAS LONGWORTH ANDERSEN (1838–92) was the youngest general in the Union Army during the Civil War. He was wounded three times and twice brevetted for bravery. His son Larz Andersen (1866–1937) became a diplomat who served in London, Rome, and Brussels, and as ambassador to Japan just before World War I. When Larz was a schoolboy at Phillips Exeter Academy and later a freshman at Harvard, his father wrote him many letters, all affectionate but not all uncritical.

August 15, 1882

If ever you are in trouble of any description whatever, come straight to me. Have implicit confidence in my love, and be certain it is the most partial tribunal you can have. I do not expect you to be perfect but I hope you will try to be loyal to us and honest with yourself.

If you are lonely, try how great a panacea letter writing is. Keep an account of your outgo and income. Love us. Read a chapter in the New Testament every night. . . .

Oct. 11, 1882

Do not fear in corresponding with me to show all your feelings as they are, fearlessly and candidly. They will not be scoffed at, be they ever so foolish; nor betrayed, be they ever so confidential. Do not be discouraged at occasional flunking. Perfection can never be attained, and your previous education has been so varied and sporadic that you cannot expect to have the same proficiency as others, even those of inferior intellect, who have received regular and thorough instruction at Exeter. . . .

Oct. 18, 1882

We were much amused in your last letter with the account of your visit to Boston. I would not like Elsie to go to a school where so much freedom is given to the girls. Your stomach seems to give you a great amount of pleasure. If your intellectual appetite were only as fond of study as your carnal appetite is of the omelettes and tenderloins of Mr. Young, you would find your pleasures more lasting. . . .

WASHINGTON, Jan. 21, 1885

I do not like to find fault, and I am exceedingly loath to interfere with your general deportment, but when your idea of college life is to pass your time on the railway train between Washington and Cambridge, I certainly object. Your Grandfather lived there four uninterrupted years; I came home once a year, and you wish to live in Washington and visit Cambridge. It is in vain for you to tell me that *tempora mutantur* and boys do otherwise now. I am old-fashioned enough to know what is right, and urge you, for your own sake more than for mine, to be true to yourself. I am sure I should like you to live a happy life and acquire learning without study, but *nul bien sans peine.*[1]

[1] *The Letters and Journals of General Nicholas Longworth Andersen* (ed. by Isabel Andersen), 239ff.

☞ *A Churchman's Private Views on Democracy and the Future Life*

CHARLES MERIVALE (1808–93) was dean of Ely Cathedral and also the author of a compendious history of the Roman Empire. Perhaps his study of the plebs of Rome influenced him as it had Gibbon, and affected his reactions in 1880 to an electoral victory of the Liberals in England, for he wrote to his grown son, Herman, whose career was chiefly as commissioner of the Court of Bankruptcy:

ELY, April 13, 1880

To me there is something very frightful in the capriciousness of the monster Democracy, which we must expect to increase more and more with the threatened extension of the franchise. You young men will have to weather a very different state of things from that which I have been privileged to live through, but no doubt you will have spirit to encounter it, which can hardly be expected of me. . . .[1]

The Dean also held unorthodox private opinions regarding immortality. Two years later, when his son's small child died, Merivale sent him this letter of consolation:

ELY, February 28, 1882

. . . I trust you have got well through the trial of yesterday and that it will have a soothing effect, as I think it is generally found to do. You will now look forward calmly to the time when the riddles of this world will be solved, and the greatest of all riddles, the prospect of another existence. That the best and wisest of mankind should be destined to a future life has always seemed a reasonable anticipation; the difficulty, I suppose, in our minds is to imagine a future for the masses who have made no mark here. But from a Socrates to a babe in arms it is impossible to draw a line between, and we must feel, I think, that the tenderness our Lord expresses toward little children is an indication of the Divine mercy towards all human beings, great and small alike. I seem to feel very sure that there is a world of spirit beyond, or behind, this material world: it is suggested to me partly by my own nature, and partly by what I believe to be a glimpse of revelation; and that in the world of spirit there is a place for all spirits with their proper sphere for all I cannot reasonably doubt.

These are thoughts which will press more and more upon us as we grow older and nearer to the solution; and the shock you have just felt may be like an unexpected step downstairs, to arrest your attention to the descent we are all making, however heedlessly. . . .[2]

[1] *Autobiography and Letters of Charles Merivale, Dean of Ely* (ed. by Judith Anne Merivale), 332.

[2] *Ibid.*, 340.

☞ *A Future War Correspondent Is Advised on Warfare*

To romantic young men at the turn of the century, Richard Harding Davis (1864–1916) represented the charms of intrigue and derring-do in far-off places. He not only wrote exciting hero-fiction, he was thought to live it, and he gave the new career of war correspondent an almost irresistible glamour. But it was not always thus, and as a freshman at Lehigh University when hazing was the fashion,

Davis had not found strife romantic. The sophomores found him worthy of their special attention, and young Davis put up a spirited resistance. When he reported the event to his father, Samuel Clarke Davis, editor of *The Philadelphia Inquirer*, the reply was brief but encouraging.

PHILADELPHIA, February 25th, 1882

OLD BOY:

I'm glad the affair ended so well. I don't want you to fight, but if you have to fight a cuss like that do it with all your might, and don't insist that either party shall too strictly observe the Markis O'Queensbury rules. Hit first and hardest so that thine adversary shall beware of you.

DAD[1]

---

[1] *Adventures and Letters of Richard Harding Davis* (ed. by C. B. Davis), 26.

☞ *"Never Tire Yourself Out," Advises a Harvard President*

No man in America placed his stamp more firmly upon American university education than Charles William Eliot (1834–1926) as president of Harvard. He developed graduate and professional studies on a high level of specialization, but established an undergraduate system that permitted each student to elect his studies from a wide range of choices. He applied both principles in his advice to his sons, urging the strong one to energetic efforts within his chosen field and advising the other to work only as hard as his health permitted. Charles William Eliot, Jr. (1859–97), then studying in Europe, was physically frail, and to him his father wrote:

April 20, '86

DEAR CHARLES,—

Don't imagine yourself deficient in power of dealing with men. Such dealings as you have thus far had with boys and men you have conducted very suitably. There is no mystery about successful business intercourse with patrons and employees. Nobody can think, and

169

at the same time pay attention to another person, as you seem to expect to do. On the contrary, exclusive attention to the person who is speaking to you is a very important point in business manners. Nothing is so flattering as that. Some audible or visible signs of close attention are of course desirable. Then there is very seldom any objection to the statement, "I should like to think that over" . . . .

I wish you were tough and strong like me. But you have nevertheless an available measure of strength, and within that measure an unusual capacity of enjoyment. . . . You get a great deal more pleasure out of your present journeyings than I could ever have. I should not have your feelings of fatigue and weakness, but neither should I have your perception of the beautiful and your enjoyment of it. When you come to professional work, you will have to be moderate in it. Where other men work eight hours a day, you must be content with five. Take all things easily. Never tire yourself out. If you feel the blues coming upon you, get a book and a glass of wine, or go to bed and rest yourself. The morbid mental condition is of physical origin. Take comfort in the thought that you can have a life of moderate labor— the best sort of life. You will have a little money of your own, and need not be in haste to earn a large income. I am strong and can work twelve hours a day. Consequently I do; and if it were not for Mt. Desert,[1] I should hardly have more time for reflection and real living than an operative in a cotton mill. . . .[2]

> But a second son, Samuel Atkins Eliot (1862–1950), had more of his father's sinewy stamina, and to him President Eliot urged more vigorous concentration, as well as the faith to leave the great mysteries to God.

August 10, 1887

DEAR SAM;—

I hope this will salute you on your birthday—the 25th! You have had a reasonably happy childhood and youth; but the best part of life is all before you—the next 25 years. Experience, knowledge, and caution will increase, but powers not much. Opportunities will multiply, but your capacity to improve them will not much enlarge—only become prompter and more facile. A man at 25 is good for about all he ever will be, so far as quickness of apprehension and power of work are concerned. You ought still to gain much in steadiness, tenacity and judgment. Tenacity involves singleness of aim—or at least one main object at a time. . . .[3]

June 7, 1887

. . . You are unreasonable in expecting to know the sense of your existence. Nobody knows the meaning of any existence—of flower, beast, man, nation, or world. Live each day usefully, innocently and happily as you can, and leave the rest to God. It is time you were married. You are too solitary. . . .[4]

Charles Eliot, Jr., despite his frailness, was on the way to leadership in the new profession of landscape architecture when he contracted spinal meningitis and died at the age of thirty-eight. Samuel Eliot became a prominent Unitarian minister and, like his father, lived for nearly a century.

[1] President Eliot spent his summer holidays at Cranberry Island and Mt. Desert on the coast of Maine.
[2] Henry James, *Charles W. Eliot*, II, 37.
[3] *Ibid.,* 39.
[4] *Ibid.,* 41.

☞ *"Learn the Secret of Tears and Ecstasy"*

NEWSPAPER editors, dealing daily with the disillusionments of life, are thought to be cynical about the higher ideals and aspirations. If so, David G. Croly, managing editor of the old *New York World,* was a notable exception, as this letter to his son, Herbert David Croly (1869–1930) then an undergraduate at Harvard, shows.

LOTUS CLUB [NEW YORK,] Oct. 31, 1886

DEAR BOY—
You said something about the divergence between my ideas and those of the philosophers whose works you are reading at college. Let me beg of you to form your own judgments on all the higher themes—religion included—without any reference to what I may have said. All that I ask is that you keep your mind open and un-

predisposed. In the language of the Scripture, "prove all things and hold fast to that which is good." Be careful and do not allow the first impressions to influence your maturer judgment. You say you are reading the controversy between Spencer and Harrison on religion. In doing so keep in mind that Spencer's matter was revised, while that of Harrison was not; and that upon the latter's protest the work was withdrawn in England. . . .

My dear son, I shall die happy if I know that you are an earnest student of philosophic themes.

Do cultivate all the religious emotions, reverence, awe and aspiration, if for no better reason than as a means of self-culture. Educate, train every side of your mental and emotional nature. Read poetry and learn the secret of tears and ecstacy. Go to Catholic and Episcopal churches and surrender yourself to the inspiration of soul-inspiring religious music.

Ever your affectionate
FATHER[1]

David Croly's advice was not wasted, although his son turned to politics rather than religion as a vehicle to express his idealism. Herbert Croly left Harvard without a degree in 1886 to become secretary to his father. But twice after his marriage and his pursuit of a journalistic career he returned to complete his course at Harvard, and in 1910 he became a Bachelor of Arts as of the Class of 1890. Then he embarked upon the founding and editing of *The New Republic*, which during and after World War I was America's most stimulating liberal weekly, of singular intellectual quality and literary distinction. Walter Lippmann, one of its leading contributors, later called Herbert Croly "the first important political philosopher who appeared in America in the twentieth century."

[1] Jane C. Croly, *Memories*, 64–65.

☞ A Scholar Deplores Intellectual Arrogance

HORACE HOWARD FURNESS (1833–1912), friend of Walt Whitman and first editor of the great Variorum Shakespeare, was one of the most respected scholars of his time. He wrote this letter to his son, Horace Howard Furness, Jr. (1865–1930), then aged twenty-three, who followed in his father's footsteps as a Shakespearean scholar and completed, with devoted industry, the Variorum.

222 WEST WASHINGTON SQUARE [NEW YORK,] 29 Jan'y 1888
DEAREST HORRIE:

. . . What you say about Wagner interests me extremely. My chiefest advice to you is to remember that the law of your being is growth, and that in passing judgment it is always best to qualify that judgment to meet the changes of that growth.

The Wagner craze that you now have I had, & had it quite as badly too, thirty-five years ago. At that time we had only Tann-hauser. He wrote Lohengrin in '56, I think, and I know very little of his music since that date, but I can see now that he has great faults, chiefest in the matter of time, the capabilities whereof in Opera, he seemed to neglect—and he lacks versatility. But there's no question about it—he can stir up the blood.

My first revulsion for Wagner came when I learned his personal characteristics. No proper criterion, I'll allow, in judging of his music. But after all, a man writes his character in his music. If, as Buffon said, *"Le style est l'homme"* very much more *"La musique est l'homme."* Wagner's life was gnarled and twisted; he dealt in problems too deep for him or for any one man; his intellectual arrogance was illimitable, and if anyone questioned his supremacy he fought, and bit, and swore. He received endless kindness from the Emperor of Austria and in return he joined the mob in 1848, and with his own hand set fire to the Conservatoire of Music in Vienna, knowing that the conflagration would burn up priceless, *priceless* treasures of music by all the old masters, which it did. It will take a good deal of harmony in Wagner to obliterate the discord of that black deed.

But what I want you to feel, dear boy, is that no one master, no one school will hold all the truth; lucky if each of them can catch a wee bit of the hem of her garment. "Many, for many virtues are excellent; None but for some and yet each different"—And we must remember that the moods of men vary, even on the upward path.

173

The earth in her annual motion has a diurnal motion also. There is a time for all things. *Vous markez mes mots,* sometime or other, in some mood or other, your demi god will be Bellini. Because an oak with its summer bravery and its winter poverty speaks a lesson to you, are you not to sympathize with Autolycus's pugging tooth when daffodils begin to appear? ...

"Talents differ. All is well and wisely put. If I can't carry forests on my back, Neither can you crack a nut," says the Squirrel to the Mountain in Emerson. And sometimes we want to crack nuts—and jokes. *Videlicet* Thackeray—with his "Ho, pretty page" and "There were three sailors in Bristol City."

Wherefore, dear boy, let everything minister to your growth that you can assimilate, and try your very hardest to assimilate the best, & highest, and purest things.

Goodbye till I see your dear smile,
Your doting old,
FATHER[1]

[1] *The Letters of Horace Howard Furness* (ed. by H. H. F. Jayne), I, 246.

☞ *"When One Has Talent One Finally Breaks Through"*

IN 1888, Camille Pissarro (1830–1903) had not yet conquered the world of art, but his neoimpressionist paintings had already impressed it. His eldest son, Lucien Pissarro (1863–1944), had early shown some talent and much desire for painting, but his mother (who had experienced the ways of artists) strongly opposed an artist's career for him. At the age of twenty Lucien left his parents' home in the country near Pontoise "to try his luck in England," where he took a position with a music publisher but continued to draw and paint landscapes. His father, unlike his mother, encouraged him.

ERAGNY [May 15, 1888]

MY DEAR LUCIEN,

I think you would do well to come here, for if you wait indefinitely for your money you will miss the good weather; come now while we have some money and prepare for your exhibition for next year and also do some illustrations. It is necessary not to be discouraged; one must get oneself accepted on the strength of incontestable, if not uncontested, talent. Renouard made his name on the strength of three or four illustrations of scenes backstage and lady painters in the Louvre, while these are far from being comparable to the works of Degas they were quite good, they lacked style but there was energy, they were not the works of a nonentity, and Renouard made his mark. I believe myself when one has talent one finally breaks through; thus when the occasion presents itself for working freely do not miss it.

I work a great deal in the studio; the leaves are burgeoning and don't give me a chance to work out a single sketch. I am making little water colors and pastels, I believe that it doesn't go too badly; in the studio I am preparing five or six canvases, I work on one after another, I'm getting used to working so.[1]

Lucien returned to France, worked with his father, and exhibited with him. But his paintings were less successful, and in time he returned to London, became a book designer, and started the Eragny Press, named for his father's home in France.

[1] Camille Pissarro, *Letters to His Son Lucien* (ed. with the assistance of Lucien by John Rewald; trans. by Lionel Abel), 125.

☞ *Paternal Adoration of a Future President*

THE Reverend Joseph Ruggles Wilson (1822–1903), long pastor of the First Presbyterian Church of Augusta, Georgia, and later professor of theology at Columbia, South Carolina, was a southern gentleman—handsome, courtly, a good scholar, and a fine preacher. He was tremendously proud of the character and career of his son, Woodrow Wilson (1856–1924), though to the end he occasionally expressed regret that Woodrow had not chosen the ministry. He did not live to see his son President of the United States, but while Woodrow was rapidly mounting the academic ladder at Wesleyan and Johns Hopkins universities as professor of politics, his father wrote to him:

CLARKESVILLE, TENN., March 6, '89

MY PRECIOUS SON—

Your most welcome letter came to hand on yesterday. I would have written you, as a break to the long silence, had I been sure of your address—but it was not known in this part of the world whether you were in M[iddletown, Connecticut] or B[altimore]. There is one thing always sure, however, and this is that you are hour by hour in my thoughts and upon my heart:—and what is just as certain is, that you deserve the place which you occupy within the house of my soul, and even a bigger place were it a bigger soul. How, in my solitude, have I longed for the presence of that dear son in whose large love I trust so implicitly and in the wealth of whose gem-furnished mind I take such delight: him in whom my affections centre as my child, and my confidences as my friend.

I can readily sympathize with you in the satisfaction you experience in getting back to Johns Hopkins once more, where intellectual life rolls its highest waves:—a satisfaction which is augmented by the fact that you are, yourself, a sort of *magna pars* where there is so much that is great. What would I not give to be in a position for hearing your lectures!—and to talk with you thereanent afterwards, perhaps, too, beforewards. I do not doubt as touching the impression they are making—and as you perceive this it must be very pleasing to your thoughts everyway. You are preaching a gospel of order, and thus of safety, in the department of political morals and conduct, such as has not heretofore been heralded, and success is therefore a personal gratification whilst it is also a public benefit. I feel very proud of you when I think of what you are doing and doing so well.[1]

[1] Ray Stannard Baker, *Woodrow Wilson: Life and Letters*, I, 40–41.

☞ *Natural Selection at Its Warmest and Best*

THOMAS HENRY HUXLEY (1825–95), man of science and expounder of Darwin's theory of natural selection, was only the most famous of a family whose wide and varied talents have endured to

176

the present generation in Julian the biologist, Aldous the literary philosopher, and others. His elder son, Leonard (1866–1933), became his biographer, as well as a poet and editor of the *Cornhill Magazine*. On Leonard's twenty-first birthday Huxley wrote:

[1881]

You will have a son some day yourself, I suppose, and if you do, I can wish you no greater satisfaction than to be able to say that he has reached manhood without ever having given you a serious anxiety, and that you can look forward with entire confidence to his playing the man in the battle of life. I have tried to make you feel your responsibilities and act independently as early as possible—but, once for all, remember that I am not only your father but your nearest friend, ready to help you in all things reasonable, and perhaps in a few unreasonable. . . .[1]

Nine years later Huxley wrote to his younger son, Henry, who had just become engaged to Miss Stobart, a letter which must then have been heart-warming to the young man:

EASTBOURNE, Jan. 30, 1890

YOU DEAR OLD HUMBUG OF A BOY—

Here we have been mourning over the relapse of influenza, which alone, as we said, could have torn you from your duties, and all the while it was nothing but an attack of palpitation such as young people are liable to and seem none the worse for after all. We are as happy that you are happy as you can be yourself, though from your letter that seems to be saying a great deal. I am prepared to be the young lady's slave; pray tell her that I am a model father-in-law, with my love. (By the way, you might mention her name; it is a miserable detail, I know, but would be interesting). Please add that she is humbly solicited to grant leave of absence for the Teneriffe trip, unless she thinks Northallerton air more invigorating. Ever your loving dad.

T. H. HUXLEY[2]

---

[1] Leonard Huxley, *Life and Letters of Thomas Henry Huxley*, II, 433.
[2] *Ibid.*, 252.

☞ *A Naturalist Defines Culture*

To many Americans at the turn of the century, John Burroughs (1837–1921) was almost a national idol—a great traveler and yet a mystic sage, a naturalist and yet a philosopher, a scientist whose prolific writings exuded morality as well as science, a man whose friendships went back to Walt Whitman and forward to Theodore Roosevelt and Henry Ford. Burroughs' scientific writings are now deemed old-fashioned as his morals, his books are seldom read, and his name means little or nothing to most members of the younger generation. His son Julian, to whom the following letters were addressed when he was a student at Harvard, later contributed a chapter to the biography of his father.

WEST PARK [NEW YORK], Mch 2 (1898)

MY DEAR BOY,

... This thought came into my head as I lay in bed this morning. You can go to college for two things, knowledge and culture. In the technical schools the student gets much knowledge and little culture. The sciences and mathematics give us knowledge, only literature can give us culture. In the best history we get a measure of both, we get facts and are brought into contact with great minds. Chemistry, physics, geology etc. are not sources of culture. But Lessig, Goethe, Schiller, Shakespeare etc. are. The discipline of mathematics is not culture in the strict sense; but the discipline that chastens the taste, feeds the imagination, kindles the sympathies, clarifies the reason, stirs the conscience and leads to self-knowledge and self-control, is culture. ...

SLABSIDES, Oct. 16, 1899

... It is now a certainty that you are fixed there in Harvard and that a wide gulf separates us. But if you will only keep well and prosper in your studies, we shall endure the separation cheerfully. Children have but little idea how the hearts of their parents yearn over them. When they grow up and have children of their own, then they understand and sigh, and sigh when it is too late. If you live to be old you will never forget how your father and mother came to visit you at Harvard and tried so hard to do something for you.

178

When I was your age and was at school at Ashland, father and mother came one afternoon in a sleigh and spent a couple of hours with me. They brought me some mince pies and apples. The plain old farmer and his plain old wife, how awkward and curious they looked amid the throng of young people, but how precious the thought and memory of them is to me! . . .[1]

[1] John Burroughs, *My Boyhood*, 190–94.

☞ *Travel Broadens the Mind—and the Joke*

SIR JOSCELYN COGHILL (1826–1905), fourth Baronet and owner of some four thousand acres in Counties Kilkenny, Cavan, and Dublin, was at the turn of the century genially risking the hazards of Mediterranean travel, but usually with spiritual or military support. On one such expedition he was accompanied by his brother-in-law, the Most Reverend William Conyngham (1828–97), D.D., L.L.D., fourth Baron Plunket, Archbishop of Dublin and Primate of Ireland; on another by his younger brother, Colonel Kendal Coghill (1832–1919), late of the Nineteenth Hussars, and by his valet, Hewitt, the son of Sam Chard, the village cobbler of Castletownshend in County Cork, the seat of Sir Joscelyn's Irish home. Perhaps this letter from Sir Joscelyn to his son, Egerton Coghill (1853–1921), busily yachting, painting, and managing the estates in Ireland, was all the more confidently comradely because Egerton was already in his forties and presumably beyond corruption by paternal jocularity. Sir Joscelyn's Italian geography seems at fault, but it is more likely that he found the possibilities of "Pisa" and "Po" more irresistible than geographical accuracy.

GRAND HOTEL, HELOUAN, EGYPT, St. Patrick's Day [1899?]
MY DEAR EGERTON,

Hewitt wants to send a pound to his father but can't get a Money Order here so asks me to write you to give the money to Sam and I will deduct it from his screw. So mote it be.

The Colonel is finely this morning and is going to dress. He is also full of his jokes and is very proud of a *mot* he has perpetrated. I would only have sent a card today except that I must send it on

179

to you. He says that on his return when anyone asks him where he spent the winter he intends to answer "I spent a part of it in a Dahabieh on the Nile and the rest of it in Diarrhoea on the Po."

That is no bad one! It is a pendant to one of mine I said to your uncle the Archbishop. We were crossing the high level bridge at Pisa one very dry season and I said "Look out, Bill, and you'll see something you won't see again. Anyone can see the po under the bed but today you can see the bed under the Po."

I am perfectly well. I had a little constipation as reaction after the attack but that has come all right. So I hope we shall both be fit for travelling per Oceana on the 25th. It is certainly a marvellous climate here and it would be perfect except for the flies and mosquitoes and for a certain heavy unpleasant smell of cookery quite peculiar to Egypt through the whole town and you can't escape it without going out into the desert. The epidemic is still raging through the house though it is on the decline. No other news.

Your affectionate dad,
J. J. COGHILL[1]

[1] By kind permission of Sir Patrick Coghill, Bt., of Savran House, Aylburton, Lydney, Gloscestershire, son of Sir Egerton.

☞ *"Avoid Any Fuss if Possible"*

THE affection of Theodore Roosevelt (1858–1919) for his children was so great that on occasion it could even induce him to advise a restraint under irritation that he himself did not often achieve. His eldest son, Theodore Roosevelt, Jr. (1887–1944), had just entered Harvard, and was at first followed everywhere by newspaper reporters, who made the freshman son of the President the victim of their attentions. To young Theodore's letter of anger and dismay the President replied:

WHITE HOUSE, October 2, 1905

BLESSED OLD TED:

The thing to do is to go on just as you have evidently been doing, attract as little attention as possible, do not make a fuss about the newspaper men, camera creatures, and idiots generally, letting it be seen that you do not like them and avoid them, but not letting them betray you into any excessive irritation. I believe they will soon drop you, and it is just an unpleasant thing you will have to live down. Ted, I have had an enormous number of unpleasant things that I have had to live down in my life at different times and you have begun to have them now. I saw that you were not out on the football field on Saturday and was rather glad of it, as evidently those infernal idiots were eagerly waiting for you, but whatever you do you will have to make up your mind that they will make it exceedingly unpleasant for you once or twice, and you will just have to bear it: for you can never in the world afford to let them drive you away from anything you intend to do, whether it is football or anything else, and by going about your own business quietly and pleasantly, doing just what you would do if they were not there, generally they will get tired of it, and the boys themselves will see that it is not your fault, and will feel, if anything, rather a sympathy for you. Meanwhile I want you to know that we are all thinking of you and sympathizing with you the whole time; and it is a great comfort to me to know that though these creatures can cause you a little trouble and make you feel a little downcast, they cannot drive you one way or the other, or make you alter the course you have set for yourself.

We are all of us, I am almost ashamed to say, rather blue at getting back in the White House, simply because we missed Sagamore Hill so much. But it is very beautiful and we feel very ungrateful at having even a passing fit of blueness, and we are enjoying it to the full now. I have just seen Archie dragging some fifty feet of hose pipe across the tennis court to play in the sand box. I have been playing tennis with Mr. Pinchot who beat me three sets to one, the only deuce-set being the one I won.

This is just an occasion to show the stuff there is in you. Do not let these newspaper creatures and kindred idiots drive you one hair's breadth from the line you had marked out in football or anything else. Avoid any fuss if possible.[1]

Theodore Roosevelt, Jr., survived that ordeal and many another test of his character and fortitude. Although he lacked some of his father's talents, he never ceased to attack life with equal courage and vigor, and throughout his life showed "the stuff in him" in ways that made his father proud. He was twice wounded and gassed in World War I; constantly active in politics and Republican candidate against Al Smith for governor of New York in 1924. He served as assistant secretary of the navy in the Harding-Coolidge administration. When the United States entered World War II, he somehow pressed his way, though over fifty years of age, into the most active possible military service. He died in a front-line camp of a heart attack induced by the exhaustion of leading his troops, regardless of great personal danger, in the invasion of Normandy. It was said that he was always trying to prove himself to himself and to be worthy of his father. If so, he did it with magnificent and unyielding determination.

[1] *The Works of Theodore Roosevelt*, XIX, 491–93.

☞ *The First Zephyrs of* The Wind in the Willows

KENNETH GRAHAME (1859–1932) was the distinguished secretary to the Bank of England, and his name is inscribed on the wall of the Bodleian Library in Oxford as one of its principal benefactors. But with his son Alastair, aged four in 1907, he was living in quite a different world, peopled by small animals who have since charmed innumerable parents as well as their children. Grahame would hurry in the evening from Threadneedle Street to the nursery of "Master Mouse" and, in the words of Alastair's nurse, invent as bedtime stories "some ditty or other about a toad." This was the genesis of *The Wind in the Willows*.

11 DURHAM VILLAS, LONDON, May 10, 1907

MY DARLING MOUSE,—

This is a birthday letter to wish you many happy returns of the day. I wish we could have been together, but we shall meet again soon and then we will have *treats*. I have sent you two picture books, one about Brer Rabbit, from Daddy, and one about other animals, from Mummy. And we have sent you a boat, painted red, with mast and sails to sail in the round pond by the windmill—and Mummy has sent you a boat-hook to catch it when it comes ashore. Also Mummy has sent you some sandtoys to play in the sand with, and a card game.

Have you heard about the toad? He was never taken prisoner by the brigands at all. It was all a horrid low trick of his. He wrote that letter himself—the letter saying that a hundred pounds must be put in the hollow tree. And he got out of the window early one morning and went off to a town called Buggleton and went to the Red Lion Hotel and there he found a party that had just motored down from London and while they were having breakfast he went into the stable-yard and found their motor car and went off in it without even saying Poop-poop! And now he has vanished and every one is looking for him, including the police. I fear he is a bad low animal.

Good-bye, from
Your loving DADDY[1]

[1] P. A. Chalmers, *Kenneth Grahame*, 122.

☞ *Aristocratic Eccentricity and Paternal Concern*

No father was ever more magnificently, and amusingly, eccentric than Sir George Reresby Sitwell (1860–1943), and no son has ever made greater literary capital of his father's unpredictabilities than his son, Sir Francis Osbert Sacheverel Sitwell (b. 1892). When Osbert was seventeen, Sir George indulged his own extravagant urge under guise of a gift to the boy, whose extravagances he at the same time condemned.

[1909]

MY DEAREST OSBERT

You will be interested that I am buying in your name the Castle of Acciaivoli (pronounced Accheeyawly) between Florence and Siena. The Acciaivoli were a reigning family in Greece in the thirteenth century, and afterwards great Italian nobles. The castle is split up between many poor families, and has an air of forlorn grandeur. It would probably cost £100,000 to build today. There is a great tower,

183

a picture gallery with frescoed portraits of the owners, from a very early period, and a chapel full of relics of the Saints. There are the remains of a fine old terraced garden, not very large, with two or three statues, a pebblework grotto and rows of flower pots with the family arms upon them. The great saloon, now divided into several rooms, opens into an interior court where one can take one's meals in hot weather, and here, over two doorways, are inscriptions giving the history of the house, most of which was rebuilt late in the seventeenth century as a "house of pleasure." The owners brought together there some kind of literary academy of writers and artists. All the rooms in the Castle have names, it seems, as the Sala of the Gonfalonieri; the Sala of the Priori—twelve of the Acciaivioli were Gonfalonieri and twelve, I think, Priorir—the Chamber of Donna Beatrice, the Cardinal's Chamber, the library, the museum. There seem to have been bathrooms, and every luxury. We shall be able to grow our own fruit, wine, oil—even champagne! I have actually bought half the Castle for £2,200; the other half belongs to the village usurer, whom we are endeavoring to get out. The ultimatum expires today, but I do not yet know the results. The purchase, apart from the romantic interest, is a good one, as it returns five per cent. The roof is in splendid order and the drains can't be wrong as there aren't any. I shall have to find the money in your name, and I do hope, my dear Osbert, that you will prove worthy of what I am trying to do for you, and will not pursue that miserable career of extravagance and selfishness which has already once ruined the family.

Ever your loving father,
GEORGE R. SITWELL[1]

A year later Sir George, while spending large sums on landscaping projects on his English estate, chided Osbert for tipping too generously.

[1910]

Thanks for the accounts. I was always struck by how much better off you are than I am. You give the footman ten shillings when five shillings at the outside is the proper thing, and porters a shilling, when I give sixpence. It is very generous, but reminds me of Jack Brale, who, when he travelled with me, bought franc cigars when he could put them down on my hotel bill, and half-penny ones when he had to pay for himself.[2]

Then came World War I, and Osbert, though ill adapted by experience, temperament, physique, or talent to life in the trenches, had just reached France as an officer in the British Expeditionary Force when he received from Sir George a letter written two days after a German warship had lightly shelled Scarborough near his country home.

WOOD END, SCARBOROUGH, December 16, 1914.
MY DEAREST OSBERT,

As I fear a line sent to Chelsea Barracks may not reach you before you leave tomorrow, I write to you care of your regiment, B.E.F., so that you may find a letter from me waiting for you when you arrive in the trenches. But I had wanted if possible to give you a word of advice before you left. Though you will not, of course, have to encounter anywhere abroad the same weight of gunfire that your mother and I had to face here—it has been my contention for many years that there were no guns in the world to compare for weight and range with the great German naval guns, and that our own do not come anywhere near them—yet my experience may be useful to you. Directly you hear the first shell, retire, as I did, to the Undercroft, and remain quietly there until all firing has ceased. Even there, a bombardment, especially as one grows older, is a strain upon the nervous system—but the remedy for that, as always, is to keep warm and have plenty of plain, nourishing food at frequent but regular intervals. And, of course, plenty of rest. I find a nap in the afternoon most helpful, if not unduly prolonged, and I advise you to try it whenever possible.

Ever your loving father,
GEORGE R. SITWELL[3]

Osbert commented on the last letter: "Undercroft was a word new to me, and it was some time before I discerned with what trisyllabic majesty the simple word cellar had clothed itself."

[1] Osbert Sitwell, *Great Morning*, 75f.
[2] *Ibid.*
[3] Osbert Sitwell, *Laughter in the Next Room*, 78.

☞ *The Best Education Comes*
from Enduring an Ill-tempered Mother

THE chief maker of modern India, Mahatma Ghandi (1869–1948) spent much of his early manhood in South Africa, whose rulers did not take kindly to his doctrines of racial equality and passive resistance. It was while he was serving his third term in prison there that he wrote to his seventeen-year-old son Manilal Ghandi (b. 1892):

March 25, 1909

MY DEAR SON, I have a right to write one letter per month and receive also one letter per month. It became a question with me so to whom I should write to. I thought of Mr. Rich,[1] Mr. Polack and you. I chose you because you have been nearest my thoughts in all my reading. . . .

How are you? Although I think you are well able to bear all the burden I have placed on your shoulders and that you are doing it quite cheerfully, I have often felt that you required greater personal guidance than I have been able to give you. I know too that you have sometimes felt that your education was being neglected. Now I have read a great deal in the prison. I have been reading Emerson, Ruskin and Mazzini. I have also been reading the *Upanishads*. All confirm the view that education does not mean a knowledge of letters but it means character building. It means a knowledge of duty. Our own (*Gujarati*) word literally means training. If this is the true view, you are receiving the best education-training possible. What can be better than that you should have the opportunity of nursing mother & cheerfully bearing her ill temper, or than looking after Chanchi & anticipating her wants and behaving to her so as not to make her feel the absence of Harilal or again than being guardian to Ramdas and Devedas? If you succeed in doing this well, you have received more than half your education. . . .

Amusement only continues during the age of innocence, i.e. up to twelve years only. As soon as a boy reaches the age of discretion, he is taught to realize his responsibilities. Every boy from such stage onward should practice continence in thought & deed, truth likewise and the not-taking of any life. This to him must not be an irksome learning and practice but it should be natural to him. It should be his enjoyment. I can recall to my mind several such boys in Rajkot. Let me tell you that when I was younger than you are my keenest enjoyment was to nurse my father. Of amusement after I was twelve, I had little or none. If you practice the three virtues, if they become part of your life, so far as I am concerned you will have completed your education—your training. Armed with them, believe me you will earn your bread in any part of the world & you will have paved the way to acquire a true knowledge of the soul, yourself and God. This does not mean that you shd not receive instructions in letters. That you shd & you are doing. But it is a thing over which you need not fret yourself. You have plenty of time for it and after all you are to receive such instruction in order that your training may be of use to others. . . .

Do give ample work to gardening, actual digging, hoeing, etc. We have to live upon it in the future. And you shd be the expert gardener of the family. Keep your tools in their respective places and absolutely clean. In your lessons you shd give a great deal of attention to mathematics and Sanskrit. The latter is absolutely necessary for you. Both these studies are difficult in after life. You will not neglect your music. You shd make a selection of all good passages, hymns and verses, whether in English, Gujarati or Hindu and write them out in your best hand in a book. The collection at the end of the year will be most valuable. All these things you can do easily if you are methodical. Never get agitated and think you have too much to do and then worry over what to do first. This you will find out in practice if you are patient and take care of your minutes. I hope you are keeping an accurate account as it should be kept of every penny spent for the household. . . .

And now I close with love to all and kisses to Ramdas, Devadas and Rami.

from
FATHER[2]

Manilal not only supported his family then, but later his father's efforts to gain freedom and unity for India. In 1930, Manilal led the famous salt march advocated by Ghandi in open defiance of British tax laws, and was arrested for it. For many years he edited *Indian Opinion* in South Africa and, back in India, carried on the protests against British rule after his father was shot and killed by a half-crazed Indian in 1948.

[1] The editor of *Indian Opinion.*
[2] Louis Fischer, *Life of Ghandi,* 90–92.

☞ *"You Have Faith— but What Else Have You?"*

IN the past century at least, sons who have felt a call to the ministry have apparently occasioned stronger parental reservations than those held regarding any other career except, perhaps, the arts. In expressing their doubts, many fathers have avoided emphasizing the purely practical disadvantages of an ecclesiastical career. One father, however, was more downright, and it may be for that reason that he elected to remain anonymous when, in 1911, he published under the protective title of "A Man of the World" his letter to a son proposing to take orders.

MY DEAR BOY:
Ever since your letter came, telling of your desire to enter the ministry, your mother has been regaling me with the most wonderful reminiscences of the ministerial intimations of your infancy. . . . I had not noticed that you were such a prodigy in the divinity department, but . . . her faith affects my reason. . . .

I believe in Christianity simply because I am a man of the world. I believe in organized Christianity because I am a man of business. And I believe that the Christian minister is meant to occupy a much more important position and exercise a mightier influence in the twentieth century than some of my business friends, and even some ministers of my acquaintance, seem to think. . . .

Just now, I am not so much concerned about the spiritual aspects of the call. I can safely leave that to your mother. But I don't think that the instincts of common sense are unchristian. The kingdom of God is not meat and drink, but without meat and drink there will be no kingdom of God on earth. You have faith—but what else have you? Have you popular gifts—gifts of speech, of persuasion, of power to manage men? And are those gifts of commercial value to the Church? Have you decided in which Church you can best invest your influence so as to secure the largest returns for truth? . . .

It's about the worst paid and the most precarious business going. And, I fancy, it will be worse before it is better. . . .

The man who wants to go into the ministry in our day, is either a fool or a hero, and heroes are scarce. Many men have been misled into the ministry who would have rendered good service to religion if they had earned their living in some other way, and devoted their spare time to the cause. . . . It's so big a business, is "the care of souls," that only the best men should go in for it. . . .

Face the facts, and *if you can't help yourself*—and I underline that —and this, *if you must enter the ministry*—well, go ahead, and God make you worth it.

Your affectionate father[1]

[1] *Letters to a Ministerial Son,* by a Man of the World, 1–4.

☞ *"You Don't Know How Much You Have to Be Thankful for"*

AFTER the president of Harvard and the dean of Princeton had declined President Woodrow Wilson's offer to become ambassador to the Court of St. James, Walter Hines Page (1855–1918), a distinguished magazine editor, accepted the post. Page was unfamiliar with both diplomacy and Europe at first hand, and during his first months in London he was depressed by the English climate and the English attitudes. Then came World War I, and Page's discomfort with the ways of the Old World increased. But as he watched England at war, he developed a strong admiration for British courage and character, and came to be regarded as a great wartime ambassador. It was after the first months of the 1914 holocaust, when Page was mystified and frustrated, that he conveyed his nostalgia for America to his youngest son, Frank Copeland Page (1887–1950), who later served in the United States Army against the Kaiser and then became a newspaper editor and the vice-president of a large electrical company.

[AMERICAN EMBASSY, LONDON,] Sunday, December 20, 1914
DEAR OLD MAN:

I envy both you and your mother your chance to make plans for the farm and the house and all the rest of it and to have one another to talk to. And, most of all, you are where you can now and then change the subject. You can guess somewhat at our plight when Kitty and I confessed to one another last night that we were dead tired and needed to go to bed early and stay long. She's sleeping yet, the dear Kid, and I hope she'll sleep till lunch time. There isn't anything the matter with us but the war; but that's enough, Heaven knows. It's the worst ailment that has ever struck me. Then if you add to that this dark, wet, foggy, sooty, cold, penetrating climate—you ought to thank your stars that you are not in it. . . .

The farm—the farm—the farm—it's yours and Mother's to plan and make and do as you wish. I shall be happy whatever you do, even if you put the roof in the cellar and the cellar on top of the house.

If you have room enough (16 by 12 plus a fire and a bath are enough for me), I'll go down there and write a book. If you haven't, I'll go somewhere else and write a book. I don't propose to be made unhappy by any house or by the lack of any house nor by anything whatsoever.

All the details of life go on here just the same. The war goes as slowly as death because it *is* death, death to millions of men. We've all said all we know about it to one another a thousand times; nobody knows anything else; nobody can guess when it will end; nobody has any doubt about how it will end, unless some totally improbable and unexpected thing happens, such as the falling out of the Allies, which can't happen for none of them can afford it; and we go round the same bloody circle all the time. The papers never have any news; nobody ever talks about anything else; everybody is tired to death; nobody is cheerful; when it isn't sick Belgians, it's aeroplanes; and when it isn't aeroplanes, it's bombarding the coast of England. When it isn't an American ship held up, it's a fool German-American arrested as a spy; and when it isn't a spy it's a liar who *knows* the Zeppelins are coming tonight. We don't know anything; we don't believe anybody; we should be surprised at nothing; and at 3 o'clock I'm going to the Abbey to a service in honour of the 100 years of peace! The world has all got itself so jumbled up that the bays are all promontories, the mountains are all valleys, and earthquakes are necessary for our happiness. We have disasters for breakfast; mined ships for luncheon; burned cities for dinner; trenches in our dreams, and bombarded towns for small-talk.

Peaceful seems the sandy landscape where you are, glad the very blackjacks, happy the curs, blessed the sheep, interesting the chin-whiskered clodhopper, innocent the fool darkey, blessed the mule, for it knows no war. And you have your mother—be happy, boy; you don't know how much you have to be thankful for.

Europe is ceasing to be interesting except as an example of how-not-to-do-it. It has no lessons for us except as a warning. When the whole continent has to go fighting—every blessed one of them—once a century, and half of them half of the time between, and all prepared even when they are not fighting, and when they shoot away all their money as soon as they begin to get rich a little, and everybody else's money too, and make the world poor, and when they kill every third or fourth generation of the best men and leave the worst to rear families, and have to start over fresh every time with a worse stock—give me Uncle Sam and the big farm! We don't need to catch any of this European life. We can do without it all as well as we can do without the judge's wigs and the court costumes. Besides, I like a land where the potatoes have some flavor, where you can buy a cigar, and get your hair cut and have warm baths.

Build the farm, therefore, and let me hear at every stage of that happy game. May the New Year be the best that has ever come to you.

Affectionately,
W. H. P.[1]

---

[1] Burton J. Hendrick, *The Life and Letters of Walter Hines Page*, I, 353ff.

☞ *"These People Think One Is Made of Stone"*

UNEASY lies the head that wears a crown, for although in England that head is no longer in physical jeopardy, the demands upon kingship make it an unenviable vocation. It is not only impossible to escape from the public routine, but improper to complain of it. George V (1865–1936) performed for twenty-six years (1910–36) royal duties especially onerous to his retiring nature, but he confessed to his son David (b. 1894) his distaste for them. David had, as Prince of Wales, embarked on his first good-will tour of the Empire. He suffered less than his father from the innumerable personal appearances, but as Edward VIII he found kingship restricting in other ways and made his dramatic escape from it into the somewhat anomalous status of Duke of Windsor.

BUCKINGHAM PALACE, Oct 12th / 19[19]

DEAREST DAVID

. . . You might take things easier during the last month of your visit & give yourself more spare time & get more rest from the ever-lasting functions & speeches which get on one's nerves. I warned you what it would be like, these people think one is made of stone & that one can go on forever; you ought to have put your foot down at the beginning & refused to do so much. . . . All I wish to say now is that I offer you my warmest congratulations on the splendid success of your tour, which is due in great measure to your own personality & the wonderful way in which you have played up. It makes me very proud of you & makes me feel very happy that my son should be received with such marvellous enthusiasm of loyalty and affection. I have had many letters from all sorts of people in Canada, as well as members of yr. Staff all singing yr. praises. . . .

Ever my dear boy
Yr. most devoted Papa
G. R. I.[1]

But some four years later the conduct of the Prince of Wales was not always equally pleasing to his royal father, who found the more conservative ways of his second son more to his liking. Three days after Prince George (1895–1952), later King George VI (1936–52), married Elizabeth Bowes-Lyon, his father sent him a note expressing more than conventional approval, with an interesting comment on the older brother.

[April 26, 1923]

You are indeed a lucky man to have such a charming & delightful wife as Elizabeth. I am sure you will both be very happy together. I trust you both will have many many years of happiness before you and that you will be as happy as Mama and I am after you have been married for 30 years. I can't wish you more.

You have always been so sensible & easy to work with & you have always been ready to listen to any advice & to agree with my opinions about people and things that I feel we have always got on very well together. Very different to dear David.[2]

[1] Edward VIII, King of England, *A King's Story: The Memoirs of H. R. H., the Duke of Windsor, K.G.,* 144.

[2] Hon. Harold George Nicolson, *King George V: His Life and Reign,* 366.

☞ *A Novelist's Comments on Undergraduate Manners*

A WRITER has a special advantage in arguments with a callow son: he can turn his literary skill into a rapier of reproof. Arnold Bennett (1867–1931), whose fictional chronicles of the Five Towns were rated more highly then than now, did not scruple to make use of that advantage in dealing with his adopted son, Richard Bennett, then an undergraduate at Cambridge. He took the boy on a tour in Scotland, after having made all the arrangements in an authoritative manner which may have accounted in part for the son's reticence or lack of enthusiasm. One evening while in Scotland together, the younger man found in his bedroom this composition by his uncle and adoptive father.

27.9 20

Report upon the Social Tactics of Richard Bennett of C[orpus] C[risti] College

At breakfast he replied to an inquiry as to his health as though the question was perfectly normal and proper; but as he responded with no similar enquiry, it is presumed that he considered enquiries about anybody else's health to be an unnecessary and futile formality.

On a remark being made he gave no sign that he had heard it, thus indicating in his opinion the absurdity of the old theory that if only for politeness a remark ought to evoke some kind of a response. On the remark being repeated he kindly gave way and condescendingly conformed to the absurd theory.

He made no conversation whatever, thus indicating his opinion that if one party had planned and paid for the holiday, he on his side was doing enough in providing the honor of his company.

He attended well to the mechanical details of the transport from Glasgow to Inverness, making very few slips and still fewer remarks.

The journey from Glasgow to Inverness comprises some of the most beautiful and historic scenery in Scotland. He made no remark on it whatever from 10. A.M. to 2:30 P.M., although he had previously been informed, and he had agreed, that it was advisable and polite not only to *feel* interest but to *show* it.

At 12 o'clock he said that the train was made up of different sorts of carriages.

At 2.20 he said the train leaked.

These were his sole voluntary remarks throughout the journey.

For three days, from lunch Wednesday to lunch Saturday, I consistently attempted beginnings of conversations, with no appreciable results. I then decided that I would for the future behave to Mr. Richard Bennett as he behaved to me. Thus very many hours passed in absolute silence, while he was continually seeing new and interesting phenomena. At noon today I decided to try again, and by intense efforts got some information about his plans for Cambridge. The process resembled prising a piece of concrete out of a road with a lever. I then, with admirable perseverance, asked him how he had done in the exam. He replied: "All right" and said no more until I did further heavy prising. The conversation then expired.

The luncheon baskets awaited us, and I said that we would eat at 1 o'clock. Mr. R. B. said nothing for some 150 minutes from noon.

At the 90th minute he began to look interestedly at the baskets, but he could not act contrary to his principles. It would have been against his conscience to make some public remark about the time, or the lunch, or about the possibility of Uncle being hungry. No hollow politeness, no initiative, at any cost! He preferred to go hungry. He did go hungry. He arrived at Inverness at 5.45 and he is in a position to say that he has accomplished the world-renowned passage through the Highlands without showing the slightest interest in it or the slightest curiosity about it.

At Inverness he once again attended to the mechanical details with efficiency, and then fell back on his grand old principle of confining his contribution to the amenities of the tour to his mere physical presence.

Marks for mechanics   90%

Marks for socialics   minus 150%

Somewhat later an addition to the text was made, as follows:

Suppl. Report

Marked abandonment of the sublime principle, and acquiescence in the traditions of civilized society.

Marks   75%[1]

[1] Arnold Bennett, *Letters to His Nephew*, 34–36.

☞ "The Final Rewards of Life Aren't Reaped in College"

THE young man in a hurry is not an uncommon character in collegiate life. He is discontented and resentful that society has not already recognized his talents, and inclined to chide his parents for his own ill-humor. John Sherman had not been long at Harvard in 1925 before he began to wallow in that morass of self-pity. His father, Stuart Sherman (1881–1926), who was just reaping the rewards of many years of literary effort, tried to make the boy see himself and the world in better proportion. Stuart Sherman's death the following year at the age of forty-five robbed the literary world of one of its most genuinely American figures.

70 MORNINGSIDE DRIVE, NEW YORK, March 30, 1925

DEAR SPUG:

. . . You lose your sense of proportion when you let yourself go like that, and make your mother feel terribly guilty. You have quite a nice group of friends, boys and girls, who like you and are interested in you. You have besides numerous acquaintances in whom you will find more friends. The *final rewards* of life aren't reaped in college anyhow. You know well enough, or ought to know, that many of the boys who play around most in college, do nothing but play around afterwards. As for the "snobbish cliques" that you talk about, no clique that is snobbish is worth getting into. If you really want to play around in Cambridge & Boston, which I don't think you do, the way to enter is to follow up the invitations you have had to visit various families, most of which you have not cared to follow up.

The help that comes from money and social prestige you somehow seem to me greatly to over-estimate. Your family backing is plenty good enough to enable you to make friends and have a good time in Cambridge. As a matter of fact, your family has no great deal to do with it—except as it has been responsible for making you what you are—a good lively agreeable youth—in my opinion, Spuggy, when you haven't lost your sense of proportion a bit. When you let off steam, your sense of humor flies out at the escape valve with the steam.

I've been glad to see you are going in for things; and tickled when you scored at anything; but heavens, we are young yet, and don't have to make all our record this spring. *Par example,* I am going on 44, and hope to do something *yet* in spite of the many targets that I've missed. At seventeen, a man's chances are simply immense. . . .

Much love from
FATHER[1]

---

[1] Jacob Zeitlin and Hoover Woodbridge, *Life and Letters of Stuart P. Sherman,* II, 722–23.

☞ *On Adjusting European Tastes*
to an Unresponsive America

AMERICA has developed few more rugged intellectual individuals and perceptive critics of its values than John Jay Chapman (1862–1933), essayist, poet, and uncompromising crusader. He followed his convictions with a courage that often defied and sometimes shocked the aristocratic American society of which he was a birthright member. As an undergraduate at Harvard he was so contrite at having struck unjustly another young man who made advances to the girl he was escorting that he held his offending hand in his coal fire until it was so badly burned that it had to be amputated. Later he often risked his friendships and sometimes his safety in defending unpopular causes. He published twenty-five books, all ardent for or against something and all vibrant with his own vivid reactions to life.

The letter that follows was sent to his son at Grenoble (members of the Chapman family spent much time in Europe). It was written on the back of typed sheets that composed an "Imaginary Obituary; E. S. Martin is No More," written by Chapman for publication in *Vanity Fair*. His friend Martin was the very-much-alive editor of the then humorous magazine *Life*. The book by Frank Harris to which Chapman's letters refers was *Contemporary Portraits*.

Nov. 26, 1919. 325 W. 82 [NEW YORK]

DEAR CHARLES

This is to amuse you. It will come out, I hope, with his picture—some months hence. I got Ned Martin to give me a photograph and told him I'd send him a copy. It will make him laugh. But he won't know what it's about.

All this reminds me that there's going to be a time in your life when you have a devilish bad time. It will be when you ultimately come back to America to settle—at whatever age you do. There's no future elsewhere, as you have an American mind, and would be an exotic anywhere else: and for anyone to hook on and get planted in here, who is American yet sees what America is, is a devilish hard job. Uncle Bob did it in middle life and with his eyes open, a rather remarkable thing to do, yet the making of him. In my days I was only abroad fifteen months—and positively had to return. But I shall

197

never forget the hardness and dryness and horror of the experience. It's so ugly and so ignorant, so bleak and unresponsive—so contented and unimaginative. I rather think it's getting better—but so little. I notice already a loss in the active-mindedness which the war brought on. The newspapers are more rigid: nothing to talk of: all shop. Business shop: art shop: charity shop. Clubdom subsiding to its normal state of a bore. Last summer we were *agace* and suffering in France. We fell into America as into a warm inn, but being here, we are here—stupid old inn. The terms of the equation are changing for the better; but its elements will remain the same for some generations—possibly centuries. . . .

What I was going to say is this: One never can find out anything about life, because the advantages are always disadvantages and the disadvantages advantages. All the European Buffet of civilization—as you see in Harris's book—tending to overfeed and belittle the clever men.—Walt Whitman did *something-or-other* just because he was ignorant. I don't like him much—only point to him as illustrating the conquest of temperament in a particular case.

Your loving,
PAPA

I read this to our Mo[ther]—who told me the story of Uncle Bob's first night in the U.S.—at 325. He saw the door knob and burst into tears—and spent a night of agony and despair. She says, however, that Europe has become dilettante and that the U.S., though rough and ignorant, has the drive and vigor of art—(this apropos of a visit to Al Jolson as contrasted with the French players here) and she says you'll be at home here—and she's pretty clever—*I must admit.*[1]

[1] M. A. DeWolfe Howe, *John Jay Chapman and His Letters*, 365–67.

☞ It's No Use Trying to Make Opposites Meet

JAWAHARLAL NEHRU (b. 1889), prime minister of India since 1950, came from a prosperous upper-class family which gave him every opportunity and a Western education at Cambridge University.

His father, Motilal Nehru (1861–1931), was himself a man of cultivation and high standing, with a desire to improve the lot of lower-caste Indians. But when his son openly defied law and authority under the British rule, Motilal could no longer approve his conduct. Nehru the son told the story:

"In 1923 I was suddenly arrested by the Nabha State authorities and later charged with various offenses, including conspiracy. My father, when he heard of this, was greatly upset, more especially as many of the Indian States of those days functioned according to no known or accepted laws. He paid me a visit in prison and was anxious to get me out. I was distressed at this because I did not want him to ask for any favour from the government"

Shortly after that visit to his son in jail, Motilal wrote to him:

September 28, 1923

MY DEAR J,

I was pained to find that instead of affording you any relief my visit of yesterday only had the effect of disturbing the even tenor of your happy jail life. After much anxious thinking I have come to the conclusion that I can do no good either to you or to myself by repeating my visits. I can stand with a clear conscience before God and man for what I have done so far after your arrest but as you think differently it is no use trying to make opposites meet.

I am sending Kapil with some notes I have jotted down. There is nothing new in them but I thought it my duty to do what I could knowing that it could not possibly be up to much in my present state of mind. I shall now be content with such news as Kapil is able to bring me. For the present I hardly know what to do with myself and shall wait here for a couple of days or so. Please do not bother about me at all. I am as happy outside the jail as you are in it.

Your loving
FATHER

Please do not think that I have written this letter either in anger or in sorrow. I have tried my best after an almost all-night consideration to take a calm and practical view of the position. I wish you not to have the impression that you have offended me as I honestly be-

lieve that the position has been forced upon both of us by circumstances over which neither has any control.[1]

[1] Jawaharlal Nehru, *A Bunch of Old Letters*, 28.

☞ *"The Arts Are Uncertain"*

LIKE Carlos Williams, Sherwood Anderson (1876–1941),
novelist, editor, and poet, put aside literary language in advising two
sons with different talents, at different stages of their development,
regarding their careers. To his son Robert, establishing himself as a
journalist but attracted to more ambitious writing, Anderson outlined
the practical problems:

[TROUTDALE, VIRGINIA, August (?), 1926]

DEAR BOB:

I have been thinking of you a good deal lately. I think that with
your energy, your quick imagination and your love of life you are
bound in the end to go toward one of the arts.

The natural thing would be for you to become, eventually, a prose
writer, a story teller.

But here, my dear fellow, you will always be under a handicap.
The great difficulty will always be that your father is one. They
would always club you with that.

When I am dead, the sons of bitches will begin to heap laurels
on me.

You would have to be almost superhuman not, in the end, to
hate me.

However, I think there is a way out, and I also think it may be
a way that finally may come natural to you.

As you know, I have never touched the stage. Why not begin
giving your mind and imagination to that?

It is, of course, a long road, but any road in the arts is long. I
think you might begin consciously to let yourself think and feel in
that way. You are a natural dramatist with a quick imagination.
Let your imagination, at odd moments, begin to play within a con-

fined space, casting people in there, and letting them in imagination play within that confined space.

And then too, Bob, I think that for us, of our tribe, it is almost necessary to have a moral balance.

There is and can be no moral balance like the long difficulty of an art.

If the idea strikes you, begin. Read what all the old and modern dramatists have done. It is entirely possible and rather nice to let your will, in part at least, control your fancy.

A man needs a purpose for real health. It is a suggestion. Think about it.

With love,[1]

To John, not yet embarked on a vocation, Anderson urged experience and caution before making a final choice, and seemed to discourage plunging into an artist's career.

[New Orleans, April 18 (?), 1926]

Dear John:

It's a problem, all right. The best thing, I dare say, is first to learn something well so you can always make a living. Bob seems to be catching on at the newspaper business and has had another raise. He is getting a good training by working in a smaller city. As for the scientific fields, any of them require a long schooling and intense application. If you are made for it, nothing could be better. In the long run you will have to come to your own conclusion.

The arts, which probably offer a man more satisfaction, are uncertain. It is difficult to make a living.

If I had my own life to live over, I presume I would still be a writer, but I am sure I would give my first attention to learning how to do things directly with my hands. Nothing brings quite the satisfaction that doing things brings.

Above all avoid taking the advice of men who have no brains and do not know what they are talking about. Most small businessmen say simply, "Look at me." They fancy that if they have accumulated a little money and have got a position in a small circle, they are competent to give advice to anyone.

201

Next to occupation is the building up of good taste. That is difficult, slow work. Few achieve it. It means all the difference in the world in the end.

I am constantly amazed at how little painters know about painting, writers about writing, merchants about business, manufacturers about manufacturing. Most men just drift.

There is a kind of shrewdness many men have that enables them to get money. It is the shrewdness of the fox after the chicken. A low order of mentality often goes with it.

Above all I would like you to see many kinds of men at first hand. That would help you more than anything. Just how it is to be accomplished I do not know. Perhaps a way can be found.

Anyway, I'll see you this summer. We begin to pack for the country this week.

With love,
DAD[2]

[1] *Letters of Sherwood Anderson* (ed. by Howard Mumford Jones), 153–54.
[2] *Ibid.*, 157.

☞ *Another Roosevelt Encounters*
Another Problem at Harvard

FRANKLIN D. ROOSEVELT (1882–1945) had not yet become President when his eldest son, James Roosevelt (b. 1907), was about to enter Harvard. The letter that follows was not addressed to James, but his father sent it to him in advance, and it may have been written as much for his eye as for that of Dean Chester Greenough of Harvard College. James protested that the letter was unjust to himself and his friends, and another letter "in a less provocative vein" was sent instead to the Dean.

MARION, MASS., August 15, 1926, Sunday

MY DEAR DEAN GREENOUGH:

This is a more or less personal note in reply to yours of August 11th regarding my oldest boy James who is about to enter the Freshman class.

He goes to Harvard with the usual advantages and handicaps of having spent six years at Groton. He did very well there in athletics and leadership, rather poorly in studies—lower half of the form—but passed all of his college Board Examinations, two with honors.

He is clean, truthful, considerate of others, and has distinct ambition to make good. He has at the same time, I think, too much love of "social good times" (like the rest of his crowd), and for that reason, although a former Overseer, etc. I hesitated for some time before letting him go to Cambridge at all. In other words, I know enough of the club and Boston life of the average private school freshman to fear the lack of individuality and the narrowness which comes to so many of them.

One of the principal troubles with most of these private school undergraduates of yours is, I am convinced after a great deal of investigation, that their parents give them a great deal too much money to go through college on. To this is added in most cases, automobiles, and all sorts of expensive toys in the holidays.

You people in authority have done and are doing a great work in aiming at a greater simplicity of college life, and incidentally your fine efforts for higher scholarship, i.e. more work, is bearing good fruit.

I, as one graduate of many, want to co-operate with you in this. During the past summer my boy has worked as a laborer in a Canadian pulp and paper mill. Most of the Groton boys will have college allowances well over 2,000 dollars a year. James and his room mate Harrison Parker Jr. will have only $1,500 or $1,600.

I should like them in addition to find some sort of employment while at college so that they could earn part of their education, even if it covered only the $300 tuition. In my own days such a thing was rare and difficult. Waiting on table at Memorial was about the only method, and the college office made very little effort to encourage boys to find jobs. I hope this phase is better handled now.

Concretely in regard to my boy I feel the following should be the objectives:

1. Better scholarship than passing marks. 2. Athletics to be a secondary not a primary objective. 3. Activity in student activities such

as debating, Crimson etc. to be encouraged. 4. Acquaintance with the average of the class, not just the Mt. Auburn Street crowd, to be emphasized. 5. Opportunity to earn part of his education.

I hope to get up to Cambridge this autumn and to have a chance to see you.

Very sincerely yours,
FRANKLIN D. ROOSEVELT[1]

James graduated from Harvard in 1930 and began a career as an insurance broker, in which many thought his father's position as President was helpful beyond the point of strict ethics. In 1938 he went into the motion picture industry, and during World War II he served in the Marine Corps, emerging with a colonel's bars and the Navy Cross. He returned to his insurance firm, but took a fling, more newsworthy than exalted, in national politics. In 1950 he was an unsuccessful candidate for the governorship of California, and he has served as a Democratic member of Congress.

[1] *The Roosevelt Letters* (ed. by Elliott Roosevelt), II, 483.

☞ *"They Cannot Destroy Our Ideas"*

No legal case in all history ever aroused and divided Americans or brought them more world criticism than the death sentences imposed, confirmed, and carried out on Nicola Sacco (1891–1927) and Bartolomeo Vanzetti. In cities abroad, mobs attacked American embassies and not only the leftish press shrieked injustice. At home class hatred was engendered and personal friendships broken. Men still differ on the justice of the case, with the liberals as usual more vocal and persuasive than the conservatives, but few would disagree on the confused idealism and pathos of Sacco's last letter to his thirteen-year-old son, Dante Sacco, written one week before his execution.

Sacco came to America from southern Italy in 1908 when he was seventeen. For eleven years he was a skilled and dependable worker in a shoe factory at Milford, Massachusetts, while he became an ardent convert to socialism and in Socialist circles made the acquaintance of Vanzetti. Then the paymaster and a guard of a shoe factory in South

Braintree were shot and killed, and Sacco and Vanzetti were charged with the murders. It was a time of bitter strikes across the country, and of drastic repressions of suspected "Reds" by an alarmed populace led by an alarmist attorney general, A. Mitchell Palmer. Many important Americans claimed that the evidence did not justify the verdict and that the judge and the jury had given way to prejudice against radicals. In Europe, men like Masaryk, Einstein, Anatole France, and Romaine Rolland signed protests, and in deference to all the objectors Governor Fuller of Massachusetts appointed a committee to consider the evidence and advise him whether to pardon the two convicted men. That committee, consisting of President A. Lawrence Lowell of Harvard, President Samuel W. Stratton of Massachusetts Institute of Technology, and the distinguished jurist, Judge Robert Grant, supported the verdict. After nearly seven years of imprisonment, ordeal, and uncertainty, Sacco and Vanzetti were executed in 1927.

CHARLESTOWN STATE PRISON, August 18, 1927

MY DEAR SON AND COMPANION:

Since the day I saw you last I had always the idea to write you this letter, but the length of my hunger strike and the thought I might not be able to explain myself, made me put it off all this time.

The other day, I ended my hunger strike and just as soon as I did that I thought of you to write to you, but I find that I did not have enough strength and I cannot finish it at one time. However, I want to get it down in any way before they take us again to the death house, because it is my conviction that just as soon as the court refuses a new trial they will take us there. And between Friday and Monday, if nothing happens, they will electrocute us right after midnight, on August 22nd. Therefore, here I am, right with you with love and with open heart as ever I was yesterday. . . .

I never thought that our inseparable life could be separated, but the thought of seven dolorous years makes it seem it did come, but then it has not changed really the unrest and the heartbeat of affection. That has remained as it was, More. I say that our ineffable affection reciprocal, is today more than any other time, of course. That is not only a great deal but it is grand because you can see the real brotherly love, not only in joy but also and more in the struggle of suffering.

Remember this, Dante. We have demonstrated this, and modesty apart we are proud of it.

Much we have suffered during this long Calvary. We protest to-day as we protested yesterday. We protest always for our freedom.

If I stopped hunger strike the other day, it was because there was no more sign of life in me. Because I protested with my hunger strike yesterday as today I protest for life and not for death.

I sacrificed because I wanted to come back to the embrace of your dear little sister Ines and your mother and all the beloved friends and comrades of life and not death. So Son, today life begins to revive slow and calm, but yet without horizon and always with sadness and visions of death.

Well, my dear boy, after your mother had talked to me so much and I had dreamed of you day and night, how joyful it was to see you at last. To have talked with you like we used to in the old days— in those days. Much I told you on that visit and more I wanted to say, but I saw that you will remain the same affectionate boy, faithful to your mother who loves you so much, and I did not want to hurt your sensibilities any longer, because I am sure that you will continue to be the same boy and remember what I have told you. I know that and what here I am going to tell you will touch your sensibilities, but don't cry Dante, because many years have been wasted, as your mother's have been wasted for seven years, and never did any good. So, son, instead of crying, be strong, so as to be able to comfort your mother, and when you want to distract your mother from the discouraging sadness, I will tell you what I used to do. To take her for a long walk in the quiet country, gathering wild flowers here and there, resting under the shade of trees, between the harmony of the vivid stream and the gentle tranquility of the mother-nature, and I am sure that she will enjoy this very much, as you surely would be happy for it. But remember always, Dante, in the play of happiness, don't use all for yourself only, but down yourself just one step, at your side and help the weak ones that cry for help, help the persecuted and the victim, because they are your better friends; they are the comrades that fight and fall and your father and Bartolo fought and fell yesterday for the conquest of the joy of freedom for all and the poor workers. In this struggle of life you will find more love and you will be loved.

I am sure that from what your mother has told me about what you said during these last terrible days when I was lying in the iniquitous death-house—that description gave me happiness because it showed you will be the beloved boy I had always dreamed.

Therefore whatever should happen tomorrow, nobody knows, but if they should kill us, you must not forget to look at your friends and comrades with the smiling gaze of gratitude as you look at your beloved ones, because they love you as they love every one of the fallen persecuted comrades. I tell you, your father that is all the life to you, your father that loved you and saw them, and knows their noble faith (that is mine) their supreme sacrifice that they are still doing for our freedom, for I have fought with them, and they are the ones that still hold the last of our hope that today they can still save us from electrocution, it is the struggle and fight between the rich and the poor for safety and freedom, Son, which you will understand in the future of your years to come, of this unrest and struggle of life's death.

Much I thought of you when I was lying in the death-house— the singing, the kind tender voices of the children from the playground, when there was all the life and the joy of liberty—just one step from the wall which contains the buried agony of three buried souls. It would remind me so often of you and your sister Ines, and I wish I could see you every moment. But I feel better that you did not come to the death-house so that you could not see the horrible picture of three lying in agony to be electrocuted, because I do not know what effect it would have on your young age. But then, in another way if you were not so sensitive it would be very useful to you tomorrow when you could use this horrible memory to hold up to the world the shame of the country in this cruel persecution and unjust death. Yes, Dante, they can crucify our bodies today as they are doing, but they cannot destroy our ideas, that will remain for the youth of the future to come.

Dante, when I said three human lives buried, I meant to say that with us there is another a young man by the name of Celestino Maderios that is to be electrocuted at the same time with us. He has been twice before in that horrible death-house, that should be destroyed with the hammers of real progress—that horrible house that will shame forever the future of the citizens of Massachusetts. They should destroy that house and put up a factory or school, to teach many of the hundreds of the poor orphan boys of the world.

Dante, I say once more to love and be nearest your mother and the beloved ones in these sad days, and I am sure that with your brave heart and kind goodness they will feel less discomfort. And you will also not forget to love me a little for I do—O Sonny! thinking so much and so often of you.

Best fraternal greetings to the beloved ones, love and kisses to your little Ines and mother. Most hearty affectionate embrace.

YOUR FATHER AND COMPANION[1]

[1] M. L. Schuster, *A Treasury of the World's Great Letters*, 443–44.

☞ *A Social Moral in Yale-Harvard Football*

JOSEPH LINCOLN STEFFENS (1866–1936), a journalist with an itch for reform, became known as a leading "muckraker" of his time. He served society and himself by exposing the graft and corruption in American cities, and blamed it primarily on the uncontrolled self-seeking and lack of social conscience of individual men. His letter to his son Peter (b. 1924) preached the need to submerge individualism in the collective aim. Steffens carried that principle so far that in his latter years he became dubious of the American system and was greatly impressed by Russian communism.

BOSTON, Nov. 26, '33

DEAR PETE:

You have had your ninth birthday. Turned the critical age of nine. Do you feel the difference? You must. There are a lot of your kid tastes that you should pass. No more stealing, no more lying; better table and other manners. For you have to clear the deck for ten. You will, of course. I am not a bit worried.

208

My trip thus far has been a surprise. No snow, no cold. Just a balmy East. But we'll soon get the weather of an Eastern winter, we are nearly through November, and December is the worst of winter.

I went to the Harvard-Yale football game yesterday. Harvard won by 19–6, and rejoiced because for two or three years Yale has always won. It was team-work that did it, teamwork, discipline and skill. One big play was a long straight pass; one man passed to a second man who ran up to where it was prearranged that the ball was to go. Perfect. Another fine play is described by the papers as a nine-yard run, but I saw it and the point I noted was that the Harvard team,—the whole team, opened the way clear for their runner and blocked the Yale players so that all their runner had to do was run. See? It was the team, not the runner, that did it.

The papers, the crowds, like and praise the individual players, but football is great because it is the teams, not the individuals, who play it when it is well played. Each individual player has to be good, skillful, perfect, but perfect only as the part of a perfect machine, which is the ideal.

Give my love to Mama, Anna, Betty Anne, Leslie and keep a teeny weeny bit for a guy named Pete. And, oh yes, if your friend Cagney is still there give him a hug for Pete' daddy.

Affectionately,
STEF.[1]

[1] *The Letters of Lincoln Steffens* (ed. by Ella Winter and Granville Hicks), II, 967.

☞ *"Don't Think You Have to Duck Anything in Life"*

WILLIAM CARLOS WILLIAMS (b. 1883), by profession a physician, is regarded by some critics as one of the finest American poets of his generation. In this letter to a son, William, nearing manhood, the language is more colloquially vivid than poetic, but like much of Williams' verse it is concerned with "the inevitable maladjustment consequent upon growing up in a more or less civilized environment." To

Williams, intellectual fortitude, more than religious faith, seems the solution.

March 13, 1935

DEAREST BILL:

This I can say for certain, you seem not far different from what I was myself at your age. I don't mind saying I went through hell . . . what with worrying about my immortal soul and my hellish itch to screw almost any female I could get my hands on—which I never did. I can tell you it is almost as vivid today as it was then when I hear you speaking of it. Everything seems upside down and one's self the very muck under one's foot.

It comes from many things, my dear boy, but mostly from the inevitable maladjustment consequent upon growing up in a more or less civilized environment. . . . But more immediately, your difficulties arise from a lack of balance in your daily life, a lack of balance which has to be understood and withstood—for it cannot be avoided for the present. I refer to the fact that your intellectual life, for the moment, has eclipsed the physical life, the animal life, the normal he-man life, which every man needs and craves. If you were an athlete, a powerful body, one who could be a hero on the field or the diamond, a *Big Hero*, many of your mental tortures would be lulled to sleep. But you cannot be that—so what? You'll have to wait and take it by a different course.

You, dear Bill, have a magnificent opportunity to enjoy life ahead of you. You have sensibility (even if it drives you nuts at times) which will be the source of keen pleasures later and the source of useful accomplishments too. You've got a brain, as you have been told *ad nauseam*. But these are things which are tormenting you, the very things which are your most valuable possessions and which will be your joy tomorrow. Sure you are sentimental, sure you admire a man like Wordsworth and his "Tintern Abbey." It is natural, it is the correct reaction of your age to life. It is also a criticism of Wordsworth as you will see later. All I can say about that is, wait! Not wait cynically, idly, but wait while looking, believing, getting fooled, changing from day to day. Wait with the only kind of faith I have ever recognized, the faith that says I wanna know! I wanna see! I think I will understand when I do know and see. Meanwhile I'm not making any final judgments. Wait it out. Don't worry too much. You've got time. You're all right. You're reacting to life in the only way an intelligent sensitive young man in college can. In another year you'll enter another sphere of existence, the practical one. The knowledge, abstract now, which seems unrelated to sense to you (at times) will get a different color. . . .

Mother and I both send love. Don't let *anything* get your goat and don't think you have to duck anything in life. There is a way out for every man who has the intellectual fortitude to go on in the face of difficulties.

Yours,

DAD[1]

[1] *Selected Letters of William Carlos Williams* (ed. by John C. Thirlwall), 153–55.

☞ *Rooseveltian Effervescence in the Depths of War*

AMERICAN fortunes were still dark and desperate in the Pacific, Hitler's forces were still holding nearly all Europe unchallenged, and D–Day seemed interminably remote in February, 1943. But American troops had landed successfully in North Africa and Roosevelt had conferred with Churchill at Casablanca. That was enough to exhilarate the President whose letter to his son John, in training with the navy at Oakland, California, typically betrayed no sign of worry.

THE WHITE HOUSE, Feb. 13, 1943

DEAR JOHNNY:

I am delighted to have your letter and to know that you are off for Oakland. I hope they won't keep you there very long for I know of your real desire to go to sea.

The Casablanca trip was grand but I want you to tell Anne that I dislike flying the more I do of it. She is dead right in her dislikes of it! . . .

I will add a bond every three months for the baby out of your allowance if that is all right with you and Anne.

I do wish I could see you to tell you all about the trip. It was really a great success and only General de Gaulle was a thoroughly bad boy. The day he arrived, he thought he was Joan of Arc and the following day he insisted that he was Georges Clemenceau. Winston and I decided to get him and Giraud to come to Casablanca and to hold a shot-gun wedding. I produced the bridegroom from Algers but Winston had to make three tries before he could get the bride.[1]

Ever so much love to all four of you,

Affectionately,[2]

John Roosevelt (b. 1916) has thus far not had a career as dramatic as that of his father. He has become an investment executive in California and New York, and his politics have not been identical with those of his father's New Deal.

[1] The "shot-gun wedding" amity between Generals De Gaulle and Giraud barely outlasted the ceremony and press photographs.

[2] *The Roosevelt Letters*, III, 456–57.

☞ *"Nine-tenths of English Children
Are the Worse for Education"*

EVEN before World War II ended, Englishmen were ardently discussing the new and finer English society they believed must be the reward of all the pains, sacrifices, and lessons of the war. But it soon became apparent that there were strong differences of opinion about what the new society should be and how it could be attained. One contributor to the public discussions of a new educational system was James Evershed Agate (1877–1947), a popular dramatic critic whose nine volumes of diaries record the books, plays, tastes, and personalities of his time. Agate's blast was, as a literary device, addressed to an imagined son.

LONDON, Sept. 9, 1944

First let me say that I have little or no belief in the power of education. I suggest that when Lady Bracknell says: "Ignorance is like a delicate exotic fruit—touch it, and the bloom is gone," Wilde meant something more than a mere witticism. In my view nine-tenths of English children are the worse for education. And for the reason that the education they are given is the wrong sort. "Educate" is derived from the Latin word "educare," meaning "to lead forth." But what is the modern system of education in this matter of leading forth? So far as I can see, it leads the child out of the darkness of healthy ignorance into the much denser night of a soul-destroying commonness. I do not believe that education in my time has had any effect except to increase the number of ways in which the young person of today can be common. You teach a young girl to read: she peruses nothing but film magazines. You teach her to write: at twenty she can hardly spell her own name. You give her music lessons: her only interest in music is in the bilge vomited by crooners and dance bands. You teach her deportment: she jitterbugs. Explore her mind and you will find nothing there except curiosity about the latest lipstick and nail-varnish. She has not learned how to speak her own language, preferring a jargon of her own. "Where was me an' Ida last night? Out Yankin'. Mine was ever such a nice boy—arst me to call 'im Texas." No one has persuaded these young women not to want to be common. The books they read, the films they see, the music they listen to—every approach to their minds is choked with commonness. And the same with the boys.[1]

[1] James Agate, *Noblesse Oblige*, 19–20.

☞ ## "We Israelites Live on a Rock Surrounded by an Ocean of Hate"

Not all American Jews feel a prejudice against them as acutely as did Dagobert David Runes (b. 1902), and his reaction is the more surprising because he elected to come to the United States as an immigrant from Austria in 1926 and was enabled by the American society he criticized to achieve a position of success and esteem. Other Jews who might agree with him would not be moved to write a similar letter to their sons. Runes was for a time a director of the

213

Institute for Advanced Education, and after 1946, while editor of the Philosophical Library, published some dozen volumes of social philosophy and criticism. In 1948 he wrote to his son, Richard Norton Runes:

As you know, I have never addressed you as "my little child" the way people are accustomed to address children. They like to create two worlds, the world of the child and the world of the man. In the world of the child virtue seems to abound, justice to flower, and kindness and tolerance to flourish. Ah, but in the world of man the ways are crooked, the designs are evil, and the interests malicious. And so they let you live your early years in the childhood world of make believe only to awaken you when maturity takes you into the reality of a most sorrowful existence. And while you still rub your eyes—were you dreaming? were you seeing things?—all the pretty, warm and playful children grow into mean, designing, envious men and women.

It was all right for you, my little man, to play with a colored girl with marbles and hoop and swing; but now if you were only to walk down the street with her hand-in-hand, they would point their fingers at you and cast you from their group like a leper.

It was all right for you, my son, to share your cot with the German lad; but now the school which he enters is closed to you and you must hunt for your learning until you find a back bench that they have put aside for you perhaps a thousand miles away.

That is why I never called you "child," my little man. I didn't want you to rise too high in the skyward climb of early dreams, only to fall on the rocky face of this infected globe.

Remember when I took you to that little town in Georgia and seated you in a classroom and you listened to a wise old teacher talk about American democracy and freedom for all and the pursuit of happiness, and how I suddenly poked you in the ribs and you began to cry and asked me why? I told you, "Don't be a dreamy fool. Just wait." And I took you across the street into the park and showed you the public fountain. Upon the stony base was engraved, "For whites only." And I told you of another park in another country where the schools were even bigger than that in Georgia and the churches more cathedral. There was a beautiful sandy beach, but in the center a huge placard said, "Jews Keep Out."

That fountain-base in Georgia, that placard in Germany, were not put up by evil-minded persons who live on the fringe of the community. These ugly deeds were perpetrated by the people in authority, by the very same people who teach their children democracy and preach the good Christian life to them in their churches.

They have made a mint of words, these people, but these words are not coins any longer. They are chips. There is neither gold in them nor silver, only some worthless plastic which they pass to each other in secret and open gentlemen's agreements—and just try to cash those chips. Let a Negro man try to ask for full value at work or at play or even at prayer. The very man who preaches that all men are God's children, equal before Him and the Holy Ghost and the loving Christ, would turn him out of the church.

If you are a Hebrew there are a thousand schools that will not accept you, a thousand homes that will not house you, a thousand bosses that will not hire you.

Democracy, equality, dignity—these are chips, my son, not coins. They may be cashed only by members, and never forget that although you and your black brother may often be guests, you can never be members. It is odd that some of these chips should bear the likeness of Christ—*Love Thy Neighbor* is the engraved motto. Others bear the motto of Moses: the *Ten Commandments* are on the reverse side. Both were Israelites; one even an African born on the Nile. Perhaps these coins were cut only in irony—how little do these people love their Israelite neighbors, and have the Commandments ever been applied to the Africans?

Since you were knee-high, my son, I have taught you the worthlessness of these coins. Six millions of your brothers and sisters were poisoned and burned, hunted, tortured, drowned and bludgeoned, butchered and choked, garroted and guillotined, denounced and strung up by seventy million well-educated Christians living in the heart of Europe. And the world of Christian men went about its business, deaf to the cries of mothers who saw their children cut up before their eyes, of children who were made to watch the agonies of their choking parents. You see, even then, in the face of these most devilish of abominations, the people of the Christian world were not concerned with the fate of your victimized brothers and sisters. They would rather forgive the skinning alive of your brothers than forget your own slightest transgression.

There are no children among the beleaguered, my son. We Israelites live on a rock surrounded by an ocean of hate, suspicion, and indifference, and we may never know when and where the next storm may come. You must be alert, my son, alert and fighting-ready. You can never really be a child in such turmoil. Never fear so long as you stand on the rock of Israel's heritage and so long as you do not let them set you to dreaming with their sirenic fables and promises. You have only one friend, my son, and that is your courage. And like that mythological figure of old, when you leave the rock of your heritage, gone is your strength and your future. Be strong, my son.

Your loving
FATHER[1]

[1] Dagobert D. Runes, *Letters to My Son*, 20–24.

☞ *Loneliness Is Natural—*
Get Used to It

IN 1947 there was published in London a small book entitled *Letters from a Civil Servant to his Son*. Although father and son remain unknown, there is no reason to doubt the authenticity of the letters or the statement that when the young man was killed in action in France in August, 1944, all his father's letters were found among his few possessions. When "Dick" was seventeen and at a public school, his father wrote this to him:

You say that, although you can let off steam to some extent with Bondfield, you are still indescribably lonely. Well, I am afraid that you must make up your mind that (subject to the one qualification which I will mention) that is an inevitable condition in the world for every intelligent man; and by intelligent I don't necessarily mean those who are bulging with obvious brains, but those who do use their brains to think about something more than their day-to-day problems and pleasures.

Now you, quite obviously, are intelligent in the sense I have mentioned. Up till a year or so ago, you were naturally, by reason of your youth, almost entirely wrapped up in your day-to-day affairs, and felt no particular sense of loneliness. Now you are beginning in your mind to go deeper, and inevitably you are beginning to find yourself more and more alone. You can communicate with others—provided they are in sympathy with you, as Bondfield at least seems to be—some of what is going on in your mind; but much of it, particularly at your time of life, when considerable mental and physical changes are taking place, cannot really be communicated at all, being rather in the shape of feelings than defined thoughts, and you are therefore thrown back on yourself.

This, as I have said, I believe to be the common and inevitable experience of all intelligent people. The "hearties," whose interests are largely confined to games, smut, food and drink, are of course perfectly happy. They find other hearties to whom they can pour out all that they have in their minds on those somewhat circumscribed topics. And between them and your (and my) type there is a considerable range of men, indeed probably a very substantial majority of the human race, who don't bother their heads about Life with a big L at all: many men, for example, with highly developed brains concentrate their interests on the higher mathematics or whatever else their line is, and apart from that they are ready to accept a ready-made creed on what I may call the things of the soul. But you and I and a number of others aren't like that; and we don't want to be like that. We demand the right to form our own judgments, and we are not prepared to accept anyone else's. It may be arrogant but there it is—that's how we're made. And the price we pay for an outlook on life which we value and in which we believe is an intellectual loneliness which we endeavor to assuage as much as possible by association with such other like-minded people as we can discover.

I said above that there was one qualification of this loneliness. That is the right kind of marriage. The value of the right kind of marriage is that it is not solely an intellectual companionship—i.e. it affords an outlet, such as friendship cannot afford, for feelings as well as thoughts. But even so, it is inevitably only partial: there must remain locked up inside every intelligent human being quite a good deal which is not communicable to others.

Regard your feeling of loneliness, therefore, as a perfectly natural phenomena, and set about getting used to it. It is troubling you now because it is *new;* you will find before long that you take it for granted and may even at times enjoy it. . . .[1]

[1] *Letters from a Civil Servant to His Son,* 65–68.

☞ *Bibliography*

Agate, James. *Noblesse Oblige*. London, Horne and Van Thal, 1944.

Allen, A. V. G. *Life and Letters of Phillips Brooks*. 2 vols. New York, Dutton, 1901.

Andersen, Nicholas Longworth. *The Letters and Journals of General Nicholas Longworth Andersen*. Edited by Isabel Andersen. New York, Fleming H. Revell, 1942.

Anderson, Sherwood. *Letters of Sherwood Anderson*. Edited by Howard Mumford Jones. Boston, Little, Brown, 1953.

Anonymous. *Letters from a Civil Servant to His Son*. London, Muller, 1947.

Anonymous. *Letters to a Ministerial Son, by a Man of the World*. London, Clarke, 1911.

Argyll, John G. E. H. D. S. Campbell, ninth Duke of (ed.). *Intimate Society Letters of the Eighteenth Century*. 2 vols. London, Stanley Paul, 1910.

Baker, C. H. C., and M. I. Baker. *James Brydges, First Duke of Chandos*. Oxford, Clarendon Press, 1949.

Baker, Ray Stannard. *Woodrow Wilson: Life and Letters*. 8 vols. Garden City, N. Y., Doubleday, Page, 1927–39. English edition, 4 vols., London, Heinemann, 1928–29.

Barrington, E. I. *Life of Walter Bagehot*. London, Longmans, Green, 1914.

Beethoven, Ludwig van. *Beethoven's Letters*. With explanatory notes by A. C. Kalischer. Translated by J. S. Shedlock. London, Dent, 1926.

———. *Letters of Beethoven*. Collected, translated, and edited by Emily Anderson. 3 vols. London, Macmillan, 1961.

Bennett, Arnold. *Letters to His Nephew*. Edited by R. Bennett. London, Heinemann, 1936.

Birks, T. R. *Memoir of Edward Bickersteth*. 2 vols. London, Seeley, 1849–52.

Blomfield, Alfred. *Memoir of Charles James Blomfield,* London, J. Murray, 1864.

Boswell, James. *London Journal, 1762–1763.* Introduction and notes by Frederick A. Pottle. New York, McGraw-Hill, 1950. (The Yale Editions of the Private Papers of James Boswell.) English edition, London, Heinemann, 1951.

Breton, Nicholas. *A Poast with a Pacquet of madde Letters.* London, Browne and Smethicke, 1606.

Bristol, John Hervey, first earl of. *Diary and Letter-Books of John Hervey, First Earl of Bristol . . . 1651–1750.* 3 vols. Wells, E. Jackson, 1894.

British Museum. Harleian MSS. Art. 39.

Brockway, W., and B. K. Winer (eds.). *A Second Treasury of the World's Great Letters.* London, Heinemann, 1950. New York, Simon and Schuster.

Browne, Sir Thomas. *Works of Sir Thomas Browne.* Edited by Geoffrey Keynes. 6 vols. London, Faber and Gwyer, 1928–31.

Browning, Andrew. *Thomas Osborne, Earl of Danby and Duke of Leeds, 1632–1712.* 2 vols. Glasgow, Jackson, 1944.

Burke, Edmund. *Correspondence of the Right Honourable Edmund Burke . . . 1744 and . . . 1797.* Edited by Charles William, Earl Fitzwilliam, and Sir Richard Bourke. London, F. and J. Rivington, 1844.

Burr, A. R. *Weir Mitchell.* New York, Duffield, 1929.

Burroughs, John. *My Boyhood.* New York, Doubleday, 1922.

Cartwright, Julia (Mrs. Henry Ady). *Castiglione: Life and Letters.* 2 vols. London, 1908.

Chalmers, P. A. *Kenneth Grahame.* London, Methuen, 1933.

Champneys, Basil. *Memoirs and Correspondence of Coventry Patmore.* 2 vols. London, Bell, 1900.

Charles I. Eikon Basilikon: The Portraiture of His Sacred Majesty. London, 1648. (Bodleian Library Pamphlet Collection, Oxford).

Charteris, Hon. Evan Edward. *The Life and Letters of Sir Edmund Gosse.* London, Heinemann, 1931.

Chesterfield, Philip Dormer Stanhope, fourth Earl of. *Letters of . . . Chesterfield.* Edited by Bonamy Dobrée. 6 vols. London, Eyre and Spottiswood, 1932.

Clarke, J. S. *Life of James II.* 2 vols. London, Longman, Hurst, 1816.

Clay, Henry. *The Works and Private Correspondence of Henry Clay.*

Edited by Calvin Colton. 10 vols. New York, A. S. Barnes, 1855–1904.

Coghill, Sir Joscelyn, Bt. Unpublished letter, in possession of Sir Patrick Coghill, Bt.

Coleridge, Samuel Taylor. *Unpublished Letters of Samuel Taylor Coleridge*. Edited by E. L. Griggs. 2 vols. London, Constable, 1932.

Connell, Brian. *Portrait of a Whig Peer*. London, Deutsch, 1957.

Crocker, Lester G. *The Embattled Philosopher: A Biography of Denis Diderot*. London, Neville Spearman, 1955.

Croly, Jane C. *Memories*. New York, Putnam, 1904.

Dahms, Walter. *Mendelssohn*. 5 vols. Berlin, Schuster and Loeffler, 1919.

David, Hans T., and Arthur Mendl (eds.). *The Bach Reader*. London, Dent, 1946.

Davis, Richard Harding. *Adventures and Letters of Richard Harding Davis*. Edited by C. B. Davis. New York, Scribner's, 1917.

Derby, James Stanley, seventh Earl of. *Private Devotions and Miscellanies of James, Seventh Earl of Derby, K. G.*, with a prefatory memoir and an appendix of documents. Edited by the Reverend F. R. Raines. 3 vols. Manchester, printed for the Chatham Society, 1867. (Added title-page: The Stanley Papers, Part III.)

Edward VIII, King of England. *A King's Story: The Memoirs of H. R. H. the Duke of Windsor, K.G.* London, Cassell, 1951.

Ellis, Sir Henry (ed.). *Original Letters Illustrative of English History*. 3 vols. London, Harding, Triphook, and Lepard, 1824.

Evelyn, John. *John Evelyn's Letter Book*. London, British Museum, Evelyn MSS 39.

Farragut, Loyall. *The Life of David Glasgow Farragut . . . embodying His Journal and Letters*. New York, D. Appleton, 1879.

Fischer, Louis. *Life of Ghandi*. New York, Harper, 1950.

Ford, Worthington C. (ed.). *A Cycle of Adams Letters, 1861–1865*. 2 vols. London, Constable, 1921. First publication, Boston and New York, Houghton Mifflin, 1920.

Franklin, Benjamin. *The Complete Works of Benjamin Franklin*. Compiled and edited by John Bigelow. 10 vols. New York, Putnam, 1887–88.

Furness, Horace Howard. *The Letters of Horace Howard Furness*. Edited by H. H. F. Jayne. 2 vols. Boston, Houghton Mifflin, 1922.

Garrison, Wendell Phillips. *William Lloyd Garrison, 1805–1879: The*

Story of His Life Told by His Children. 4 vols. New York, Century, 1885–89.

Graham, William A. *Papers of William A. Graham.* Edited by J. G. de Roulhac Hamilton. 4 vols. Raleigh, North Carolina State Department of Archives and History, 1957.

Harris, William. Unpublished letter, Bodleian Library, Oxford. Rawlinson MSS Letters, c.56, f.2.

Hazlitt, William. *The Complete Works of William Hazlitt.* Edited by P. P. Howe. 21 vols. London, Dent, 1930–34.

Hendrick, Burton J. *The Life and Letters of Walter Hines Page.* 3 vols. New York, Doubleday, Page, 1925–26.

Henry, Rev. Philip. Unpublished letter, Bodleian Library, Oxford. English Letters, e.29, f.30.

Herbert, Lord (ed.). *Pembroke Papers (1780–1794): Letters and Diaries of Henry, Tenth Earl of Pembroke, and His Circle.* London, Cape, 1950. (A continuation of *Henry, Elizabeth, and George ...,* 1939.)

Hinton, James. *Life and Letters of James Hinton.* Edited by Ellice Hopkins. London, Kegan Paul, 1878.

Hopkins, Gerard Manley. *Further Letters of Gerard Manley Hopkins.* Edited by C. C. Abbott. 2nd ed., revised and enlarged. London and New York, Oxford University Press, 1956.

Houston, Sam. *The Writings of Sam Houston.* Edited by Amelia W. Williams and Eugene C. Barker. 8 vols. Austin, University of Texas Press, 1938–43.

Howe, M. A. deWolfe. *John Jay Chapman and His Letters.* Boston, Houghton Mifflin, 1937.

[Hugo, Adèle ("Mme Victor Hugo")]. *Victor Hugo: A Life.* Related by one who has witnessed it. 2 vols. London, Allen, 1863.

Hunt, Charles Havens. *Life of Edward Livingston.* New York, Appleton, 1864.

Huxley, Leonard. *Life and Letters of Thomas Henry Huxley.* 2 vols. London, Macmillan, 1900.

Ingpen, Roger. *Shelley in England.* London, Kegan Paul, Trench, Trubner, 1917.

Jackson, Andrew. *Correspondence of Andrew Jackson.* Edited by J. S. Bassett. 6 vols. Washington, Carnegie Institution, 1926–33.

James, Henry. *Charles W. Eliot.* 2 vols. Boston, Houghton Mifflin, 1930.

James, Marquis. *Andrew Jackson: Portrait of a President*. Indianapolis, Bobbs-Merrill, 1937.

Johnston, William Preston. *The Life of Gen. Albert Sidney Johnston*. New York, D. Appleton, 1878.

Kingsley, Charles. *Charles Kingsley: His Letters and Memories of His Life*. Edited by his wife. 2 vols. London, H. S. King, 1879.

Lawrence, Amos. *Extracts from the Diary and Correspondence of the Late Amos Lawrence*. Edited by his son, William R. Lawrence, M.D. Boston, Gould and Lincoln, 1855.

Lee, Robert E., Jr. *Recollections and Letters of General Robert E. Lee*. By his son Captain Robert E. Lee. 2d ed., Garden City, N. Y., Doubleday, Page, 1924.

Lee, Sir Sidney. *King Edward VII: A Biography*. 2 vols. London, Macmillan, 1925–27.

Lewisohn, Ludwig. *Goethe: The Story of a Man*, as told in his own words and the words of his contemporaries. 2 vols. New York, Farrar, Straus, 1949.

Lingard, R. *A Letter of Advice to a Young Gentleman Leaving the University*. London, Tooke, 1673.

Lowell, John. Letter in Harvard University Archives, Hud 811.51.

Marx, Karl. "Karl Marx Papers," *Neue Zeit*, Vol. I, No. 1 (Berlin, 16th year, n.d.).

Maurois, André. *The Titans: A Three-Generation Biography of the Dumas*. Translated by Gerard Hopkins. New York, Harper, 1957.

Melville, Lewis (pseudonym for Lewis Saul Benjamin). *The Life and Letters of William Cobbett in England and America*. 2 vols. London, John Lane, 1913.

Meredith, George. *Letters of George Meredith*. Collected and edited by his son [W. H. Meredith]. 2 vols. London, Constable, 1912.

Merivale, Charles. *Autobiography and Letters of Charles Merivale, Dean of Ely*. Edited by Judith Anne Merivale. London, Arnold, 1899.

Monypenny, W. F., and G. E. Buckle. *The Life of Benjamin Disraeli, Earl of Beaconsfield*. 6 vols. London, J. Murray, 1910–20.

Montgomery, James. *The Christian Correspondent*. 3 vols. London, Ball, 1837.

Morley, John. *Diderot and the Encyclopaedists*. 2 vols. London, Macmillan, 1886.

————. *The Life of William Ewart Gladstone.* 2 vols. London, Lloyd, 1908.

Morse, Samuel F. B. *Samuel F. B. Morse: His Letters and Journals.* Edited and supplemented by his son, Edward Lind Morse. 2 vols. Boston, Houghton Mifflin, 1914.

Mozart, Amadeus Wolfgang. *Letters of Mozart and His Family.* Translated and edited by Emily Anderson. London, Macmillan, 1938.

Nehru, Jawaharlal. *A Bunch of Old Letters.* Bombay and London, Asia Publishing House, 1958, 1960.

Nicolson, Hon. Harold George. *King George V: His Life and Reign.* London, Constable, 1952.

Ormsby, R. (ed.). *Memoirs of J. R. Hope-Scott.* 2 vols. London, J. Murray, 1884.

Osborne, Francis. *Advice to a Son.* Bodleian Library Pamphlet Collection, c.1656.

Payne, Robert. *The Gold of Troy.* New York, Funk and Wagnalls, 1959.

Peel, Sir Robert. *The Private Letters of Sir Robert Peel.* Edited by George Peel. London, J. Murray, 1920.

Pepys MSS. Royal Historical Manuscripts Commission. London, Stationers Office, 1911. (Vol. LXX of Historical Manuscripts Collection Series.)

Pissarro, Camille. *Letters to His Son Lucien.* Edited with the assistance of Lucien and John Rewald. Translated by Lionel Abel. London, Kegan Paul, 1944.

Quincy, Josiah. *Memoir of the Life of Josiah Quincy, Jun., of Massachusetts.* By his son. Boston, Cummings, Hilliard, 1825.

Raleigh, Sir Walter, and others. *Instructions for Youth.* London, Minshull, 1722.

Reid, Stuart J. *Life and Letters of the First Earl of Durham, 1792–1840.* 2 vols. London, Longmans, Green, 1906.

Roosevelt, Franklin Delano. *The Roosevelt Letters.* Edited by Elliott Roosevelt. 5 vols. London, Harrap, 1949–52. First published in the U.S. as *FDR: His Personal Letters.* 4 vols. New York, Duell, Sloan and Pearce, 1947–50.

Roosevelt, Theodore. *The Works of Theodore Roosevelt.* 20 vols. New York, Scribner's, 1926.

Rowland, Kate Mason. *The Life of Charles Carroll of Carrollton, 1737–1832.* 2 vols. New York, Putnam, 1898.

Runes, Dagobert David. *Letters to My Son.* New York, Philosophical Library, 1949.

Russell, John, Earl of Bedford. *Life of William, Lord Russell.* 2d ed. 2 vols. London, Longman, Hurst, 1820.

Rush, Benjamin. *Letters of Benjamin Rush.* Edited by L. H. Butterfield. 2 vols. Princeton, published for the American Philosophical Society by Princeton University Press, 1951.

Ruskin, John. *Works of John Ruskin.* Edited by E. T. Cook and Alexander Wedderburn. 39 vols. London, Allen, 1903–1912.

Rymer, Thomas. *Foedera.* Record edition. 4 vols. London, n.d.

Sacco, Nicola, and Bartolomeo Vanzetti. *Letters of Sacco and Vanzetti.* Edited by Marion Denman Frankfurter and Gardner Jackson. New York, Viking, 1928.

Schuster, M. L. *A Treasury of the World's Great Letters.* London, Heinemann, 1941.

Scoones, W. Baptiste (ed.). *Four Centuries of English Letters.* London, Kegan Paul, 1880.

Scott, Sir Walter. *The Letters of Walter Scott.* Edited by H. J. C. Grierson and others. 12 vols. London, Constable, 1932–37.

Sedgwick, Charles. *Letters of Charles Sedgwick.* Edited by his sister. Boston, privately printed, 1870.

Semmes, J. E. *John H. B. Latrobe and His Times.* Baltimore, Norman, Remington, 1917.

Shelburne, William Petty, Earl of. Unpublished letter. Shelburne Papers, The William L. Clements Library, University of Michigan.

Simms, William Gilmour. *Letters of William Gilmour Simms.* Collected and edited by Mary C. Simms Oliphant, Alfred Taylor Odell, and T. C. Duncan Eaves. 5 vols. Columbia, S. C., University of South Carolina Press, 1952–56.

Sitwell, Sir Osbert. *Great Morning.* London, Macmillan, 1947.

———. *Laughter in the Next Room.* London, Macmillan, 1948.

Spurr, H. A. *The Life and Writings of Alexander Dumas.* London, Dent, 1902.

Steffens, Lincoln. *The Letters of Lincoln Steffens.* Edited by Ella Winter and Granville Hicks. New York, Harcourt, Brace, 1938.

Strafford, Thomas W., first Earl of. *The Earl of Strafford's Letters and Dispatches.* Somers Tracts (edited by W. Scott), Quarto IV. London, 1810.

Stuart-Wortley, E. *A Prime Minister to His Son*. London, J. Murray, 1925.

Tennyson, Hallam. *Alfred Lord Tennyson: A Memoir*. 2 vols. London, Macmillan, 1897.

Thayer, Alexander Wheelock. *The Life of Ludwig van Beethoven*. 3 vols. New York, Beethoven Association, 1921.

Thompson, Lawrance. *Young Longfellow (1807–1843)*. New York, Macmillan, 1938.

Trenchfield, Caleb. *A Cap of Grey Hairs for Green Heads*. London, Baldwin, 1777.

Venn, Henry. *Life of the Rev. Henry Venn*. London, Hatchard, 1834.

Verney Family. Letters and Papers . . . down to the End of the Year 1639. Edited by John Bruce. London, Camden Society, 1853. (Volume 56 of Camden Society Series.)

Webster, Daniel. *The Private Correspondence of Daniel Webster*. Edited by Fletcher Webster. 2 vols. Boston, Little, Brown, 1857.

Wilberforce, William. *Private Papers of William Wilberforce*. Collected and edited by A. M. Wilberforce. London, Unwin, 1897.

Wilberforce, Robert Isaac and Samuel. *The Life of William Wilberforce*. by his sons. London, J. Murray, 1838.

Williams, C. T. *Memoir of Bishop Atterbury*. London, 1867.

Williams, William Carlos. *Selected Letters of William Carlos Williams*. Edited by John C. Thirlwall. New York, McDowell, Obolensky, 1957.

Winthrop Papers. Boston, Massachusetts Historical Society, 1892.

Worth, Jonathan. *The Correspondence of Jonathan Worth*. Collected and edited by J. G. de Roulhac Hamilton. 2 vols. Raleigh, 1909. Publications of the North Carolina Historical Commission.

Zeitlin, Jacob, and Hoover Woodbridge. *Life and Letters of Stuart P. Sherman*. 2 vols. New York, Farrar and Rinehart, 1929.

☞ Index

Adam, Mr. (of Wintringham, England): 78
Adams, Charles Francis: 145; letter from, 145–46
Adams, Charles Francis, Jr.: 145; letter to, 145–46
Adams, Henry: 145
Adams, President John: 144
Adams, President John Quincy: 144
Agate, James Evershed: 212; letter from, 212–13
Albert Francis Charles Augustus Emmanuel, Prince, of Saxe-Coburg-Gotha (consort of Queen Victoria): letter from, 138–39
Andersen, Larz: 166; letters to, 166–67
Andersen, General Nicholas Longworth: 166; letters from, 166–67
Anderson, John: 201; letter to, 201–202
Anderson, Robert: 200f.; letter to, 200–201
Anderson, Sherwood: 200f.; letters from, 200–202
Anne, Queen (of England): 46, 51
Arabella Stuart: 18
Argyll, George Campbell, Duke of: 87f.
Argyll, John Campbell, Duke of: letters from, 88–89
Argyll, John Douglas Edward Henry Campbell, Duke of: 87; letters to, 88–89
Atterbury, Francis (Bishop of Rochester): 43f.; letter to, 43–44
Atterbury, Rev. Lewis: 43; letter from, 43–44

Bach, Johann Gottfried Bernhard: 52; letter concerning, 52–54
Bach, Johann Sebastian: 52; letter from, 52–54
Bagehot, Thomas Watson: 135; letter from, 135–36
Bagehot, Walter: letter to, 135–36
Bedford, William Russell, Duke of: 33; letter from 33–34
Beecher, Henry Ward: 151
Beethoven, Karl van: 113ff.; letters to, 114–15
Beethoven, Ludwig van: 113f.; letters from, 114–15
Bennett, Arnold: 193; letter from, 193–95
Bennett, Richard: letter to, 193–95
Bickersteth, C.: letter to, 124
Bickersteth, Rev. Edward: 123f.; letter from, 124
Blomfield, Alfred (Bishop Suffragan of Colchester): letter to, 134–35

227

Index

Verney, Sir Edmund: 25f.; letter from, 25–26
Verney, Sir Ralph: 25f.; letter to, 25–26
Victoria, Queen (of England): letter from, 138–39

Wagner, Wilhelm Richard: 173
Walpole, Horace, Earl of Orford: 49
War: 21, 37, 185, 190–91
Warwick, John Dudley, Earl of: 11f.; letter to, 11
Webster, Daniel: 124f.; letter from, 124–25
Webster, Daniel Fletcher: 124f.; letter to, 124–25
Weld, Henry: 107
Wentworth family: *see* Strafford
Westmoreland, John Fane, Earl of: 83f.
Westmoreland, Lady Sarah Jane (Child) Fane: 82ff.
Wilberforce, Samuel (Bishop of Oxford and of Winchester): 100; letters to, 100–102
Wilberforce, William: letters from, 100–102
William of Orange (King William III of England, joint sovereign with Mary II): 37f., 44, 51
Williams, William: letter to, 210–11
Williams, William Carlos: 200, 209–10; letter from, 210–11
Wilson, Joseph Ruggles: 175; letter from, 176
Wilson, President Woodrow: 175, 189; letter to, 176
Windsor, Duke of: *see* Edward VIII
Wine: 13–14
Winthrop, John: letter to, 51
Winthrop, General Wait: 50f.; letter from, 51
Witherspoon, Dr. John: 91
Work: 18, 169f.
Worth, David G.: letter to, 143–44
Worth, Governor Jonathan: 143; letter from, 143–44

Yankees: 117, 127

237

Fathers to Sons has been set in several sizes of the Linotype recutting of Caslon, an eighteenth-century typeface designed by William Caslon. The long and honorable tradition in type founding which the house of William Caslon and Son enjoyed in England imparts a flavor which complements this collection of letters from fathers to sons.

UNIVERSITY OF OKLAHOMA PRESS

Norman